Effective College and University Teaching

In memory of Victor Anthony Benassi, Sr.

—Victor Benassi

For Harper Aurelia Payne: May all your teachers be excellent.
—William Buskist

Effective College and University Teaching

Strategies and Tactics for the New Professoriate

William Buskist
Auburn University

Victor A. Benassi
University of New Hampshire

Los Angeles | London | New Delhi
Singapore | Washington DC

Los Angeles | London | New Delhi
Singapore | Washington DC

FOR INFORMATION:

SAGE Publications, Inc.
2455 Teller Road
Thousand Oaks, California 91320
E-mail: order@sagepub.com

SAGE Publications Ltd.
1 Oliver's Yard
55 City Road
London EC1Y 1SP
United Kingdom

SAGE Publications India Pvt. Ltd.
B 1/I 1 Mohan Cooperative Industrial Area
Mathura Road, New Delhi 110 044
India

SAGE Publications Asia-Pacific Pte Ltd
33 Pekin Street #02-01
Far East Square
Singapore 048763

Acquisitions Editor: Christine Cardone
Editorial Assistant: Sarita Sarak
Production Editor: Catherine M. Chilton
Copy Editor: Brenda Weight
Typesetter: Hurix Systems Pvt. Ltd.
Proofreader: Sarah J. Duffy
Indexer:
Cover Designer: Bryan Fishman
Marketing Manager: Liz Thornton
Permissions: Karen Ehrmann

Copyright © 2012 by SAGE Publications, Inc.

Printed in the United States of America.

Library of Congress Cataloging-in-Publication Data

Effective college and university teaching : strategies and tactics for the new professoriate / William F. Buskist, Victor Benassi, editors.

    p. cm.

    Includes bibliographical references and index.

    ISBN 978-1-4129-9607-5 (pbk. : alk. paper)

    1. College teaching—United States. 2. Professional learning communities—United States. 3. Effective teaching. I. Buskist, William. II. Benassi, Victor.

  LB2331.E385 2012
  378.1'250973—dc23   2011019183

This book is printed on acid-free paper.

11 12 13 14 15 10 9 8 7 6 5 4 3 2 1

Contents

Preface

❖

We have devoted the bulk of our academic careers to the professional development of graduate students and new faculty, especially in the area of teaching and learning at the college and university level. Combined, we have about 50 years of professional development experience related directly to improving college and university teaching. Countless hours of that half-century of work have been involved with creating, designing, and leading classes and workshops for graduate students and new faculty on "best practices" in college and university teaching. We have probably spent almost as many hours directly observing these individuals in the classroom and providing them feedback about their teaching. If there is one thing that we have learned with absolute certainty from this labor of love, it is that with proper training and practice, graduate students and new faculty can become highly skilled teachers—and in some cases, even excellent teachers.

Preparing graduate students and new faculty for their teaching duties often has an impact on these individuals that transcends the development and refinement of their pedagogical skills. To be sure, although many of these individuals were once certain that they wanted solely a research career or a nonacademic career, some of them discovered that they truly enjoy teaching, and for the first time in their new careers, they contemplated an academic career in which teaching plays a central role in defining their work. These individuals discovered the transformative power of teaching in guiding their professional lives and in shaping the lives of their students. In short, through their formal pedagogical training, these individuals discovered that college and university teaching is worthy of the time it takes to become proficient at it.

We crafted this volume in part to share this message with our readers, be they graduate students, new faculty, faculty developers, or experienced teachers. The larger part of our purpose, though, is to share with our readers what is known about effective teaching and what is known about teaching that information to others. Thus, this book is intended for graduate students who aspire to academic careers, new faculty making the transition to the professoriate, program directors and supervisors of graduate student teacher training, directors of teaching and learning centers, and seasoned faculty who may wish to update or otherwise improve their pedagogical knowledge and teaching.

To help us accomplish our goals, we enlisted the help of leading pedagogical scientists, faculty developers who train graduate students and faculty for teaching, supervisors of graduate teaching assistant programs, new faculty, and even a few graduate students who have recently undergone training for teaching. Their collective efforts nicely summarize cutting-edge data and theory in the scholarship of teaching and learning and in current best practices for putting this knowledge into action online and in the classroom.

As you may notice when you read through the biographical sketches of our contributors, the vast majority of our authors come from psychology departments or have academic backgrounds predominately in psychological science. This collection of particular authors is no accident. Psychology has long been interested in the empirical analysis of pedagogical practices and exporting what is practically useful from this inquiry to the classroom. Psychology is, after all, the study of human behavior, which includes, among other things, learning, thinking, communicating, and social interaction—all of which occur in the classroom, and for that matter, in online teaching. In fact, there is a small legion of psychologists whose professional identities center on the teaching of psychology and who take it as their raison d'etre to engage in the scholarship of teaching and learning as it applies to improving teaching at all levels and across all disciplines.

As editors, we believe that our authors have much to offer our colleagues across the academy. As you will discover as you read the chapters in this volume, our authors address the gamut of issues central to college and university teaching in the 21st century, but do so in broad strokes, using language, ideas, and examples that apply to teachers interested in improving their teaching or helping others develop their teaching, regardless of subject matter or professional academic interest. For their excellent work and timely and insightful contributions, we thank each of our authors.

We would also like to thank the many good people at Sage. First and foremost, we would like to thank Senior Acquisitions Editor Christine Cardone for her belief in this book and for her support during every phase of the project. From reading our prospectus to discussing issues related to the development of the project to even working with us to tweak our title, Chris was by our sides—and for her good work and good humor we extend to her our heartfelt gratitude. Chris's editorial assistant, Sarita Sarak, skillfully handled the innumerable behind-the-scenes details that were involved in creating, developing, and publishing this volume. Thank you, Sarita, for everything. We owe no small debt of gratitude to Marketing Manager Liz Thornton for her excellent work in getting the good word out to people like yourself about this volume. Brenda Weight did a marvelous job in her copyediting. To all of you at Sage, thank you again.

Last, but far from least, we would like to thank our wives for their patience and support for us as we solicited, edited, and submitted manuscripts for this volume. Their good cheer at the end of the day made it possible for us to see the work through to fruition. Connie and Peg—you're the best.

—Bill Buskist
Auburn, Alabama

—Victor Benassi
Durham, New Hampshire
February 2011

Acknowledgments

❖

SAGE Publications would like to thank the following reviewers:

Stephen F. Davis
Morningside College

Sandra Goss Lucas
University of Illinois at Urbana-Champaign

Regan A. R. Gurung
University of Wisconsin–Green Bay

Rodolfo Mendoza
University of California–Berkeley

Steven Meyers
Roosevelt University

Stephen Prentice-Dunn
University of Alabama

Loreto R. Prieto
Iowa State University

Chapter 1

Preparing the New Professoriate to Teach

❖

Victor A. Benassi and William Buskist

Professor 1:   Do you provide doctoral students in your graduate program the opportunity to teach a course as the instructor of record?

Professor 2:   Of course not. They don't yet have the terminal degree, so they're not qualified.

Professor 1:   So you think a terminal degree in your discipline is a *necessary* requirement to teach a college course in the area. Others may not agree with that view. However, *surely* you are not suggesting that the mere possession of the terminal degree is a *sufficient* qualification for teaching in your discipline.

Professor 2:   Well, I *surely* am making that claim! In my discipline, you are qualified to teach at the college level when you've earned the PhD, and not before. That's not the way it is in your discipline?

How representative is Professor 2's view? We have talked with colleagues from a broad range of fields and disciplines, and we can attest to the breadth and depth of at least the second part of Professor 2's claim—that the terminal degree is considered sufficient qualification for teaching at the college or university level (see also Howard, Buskist, & Stowell, 2007).

In fact, a respondent in a survey of department chairs and new faculty that one of us (VAB) conducted replied with a note stating that graduate students who were trained in teaching were the *least* accomplished when they taught their own courses. Although this respondent's opinion may be rarely held, preparation of doctoral students for teaching duties is often low on the priority list of graduate faculty in terms of the skill sets they wish to have their graduate students develop while earning their PhDs. Given the low priority assigned to teaching relative to research in many of the doctoral programs, we are not surprised to hear graduate students say that teaching preparation is deemphasized or even ignored in their graduate programs. As an editor noted in a comment in the American Historical Society's *Perspectives*, "Academics have long been concerned by the fact that research universities often produce topflight scholars who cannot, however, translate their scholarship into effective classroom instruction" (editor's note in Rayson, Farmer, & Frame, 1999; see also Caplinger, 2004; Utecht & Tullous, 2008).

Robert Boice (1992), in his classic *The New Faculty Member*, documented in stark terms the toll taken on many faculty during their first several years on the job, especially inexperienced faculty (those who lack teaching experience or who did not receive any sort of preparation for teaching while in graduate school). Boice examined the experiences of new tenure-track faculty members at a comprehensive public university and at a research university. He found that the first several years on the job were stressful and difficult for many of these new faculty members—not a surprising finding for those who work in academic departments. He also reported that many of the new faculty indicated that they spent large amounts of time on their teaching duties. For many of these faculty, the large time commitment to their teaching did not pay off. They often reported feeling stressed and expressed resentment toward students and senior faculty (who gave them little direction or support). End-of-semester student evaluation reports gave many of them discouraging news. Not surprisingly, these faculty worried about their teaching, but they also worried about not having sufficient time to complete their research or other scholarly work. Some of the faculty members were sure the situation would improve:

> Yes, I know that you're worried about me. And I often worry, too. But I'll get to writing later, when conditions are right. I've been too busy [teaching] to do a proper job of it so far. Once I settle down to writing, I'll be able to get a lot done in a hurry. So you don't need to worry. (Boice, 1992, pp. 90–91)

Although some faculty remained optimistic that they would make progress in their research and writing, others continued to report they were worried that time was running out. As one third-year faculty member from the research university put it, "I guess it must be obvious to you that I'm no great producer. I certainly have not spent my time the way I had planned. I really don't understand it. I certainly didn't expect to devote almost all of my time to teaching— I'm not even enjoying teaching" (Boice, 1992, p. 88; note that the nominal teaching load at the research university was two courses per semester).

Fortunately, many faculty members in Boice's (1992) study were ultimately successful in setting their teaching and research on a positive trajectory. Unfortunately, the situation did not improve for some, resulting in a poor overall pre-tenure record of teaching and/or scholarship. We are not suggesting that the new faculty in Boice's study would have had clear sailing if they had been better prepared as graduate students for their teaching duties. However, we know that very few reported any formal preparation in teaching while in graduate school (Boice, 1992, pp. 54–55). We agree with Seidel, Benassi, Richards, and Lee's (2006) view that "being teaching-ready upon appointment [as a faculty member] . . . should decrease the likelihood that new faculty members will defer their scholarly growth until they have achieved an advanced level of teaching competence" (p. 230; see also Seidel & Caron, 2007; Silvestri, Cox, Buskist, & Keeley's Chapter 4 of this volume).

To be sure, during the past two decades, academic leaders, representing many fields and disciplines, have recognized the need to prepare their faculty and future faculty to become effective teachers (Adams, 2002; Gaff, Pruitt-Logan, Sims, & Denecke, 2003; Pruitt-Logan, Gaff, & Jentoft, 2002). Many colleges and universities have established teaching and learning centers for the professional development of their faculty and graduate students. Likewise, many academic departments also provide some sort of preparatory or training experiences for new faculty and new graduate teaching assistants (GTAs).

However, the nature and extent of these preparatory experiences vary tremendously in their content, quality, and duration (see, e.g., Buskist, Tears, Davis, & Rodrigue, 2002). Moreover, they are often aimed at graduate student teaching assistants (see, e.g., Howard et al., 2007), not graduate student instructors of record. They range from half-day pre-semester workshops to year-long courses on the teaching of discipline-specific content. They may address a vast array of issues and topics, including course design, creating syllabi, classroom management practices, active learning techniques, lecture preparation, teaching ethically, student assessment, and course evaluation.

In *What Colleges and Universities Want in New Faculty*, Adams (2002, p. 4) offered several excellent recommendations to graduate faculty for preparing graduate students for college and university teaching:

- "Graduate programs must provide their doctoral students with a variety of teaching experiences and successively more independent teaching in order to prepare them for academic careers. These experiences should begin during the first year of graduate school and continue throughout graduate study."

- "Students need to be introduced to new pedagogies, becoming involved with and knowledgeable about such areas as active learning, field-based learning, diversity, and technology."

- "Students need more than just the experience of teaching classes. New teachers also should receive constructive feedback about their performance and participate in group discussions about creative teaching possibilities, problem solving, and advising."

These recommendations are as timely today as when they were published a decade ago. We suggest that by implementing these and related recommendations, graduate faculty will help prepare graduate students to take on the full array of roles and responsibilities they will be expected to perform as faculty.

One purpose for creating this book is to draw more attention to the need to provide consistent and thorough training for GTAs and graduate teachers of record across disciplines. Additionally, we want to share with faculty from other fields and disciplines what has been learned in psychology regarding teaching others about effective teaching and learning. As a discipline, psychology has long been a leader in providing support and resources for teaching at the college and university level (Puente, Matthews, & Brewer, 1992). The Society for the Teaching of Psychology, founded in the mid-1940s, provides a tremendous array of resources to psychology teachers through its Office of Teaching Resources in Psychology (http://teachpsych.org/otrp/index.php) and its various electronic publications (http://teachpsych.org/resources/e-books/index.php). Also, the first comprehensive approach to preparing PhD students for college and university teaching may have been implemented in the psychology department at the University of New Hampshire in the mid-1960s (Benassi & Fernald, 1993; Benassi & Fuld, 2004).

In this book, our contributors have reviewed and discussed the best practices that currently exist for preparing graduate students and new faculty to become effective in their duties as teaching assistants and in readying them to become teachers of record for undergraduate courses. Our goal was to cover the full range of topics central to developing efficacious training practices aimed at the professional development of the next generation of college and university teachers. The volume is primarily intended to be a resource for helping GTA supervisors and other faculty teach graduate students how to teach. However, for those graduate students and new faculty who do not have the opportunity to benefit from a formal GTA training program, we are confident that they can read and benefit from the book's contents on their own.

In addition to this book (and the sources cited in Stiegler-Balfour and Overson's Chapter 23), we urge readers to consult the burgeoning array of resources that are available through reliable Internet sites. Some examples include the following:

- Training for Teaching Assistants at Duke in Mathematics (http://www.math.duke.edu/~bookman/grsttr.html)
- The Colleges of Worcester Consortium's Certificate in College Teaching (http://www.cowc.org/college-student-resources/certificate-college-teaching)
- The Teaching Fellows Program at Auburn University (http://www.auburn.edu/~buskiwf/teaching_fellows.htm)
- The Academic Program in College Teaching at the University of New Hampshire (http://www.unh.edu/teaching-excellence/Academic_prog_in_coll_teach/index.html)
- The Higher Education Academy in the UK (http://www.heacademy.ac.uk/)
- The Teaching Assistant Training and Teaching Opportunity (TATTO) program at the Emory University Laney Graduate School (http://www.gs.emory.edu/resources/professional.php?entity_id=20)
- Services for GTAs at the University of Washington's Center for Instructional Development and Research, one of the early leaders in preparing graduate students for teaching duties (http://depts.washington.edu/cidrweb/consulting/ta.html)

Overview of This Book

Several of our chapters address topics that do not directly involve teaching but are relevant to it—working relationships between faculty and teaching assistants (Chapter 2), addressing graduate students' fears about teaching (Chapter 3), GTAs' perceived preparedness for teaching duties (Chapter 4), professional development and work–private life balance (Chapter 5), and preparing graduate students for the political nature of academic institutions (Chapter 21). We also include several chapters that focus on work that needs to be completed by graduate students as they prepare for teaching duties, especially when they are going to be the teachers of record—learning how to design a course (Chapter 7) and developing a teaching philosophy statement (Chapter 8). Of course, there are also the expected chapters that address different approaches to teaching—use of lectures (Chapter 10), active learning methods (Chapter 11), discussions (Chapter 12), and the appropriate use of technology (Chapter 18). What occurs during and outside of class time can have a large impact on whether a course is successful, and so we include several chapters that address this general topic—building classroom rapport (Chapter 9), addressing ethical issues in teaching (Chapter 14), identifying and addressing incivility in and out of class (Chapter 15), addressing issues related to diversity in teaching (Chapter 16), and teaching controversial issues in the context of a liberal education (Chapter 17). We address the topic of assessment from three perspectives—assessment of student learning (Chapter 13), assessment of courses and their teachers by students (Chapter 19), and assessment of GTA training programs (Chapter 20). In an effort to inform GTAs and faculty who prepare GTAs about a large, and growing, body of scholarship on the science of instruction and of learning (Mayer, 2010) and its applications to teaching and learning in college and university courses, we include a chapter that describes some powerful principles that teachers can easily apply to a wide variety of teaching and learning contexts (Chapter 6). For those faculty interested in introducing undergraduates to college and university teaching, we include a chapter on teaching with undergraduate teaching assistants (Chapter 22). Finally, we include "Useful Resources for Preparing the New Professoriate" (Chapter 23).

Should All Graduate Students Receive Preparation for Their Teaching Duties?

The short answer to this question is yes (see also Adams, 2002). Putting unprepared GTAs (or new faculty who have not been prepared for teaching) in charge of a class of college students is, to us, indefensible. However, this reply is also the easy answer. It may be more constructive to consider this question in historical context. As Seidel et al. (2006, p. 226) observed,

> In virtually every professional field, the development of formal academic programs to prepare individuals has followed long after the emergence of a specific profession. For instance, the practices of medicine, law, nursing, and journalism predated medical schools, law schools, colleges of nursing, and university-based journalism programs. So, too, the professoriate came into existence long before the development of formal academic programs in college teaching. As has been the case with these other professional fields, it is to be expected that the development of formal academic programs in college teaching will lead increasingly to practice expectations being based upon research and scholarship.

As evidenced by the scholarship included in this book and that is readily available in many scholarly publications, we believe that there is a strong body of knowledge on the full range of topics and issues related to teaching and learning at the college and university level. This body of knowledge and the implications it raises for practice constitute "college teaching as a professional field of study" (Seidel et al., 2006, p. 225; see also Seidel & Caron, 2007, for an example in doctoral education in health administration).

Perhaps one reason many graduate programs do not include a systematic and thorough component on preparation of graduate students who aspire to faculty positions is that faculty and other academic leaders do not know about or perceive the value of the body of knowledge that constitutes the professional field of study in college teaching. Some faculty and administrators may also hold the view that learning to teach is done by teaching—"That's how I did it. That's how my advisor did it. We turned out okay."

Today, that view simply does not wash. We started this chapter with a brief discussion of Boice's (1992) work and the price that ill-prepared new faculty can pay. Fortunately, today we know a lot about how students learn, how teachers effectively assess what they learn, how to create engaging classroom environments that can foster student motivation and learning, and how to maximize the effectiveness of technology in teaching and learning. Although it is true that new teachers can, through trial and error, become effective instructors, it is also true—as this book will show—that preparing the future professoriate for teaching through formal academic programs in college teaching can have immediately positive and powerful effects on enhancing teaching quality and improving student learning.

References

Adams, K. A. (2002). *What colleges and universities want in new faculty.* Washington, DC: American Association of Colleges and Universities, Preparing Future Faculty (PFF) Occasional Paper Online. Retrieved from http://www.aacu.org/pff/pdfs/PFF_Adams.PDF

Benassi, V. A., & Fernald, P. S. (1993). Preparing tomorrow's psychologists for careers. *Teaching of Psychology, 20,* 149–155.

Benassi, V. A., & Fuld, K. (2004). University of New Hampshire's preparing future psychology faculty program. In W. Buskist & B. Beins (Eds.), *Preparing the new psychology professoriate: Helping graduate students become competent teachers.* Society for the Teaching of Psychology. Retrieved from http://www.teachpsych.org/teachpsych/pnpp/

Boice, R. (1992). *The new faculty member: Supporting and fostering professional development.* San Francisco: Jossey-Bass.

Buskist, W., Tears, R., Davis, S. F., & Rodrigue, K. M. (2002). The teaching of psychology course: Prevalence and content. *Teaching of Psychology, 29,* 140–142.

Caplinger, C. (2004, September 10). Graduate students as future teachers. *The Chronicle Review, 51*(3), A55. Retrieved from http://chronicle.com/article/Graduate-Students-as-Future/32921/%5bAu

Gaff, J. G., Pruitt-Logan, A. S., Sims, L. B., & Denecke, D. D. (2003). *Preparing future faculty in the humanities and social sciences: A guide for change.* Washington, DC: Association of American Colleges and Universities.

Howard, C., Buskist W., & Stowell, J. (2007). *The STP guide to graduate student training in the teaching of psychology.* Retrieved from http://teachpsych.org/resources/e-books/gst2007/gst07.php

Mayer, R. E. (2010). *Applying the science of learning.* Upper Saddle River, NJ: Pearson.

Pruitt-Logan, A. S., Gaff, J. G., & Jentoft, J. E. (2002). *Preparing future faculty in the sciences and mathematics: A guide for change.* Washington, DC: Association of American Colleges and Universities.

Puente, A. E., Matthews, J. R., & Brewer, C. L. (1992). *Teaching in psychology: A history.* Washington, DC: American Psychological Association.

Rayson, D., Farmer, E. L., & Frame, R. (1999, January). Preparing future faculty: Teaching the academic life. *Perspectives.* American Historical Association. Retrieved from http://www.historians.org/perspectives/issues/1999/9901/9901TEC.CFM

Seidel, L. F., Benassi, V. A., Richards, H. J., & Lee, M. J. (2006). College teaching as a professional field of study. *Journal on Excellence in College Teaching, 17,* 225–239.

Seidel, L. F., & Caron, R. M. (2007). Can they teach? Evidence-based pedagogy as a doctoral competency. *Journal of Health Administration Education, 24,* 221–234.

Utecht, R. L., & Tullous, R. (2008). Countdown to teaching. *Proceedings of the Allied Academies, 15*(2), 163–172. Retrieved from http://sbaer.uca.edu/research/allied/2008-Reno/International%20Conference/50.pdf

Chapter 2

Creating Effective Working Relationships Between Faculty and Graduate Teaching Assistants

❖

Steven A. Meyers

Most resources on preparing graduate teaching assistants (GTAs) for their responsibilities have emphasized the technical matters of training, such as which formats to use, topics to address, or methods to employ (Prieto & Meyers, 2001). Others have described effective teaching practices to guide GTAs, such as how to deliver a well-organized lecture, lead an engaging discussion, or design a fair test (Davis, 2009). Fewer authors, however, have discussed how training occurs within an interpersonal context, and that the relationship between faculty members and graduate students needs to be cultivated because it significantly impacts GTAs' performance and emerging sense of competence. Professors mentor, encourage, and empower GTAs when a responsive supervisory relationship is intentionally formed. On the other hand, professors raise GTAs' anxiety, create self-doubt, and promote frustration when they disregard rapport development or derogate graduate students.

Nevertheless, focusing on relationships may be uncertain territory for some supervising faculty members. Many faculty may be more comfortable considering other aspects of GTA training rather than personal areas that require self-reflection. I pose and discuss the following questions to enhance such working relationships: Am I clarifying GTAs' responsibilities and providing them with structure? Am I being attentive to GTAs' changing developmental level and needs? Do I display sensitivity and respect for GTAs as professionals in training? Do I provide feedback and manage conflict in constructive and supportive ways?

Clarify GTAs' Responsibilities and Provide Structure

Graduate students' responsibilities vary widely depending on the nature of their teaching assistantship. Some GTAs mainly provide administrative support for classes and/or proctor and score exams. Other GTAs have greater instructional responsibilities and conduct discussion or laboratory sections. Still others assume full course responsibility and teach classes under the supervision of faculty members. Given this range, graduate students are often initially uncertain about the scope of their work (Wilson & Stearns, 1985). Moreover, faculty members have their own unique expectations for GTAs whom they supervise, which can add to the ambiguity with respect to GTAs' roles and responsibilities.

A clear delineation of graduate students' tasks reduces their anxiety and potential confusion, which maximizes the likelihood that GTAs understand the professor's expectations for their work and provides criteria for subsequent evaluation, feedback, and remediation. Clarifying these responsibilities essentially structures the relationship between the faculty supervisor and the TA.

Professors can begin explaining GTAs' duties in an initial meeting before the start of the semester. In this discussion, faculty members outline their expectations in concrete and detailed ways. For example: Are GTAs expected to hold office hours? Where should they be held and for how long? Are GTAs required to attend every class led by the professor? Will GTAs be expected to read all texts for the class? If GTAs grade assignments, will they be provided with grading criteria? What is the desired turn-around time for completing such work? If GTAs lecture to the class, how often will they do so? Will the professor be present to provide feedback afterward, or will the TA lead class in the professor's absence?

This level of detail may appear excessive. However, the relationship between GTAs and faculty members can be strained on both sides when needs are unstated and, as a consequence, are unfulfilled. Some supervisors create written job descriptions for GTAs to assist with this clarification.

Discussions of GTAs' responsibilities should continue as the semester progresses. It is difficult for supervising faculty members to anticipate all questions that graduate students may have, and unexpected situations often arise during the term. Teachers can continue to support GTAs through regularly scheduled supervision meetings as well as through impromptu conversations.

Finally, faculty members should consider and explain how they will actively assist GTAs during the semester. The guiding principle of mutual obligation challenges the notion held by some faculty members that GTAs are "theirs" because students receive funding that supports their duties (McNaron, 2002). Balanced and productive relationships are formed when professors appreciate that they are mentoring future faculty members and are willing to share their expertise. Professors can emphasize their availability and commitment, genuinely collaborate with GTAs and consider their input, answer questions thoroughly and thoughtfully, and remain cognizant that they are role models.

Be Observant and Attentive to GTAs' Developmental Level and Needs

Clarifying roles does not imply being rigid about them. Graduate students' abilities and needs change as they gain experience both in their field and in the classroom. This development has implications for the relationship between supervising faculty members and GTAs at the different points of students' professional development.

Nyquist and colleagues (e.g., Nyquist & Sprague, 1998; Nyquist & Wulff, 1996) proposed three stages through which GTAs progress, each differentiated by GTAs' concerns, their communication style, how they approach authority, and how they relate to their students. At the outset of their experience, GTAs are best characterized as "senior learners," who tend to personalize their interactions with undergraduates and are preoccupied by whether students will like them. They are more dependent on their supervisors and generally provide students with simplistic explanations because of their limited graduate coursework and knowledge.

With greater experience, GTAs are more appropriately considered "colleagues-in-training," who likely want greater autonomy from their supervisors. At this point, GTAs increasingly embrace their emerging identities by using the technical language of their fields (sometimes to excess) and focus more on the mechanical skills of instruction.

The working relationship between professors and GTAs shifts again when graduate students become "junior colleagues." GTAs in this stage begin to relate to faculty as collaborators. They have a more nuanced view of the learning process and are more focused on undergraduates' educational outcomes. Graduate students are increasingly comfortable at this point with their professional socialization, and they can use technical discourse as well as explain concepts in understandable ways.

Given this development, supervising faculty members need to be adept at gauging the appropriate amount of support that they should provide. Although there is individual variability depending on the abilities, needs, and personalities of the particular graduate student, Nyquist and Wulff (1996) highlighted that professors generally should alter their supervision style from the role of manager to that of mentor. At each step, instructors need to reevaluate their expectations, provide appropriately challenging responsibilities, and grant GTAs increasing authority and independence.

Prieto (2001) added nuance to this progression in his Integrated Developmental Model of Supervision for Graduate Teaching Assistants (IDM-GTA). He proposed that graduate students move through three similar stages of development (i.e., beginning GTAs, advanced GTAs, and junior faculty members). A different level of motivation, point of focus (i.e., students vs. self), and desire for autonomy characterize each stage. However, the IDM-GTA emphasizes that these dimensions and categorizations vary across seven different teaching domains (i.e., presentation skills, assessment skills, academic ethics, organizational skills, sensitivity to students' individual differences, interpersonal skills, and networking abilities). A GTA may be adept and autonomous in one area, but depend on assistance in another area at the same point in time. Thus, supervising faculty members must be highly attuned to the varied skill levels of GTAs, closely monitor changes in each domain across time, and adjust their supervision as needed.

Display Sensitivity and Respect for GTAs as Professionals in Training

Faculty members who are committed to establishing effective working relationships with GTAs also need to monitor whether they are conveying respect in their interactions. Consider these contrasting quotes from two graduate students, cited by Meyers (1995), as they described their supervising faculty:

> The professor I worked for separates people into two categories—those with a PhD and those without. He feels that those without deserve no respect and should feel privileged to work for those who have one. His way of teaching GTAs is to yell at them when a problem arises in a lab.

> The attitude he had was that this was a collaborative experience—that we were in it together and could both share and learn from the experience. The respect he had for what I did and the appreciation he showed for the work done was also very important.

Professors enhance their working relationships with GTAs when they are intentional about developing students' feelings of competence and confidence. They should consider praising GTAs for their accomplishments, conveying a genuine interest in their activities and professional growth, and remaining pleasant and upbeat in their interactions. Professors also accomplish this goal when they solicit GTAs' input into decision making at an appropriate level and respectfully listen to graduate students' opinions.

Respect and sensitivity are important hallmarks of effective relationships between professors and GTAs. Prieto, Scheel, and Meyers (2001) assessed the extent to which GTAs valued three supervisory styles exhibited by professors. These included professors' collegiality (e.g., characterized by traits such as flexibility and openness), interpersonal sensitivity (e.g., featuring traits such as perceptiveness and intuitiveness), and task centeredness (e.g., emphasizing goal accomplishment by being evaluative or prescriptive). Their results generally documented that GTAs significantly favor a supervisory style that is collegial in nature, but that also incorporates some interpersonally sensitive elements.

These findings are echoed by Meyers (1996), who asked GTAs across a range of disciplines to characterize their professors' supervision styles as "democratic" (i.e., frequently encouraged verbal give-and-take, promoted discussion of expectations, provided clear but flexible standards, appreciated differences of opinions), "authoritarian" (i.e., did not permit GTAs to question decisions, required compliance to requests, became upset during disagreements), or "permissive" (i.e., seldom provided guidance or expectations, allowed GTAs to have their way as they pleased, allowed independent decision making). Graduate students' ratings of democratic relationships with their professors were significantly associated with higher satisfaction levels and higher ratings of their effectiveness as a GTA. In contrast, ratings of professors' authoritarian behavior were associated with lower self-rated satisfaction and competence. Ratings of professors' permissiveness had generally weaker associations with GTA outcomes.

Notably, the commitment to enhancing the working relationship with GTAs has to originate with faculty members because of the power imbalance that exists between the two parties. Faculty members can treat students who serve as GTAs in disrespectful ways often without consequence because of the level of influence they have within graduate programs.

Successful faculty members are actively invested in both the short-term and long-term success of GTAs. They realize that they are preparing future faculty, and they optimize their relationship toward this end. Supportive interpersonal connections increase the probability of graduate students' success and completion of their programs (Wulff & Austin, 2004). However, almost half of the respondents in a national survey of 32,000 current and recent doctoral students reported that they lacked sufficient supervision of their teaching responsibilities (Fagen & Suedkamp Wells, 2004). This mentorship deficit was most pronounced among underrepresented groups, especially for students of color.

Provide Feedback and Manage Conflict in Constructive and Supportive Ways

Effective working relationships between faculty members and graduate students are vital when providing GTAs with feedback to help them refine their instructional skills. Without a sense of trust and openness, GTAs are more likely to conceal their struggles and avoid approaching their supervisors for needed assistance because they fear criticism, blame, or negative evaluations.

Boehrer and Sarkisian (1985) emphasized how vulnerable graduate students feel when they first assume their teaching responsibilities. Some GTAs are anxious because they are daunted by public speaking or teaching material that they find novel. Other GTAs doubt or blame themselves for their students' poor performance or apathy in class. Faculty members must be mindful that many graduate students feel as if they are taking a risk by being candid and exposing their difficulties. A supportive relationship provides graduate students with the reassurance to display vulnerability and to disclose their problems.

In their survey of supervisors and GTAs, Myers, Douglas, Madden, and Briggs (2002) found that maximizing collaboration and empathy within the context of evaluation was essential. Teaching assistants were most likely to accept feedback when they played an active role in the evaluation process by providing supervisors with background information about their class session, their instructional goals, and their own areas of concern. Planning meetings can allow graduate students to suggest emphases of the evaluation and how best to collect information (Black & Kaplan, 1998). A collaborative framework can also be used in a post-observation session to identify areas of strength and to develop concrete goals, strategies, and follow-up plans to enhance performance (Black & Kaplan, 1998).

Strategies that build the relationship between faculty members and graduate students are also needed when conflicts emerge. Significant problems and disagreements sometimes occur with GTAs. These situations may relate to a teaching deficit; however, conflicts may also focus on issues of deportment (e.g., communicating respect to supervising professors) or responsibility (e.g., appearing on time to lead a discussion or lab section; grading papers in a timely fashion).

Many of the approaches outlined earlier have the potential to improve such situations. Research on conflicts between professors and students can be instructive (Meyers, Bender, Hill, & Thomas, 2006). The interventions that have been shown to be the most effective begin with professors respectfully broaching the issue and acknowledging the student's circumstance and emotions. With a shared, concrete understanding of the problem and each person's concerns, faculty supervisors can ask GTAs to help solve the problem rather than solely dictate a remedy. Through this approach, conflicts are addressed through the lens of mutual respect, common interest, clarified structure, and developmentally appropriate power sharing.

Conclusions

The working relationship between faculty members and GTAs is a critical ingredient of training. Its development needs to be as purposeful as the implementation of other formats and methods that supervisors use to cultivate graduate students' teaching skills. However, there are several hurdles in this process. First, supervisors need to realize that the relationship itself is important and can moderate the effectiveness of the other elements of training. In other words, GTAs are more likely to successfully implement their skills when they are encouraged and monitored by a supportive faculty member.

The second hurdle is that addressing the faculty-GTA relationship is an inherently personal practice. Faculty members need to be introspective and self-aware as they ask themselves difficult questions such as "How do I exercise power in professional settings?" or "How much patience do I display?" or "To what extent do I consider the needs and views of others as I supervise GTAs?" These can be hard for some professors to answer with candor and conviction if changes are needed.

Finally, supervisors need to understand that effective relationships with GTAs start with "being nice," but then exceed this benchmark. Professors must provide structure and role clarity for GTAs. They also have to monitor GTAs' changing level of professional development and alter their expectations to allow graduate students to grow into their potential as future faculty members.

References

Black, B., & Kaplan, M. (1998). Evaluating TAs' teaching. In M. Marincovich, J. Prostko, & F. Stout (Eds.), *The professional development of graduate teaching assistants* (pp. 213–234). Bolton, MA: Anker.

Boehrer, J., & Sarkisian, E. (1985). The teaching assistant's point of view. In J. D. W. Andrews (Ed.), *Strengthening the teaching assistant faculty* (pp. 7–20). San Francisco: Jossey-Bass.

Davis, B. G. (2009). *Tools for teaching* (2nd ed.). San Francisco: Jossey-Bass.

Fagen, A. P., & Suedkamp Wells, K. M. (2004). The 2000 national doctoral program survey: An on-line study of students' voices. In D. H. Wulff, A. E. Austin, & Associates (Eds.), *Paths to the professoriate: Strategies for enriching the preparation of future faculty* (pp. 74–91). San Francisco: Jossey-Bass.

McNaron, T. A. H. (2002). Here today, not gone tomorrow. In W. Davis, J. Smith, & R. Smith (Eds.), *Ready to teach: Graduate teaching assistants prepare for today and tomorrow* (pp. 5–9). Stillwater, OK: New Forums Press.

Meyers, S. A. (1995). Enhancing relationships between instructors and teaching assistants. *Journal of Graduate Teaching Assistant Development, 2,* 107–112.

Meyers, S. A. (1996). Consequences of interpersonal relationships between teaching assistants and supervising faculty. *Psychological Reports, 78,* 755–762.

Meyers, S. A., Bender, J., Hill, E. K., & Thomas, S. Y. (2006). How do faculty experience and respond to classroom conflict? *International Journal of Teaching and Learning in Higher Education, 18,* 180–187.

Myers, C., Douglas, F., Madden, C., & Briggs, S. (2002). Observation and feedback for improving TA instructional development: A comparative study. In W. Davis, J. Smith, & R. Smith (Eds.), *Ready to teach: Graduate teaching assistants prepare for today and tomorrow* (pp. 109–115). Stillwater, OK: New Forums Press.

Nyquist, J. D., & Sprague, J. (1998). Thinking developmentally about TAs. In M. Marincovich, J. Prostko, & F. Stout (Eds.), *The professional development of graduate teaching assistants* (pp. 61–88). Bolton, MA: Anker.

Nyquist, J. D., & Wulff, D. H. (1996). *Working effectively with graduate assistants.* Thousand Oaks, CA: Sage.

Prieto, L. R. (2001). The supervision of teaching assistants: Theory, evidence, and practice. In L. R. Prieto & S. A. Meyers (Eds.), *The teaching assistant training handbook: How to prepare TAs for their responsibilities* (pp. 103–129). Stillwater, OK: New Forums Press.

Prieto, L. R., & Meyers, S. A. (Eds.). (2001). *The teaching assistant training handbook: How to prepare TAs for their responsibilities.* Stillwater, OK: New Forums Press.

Prieto, L. R., Scheel, K. R., & Meyers, S. A. (2001). Psychology graduate teaching assistants' preferences for supervisory style. *Journal of Graduate Teaching Assistant Development, 8,* 37–40.

Wilson, T., & Stearns, J. (1985). Improving the working relationship between professor and TA. In J. D. W. Andrews (Ed.), *Strengthening the teaching assistant faculty* (pp. 35–45). San Francisco: Jossey-Bass.

Wulff, D. H., & Austin, A. E. (2004). Future directions: Strategies to enhance paths to the professoriate. In D. H. Wulff, A. E. Austin, & Associates (Eds.), *Paths to the professoriate: Strategies for enriching the preparation of future faculty* (pp. 267–292). San Francisco: Jossey-Bass.

Chapter 3

Allaying Graduate Student Fears About Teaching

❖

Sandra Goss Lucas

Nothing substitutes for knowledge and experience—and that is especially true as graduate students face their first teaching experience. In this chapter I will focus on what new graduate student teachers fear and five practices that can be implemented to address those fears.

In an ideal world, graduate students would know of their teaching assignment well before the term begins and have time to prepare by reading the relevant research-based literature (but see Benassi's Chapter 7 for an exception; see also Stiegler-Balfour & Overson's Chapter 23 for an annotated bibliography). In a less ideal world, new graduate teaching assistants (GTAs) who find out their assignments immediately before the term begins are so overwhelmed that they often feel that they do not have the time to read such preparation materials.

In our ideal world, graduate students also would begin their teaching assignments as "true GTAs" and not as "the teacher of record." Being a "true GTA" provides opportunities for new GTAs to observe the teaching of veteran instructors (GTAs and faculty) and to ask questions about their teaching decisions and behaviors. "True GTAs" would also participate in discussions about teaching, either informally, with veteran instructors and/or other GTAs, or more formally, in a class focused on preparing to teach or in mentoring communities (Thomas, 2006).

However, regardless of when graduate students receive their assignment or whether they are "true GTAs," most new teachers share some common fears about teaching.

New Graduate Student Instructors' Fears

For almost 20 years, I have been involved in my department's New TA Orientation Program. At our first meeting and after introductions, I have the new GTAs write on an index card (anonymously) what they are most anxious about in terms of their teaching assignment and to rate their anxiety on each of these issues on a 1 (low anxiety) to 5 (high anxiety) scale. Then they flip their card and write what they are most excited about in their teaching. I collect the cards, shuffle them, and randomly redistribute them to the students so that no one gets his or her own card back. Those GTAs who receive a card with a "5" read it aloud to the group. They are eager to do so because they are NOT disclosing their own fears—they are merely conveying someone else's fears. This exercise brings out the most common fears and anxieties and it begins a discussion to address them. Students speak up because they are not being judged on what they say (read), which also models a method for new GTAs to use in promoting discussion in their own classrooms. I gather all the cards at the end of the day.

These concerns vary little from year to year and, although some center on the "nuts and bolts" of teaching (grading, etc.), most of the concerns fall into five general categories:

1. How competent am I to teach this course?

2. How do I decide what to present, how to present it, and what level to present it at?

3. How will I relate to my students and they to me?

4. How can I balance my teaching with my research and coursework?

5. How helpful will my faculty supervisor be?

How Competent Am I to Teach This Course?

Beginning teachers often worry that they do not know the material as well as they should (Gardner & Leak, 1994; Huston, 2009; Lucas & Murry, 2002; Thomas, 2006). They worry about not knowing the answer to students' questions, "freezing up" in class, providing an incorrect answer, and "sounding like an idiot." They worry about keeping one step ahead of the students in learning or relearning the content (Bobrick, 1999; Gardner & Leak, 1994;

Huston, 2009). Beyond worrying about what they know, they also worry about how to present what they know (Fish & Fraser, 2001; Showalter, 2003).

How Do I Decide What to Present, How to Present It, and at What Level to Present It?

Most new GTAs do not know what content to present, especially given "the infinite amount of . . . knowledge and the finite amount of academic time" (Showalter, 2003, p. 12). They worry about the level at which they should present the content—a very valid concern because teaching often entails presenting the "big" picture (especially in basic survey courses that most GTAs help teach), whereas graduate school focuses on the details that are important in conducting and presenting research. New GTAs want to present well; they do not want their students to be bored. They worry about the pace of their presentation—will they cover the material too quickly for most students? New GTAs worry about using PowerPoint (and other technology) in pedagogically sound ways (Davis, 2009; Huston, 2009; Svinicki & McKeachie, 2011). They also worry about learning course management systems, and using discussion boards and student response systems (Austin, 2002). Technology adds an additional layer of anxiety for new GTAs, who are primarily worried about just presenting information accurately.

How Will I Relate to My Students and They to Me?

Because new GTAs fear being incompetent, they worry about what their relationship should be with their students. They fear that their students will perceive them as being too easy or too difficult. Because they are often close to the age of their students, they have special issues of being perceived as authoritative. They worry about "convincing students that I am qualified to teach," keeping student interest, motivating students, and getting them to participate in class. They wonder how to get students to respect them. They worry about how they will deal with problem students. Most new GTAs also obsess over being liked by their students (Svinicki & McKeachie, 2011).

How Can I Balance My Teaching With My Research and Coursework?

All new GTAs are graduate students. They conduct research and take classes. They worry about balancing their commitments and having time to complete all their tasks well (Austin, 2002; Nyquist et al., 1999). They know that being a good teacher entails time commitments in preparing for teaching, developing classroom presentations, working with students individually, and developing assessment instruments. But GTAs also know that, although teaching is "verbally valued," the reality is that the institutional reward structure does not favor teaching expertise (Austin, 2002; Fraser, Houlihan, Fenwick, Fish, & Moller, 2007; Lucas & Murry, 2002; Nyquist et al., 1999; Showalter, 2003). Or as one graduate student put it, "I have professors telling me, 'Spend as little time as possible on your teaching, and make sure you're a good researcher'" (Showalter, 2003, p. 11). In this environment, it is understandable that graduate students are confused about how to properly balance teaching and research.

How Helpful Will My Faculty Supervisor Be?

New GTAs worry about the guidance they will receive from their faculty supervisor. Most GTAs worry that their faculty supervisor will not be available or will be psychologically unengaged in helping them learn how to teach (Austin, 2002). A few worry that they will be "micromanaged" by their faculty supervisors and will not have the freedom and support to develop their own teaching strategies and tools.

Except for concerns about faculty supervisors and coursework, new graduate student teachers worry about many of the same issues that veteran instructors worry about—preparing lessons, presenting in the classroom, and balancing their teaching and research (Fish & Fraser, 2001; Fraser et al., 2007; Gardner & Leak, 1994; Showalter, 2003). Because these same issues arise year after year, departments should be able to develop ways to address GTAs' concerns. After many years of working with new GTAs, I have some suggestions.

Core Elements in Allaying New GTAs' Fears About Teaching

There are core elements that are essential for new GTAs to have a good first teaching experience. Together, these elements can provide new GTAs with the support they need so they can become effective classroom instructors.

Acknowledge Fears and Concerns

The first element is a simple acknowledgment that concerns and fears exist about the initial (and possibly subsequent) teaching experience(s) and that such concerns are justified. All too often graduate students are "pacified" by senior faculty who tell them "all will be well" without giving them the tools necessary to do well or who deemphasize the importance of their teaching experience altogether. New GTAs who are involved in an orientation or class with other new GTAs will realize that they are not alone in this new endeavor and will have opportunities to ask questions and work on their pedagogical knowledge base (Austin, 2002; Nyquist et al., 1999). But even if there is no organized program, the department, through the supervising faculty member and/or a designated department person, should acknowledge the legitimate concerns new GTAs have about the teaching experience and establish clear lines of communication about such concerns. New GTAs will not approach faculty who have brushed off their fears about teaching.

Have an Accessible and Supportive Departmental Representative

The second essential element in allaying new GTAs' fears about teaching is having an accessible and supportive departmental representative with whom to talk. Having a designated representative who genuinely cares about graduate students' teaching experiences provides a departmental structure to nurture new GTAs, thus allowing new and continuing GTAs to broach issues they would not raise with their supervising faculty members (Austin, 2002). Having a departmental representative to whom GTAs can bring issues and problems, as well as share positive classroom experiences, is especially important if there is no structured course that accompanies GTAs' first teaching experience. This departmental representative should have teaching experience, possess credentials that provide him or her with validated "wisdom" about teaching, and, in general, be recognized as a good if not excellent teacher.

Such a representative will also accrue a significant amount of information about the teaching experiences specific to the new GTAs in his or her department. This information could be used to examine departmental policies in an effort to be more supportive of teaching or to develop one-time seminars focused on common teaching concerns, or help the department evaluate teaching assignments and responsibilities (Austin, 2002; Nyquist et al., 1999).

Departments with well-established and effective new GTA orientation programs and/or structured courses on teaching generally have a departmental person who is available throughout the year to consult with GTAs on preparing to teach (vetting syllabi, course policies, etc.), dealing with issues that arise while teaching (classroom management considerations, classroom climate/dynamics, teacher-student rapport, etc.), and guiding reflection and evaluation of teaching at the end of the term. Having someone who listens to GTA concerns and is supportive and helpful in designing solutions will help alleviate many GTA fears about teaching.

Mentoring by Senior GTAs

The third essential element in allaying new GTAs' fears about teaching is to provide mentoring by senior GTAs. As important as the supervising faculty member and the departmental representative are, nothing replaces the information that can be shared among graduate students (Austin 2002; Nyquist et al., 1999; Thomas, 2006). Ideally, the graduate student mentor would be someone who had previously taught the course. In my department's new TA orientation program, every new GTA receives information about his or her teaching assignment from the GTA who last "TA'd" the course. The information provided describes GTAs' responsibilities (e.g., grading, leading discussions, lecturing, lab demonstrations, writing quizzes and/or exams, attending lectures, taking notes, meeting with students), lists all required and recommended material or equipment GTAs will need (e.g., books, lab supplies) and how they can acquire them, provides information important for new GTAs to have (e.g., useful websites, ancillary materials such as instructor resource manuals, class demonstrations), offers words of wisdom and advice for being a successful GTA in the course, supplies information about who the faculty supervisor is and where and how he or she can be contacted, provides information about whether regular meetings will take place and when and where the meetings will occur, and provides the latest syllabus for the course.

In the large introductory-level course that I supervised, we paired new GTAs with veteran GTAs, trying to "match personalities" whenever possible. The veteran GTAs received credit for the mentoring (an important component, I believe) through our campus's Graduate Teaching Certification program. Beyond these sorts of "mentoring communities," Thomas (2006) suggested instituting informal teaching groups that have only a facilitator (not a leader) and which teachers at all levels of experience could attend to share information and to be supported in their talk about teaching behaviors.

Although veteran TAs can provide support and general knowledge about the content that is being taught, often their teaching advice is "anecdotal," based on situations they have encountered, which leads me to the fourth essential element—providing research-based information about issues in teaching.

Provide Research-Based Information About Teaching

New GTAs need to know that a respectable research base exists about teaching at the college level. This research-supported information about teaching and learning can (and should) be made available to new GTAs in a variety of ways. The designated departmental representative should have many of these resources available for GTAs to read and use. These resources might include Nilson's (2010) *Teaching at Its Best: A Research-Based Resource for College Instructors;* Goss Lucas and Bernstein's (2005) *Teaching Psychology: A Step by Step Guide;* Davis's (2009) *Tools for Teaching;* and Forsyth's (2003) *The Professor's Guide to Teaching: Psychological Principles and Practices.* One-time seminars could be structured to include the research base to address common teaching concerns. GTAs could also be given an annotated bibliography of books and journal articles that provide the research base for teaching practices.

In the course I supervised, I developed such a resource library. I was careful to choose items that provided research evidence for teaching practices. We made the resources available to all GTAs. In addition, my campus's Center for Teaching Excellence (CTE) maintains a website addressing common teaching concerns and providing research-based resources to address them. Our CTE has an active Scholarship of Teaching and Learning (SoTL) research group, composed of faculty and graduate students from across campus who are engaged in classroom research.

Practice Teaching

The fifth and final essential element for allaying GTAs' fears about teaching addresses the experience/practice aspect with which I began the chapter. Although fear of public speaking may be part of new teachers' fears about teaching, such is not usually the case. In my experience, many new teachers are less concerned about speaking in front of a group and more concerned about being able to transmit content and keeping the class on task. This fear of public speaking in a teaching context can be ameliorated by practice, before new GTAs are in front of a classroom full of undergraduates. Providing new GTAs with the opportunity to give a "mini-lecture" (often 10 minutes) on a topic they will be teaching, and videotaping the mini-lecture, can be a great investment in allaying teaching anxiety. In my many years of working with new GTAs, I found that having GTAs prepare a lesson (with guidance and feedback from experienced instructors) and present that lesson (while peers act as students) helps them figure out some of the nuts and bolts of teaching (e.g., pacing of content, how to move around the classroom, what voice level and inflection to use). In addition, watching a video of their teaching and receiving feedback from both peers (acting as students) and a veteran instructor on their lesson presentation provides new GTAs more stress relief than anything else we have done. New GTAs are often astounded that their videotaped presentation, documenting what actually came out of their mouth, was much more organized and coherent than it seemed when they were actively teaching and had all the "teacher talk" going on in their heads. They also are able to see mannerisms that might detract in the classroom (e.g., repeated "ums") before they go into their actual classroom.

In our technologically savvy world, videotaping is accomplished relatively easily. We encourage new GTAs to be videotaped throughout their first term of teaching to note changes in their teaching behaviors and incorporation of suggestions from faculty supervisors and veteran instructors.

Conclusions

The goal of this chapter was to outline common fears about teaching expressed by new GTAs and to suggest ways of allaying these fears in a departmental structure. The overriding message is that many GTAs need structured support if they are to become effective classroom teachers (Austin, 2002; Nyquist et al., 1999; Thomas, 2006). Interestingly, the research literature on teaching anxiety is primarily based on current professors' experiences with one constant feature—they felt they did not get enough information, feedback, or mentoring in regard to their teaching as GTAs (Bobrick, 1999; Fish & Fraser, 2001; Fraser et al., 2007; Gardner & Leak, 1994; Showalter, 2003). As Showalter (2003, p. 4) noted, lamenting the lack of teacher training in graduate school, "The most profound anxiety of teaching is our awareness that we are making it up as we go."

If we are to help our graduate students in their development toward becoming good faculty members, and thus effective teachers, then we must take seriously and address their anxieties about teaching. By providing a more supportive and structured environment for our new GTAs and new teachers, departments can alleviate their fears and support them, so they won't have to "make it up as they go" when they become faculty members. I wish all new graduate student teachers a wonderful first teaching experience and hope the suggestions from this chapter will resonate with both new GTAs and faculty interested in alleviating GTAs' teaching anxieties.

References

Austin, A. (2002). Preparing the next generation of faculty: Graduate school as socialization to the academic career. *Journal of Higher Education, 73*(1), 94–122.

Bobrick, E. (1999, September 1). Fear 101: Seasonal teaching anxiety reduces the most experienced professors to raw nerves and nightmares. *Salon.com*. Retrieved from http://www.salon.com

Davis, B. (2009). *Tools for teaching* (2nd ed.). San Francisco: Jossey-Bass.

Fish, T., & Fraser, I. (2001). Exposing the iceberg of teaching anxiety: A survey at three New Brunswick universities. *Perspectives (Electronic Journal of the American Association of Behavioral Sciences), 4.* Retrieved from http://aabss .org/Perspectives2001/Fish2001.jmm.html

Forsyth, D. (2003). *The professor's guide to teaching: Psychological principles and practices.* Washington, DC: American Psychological Association.

Fraser, I., Houlihan, M., Fenwick, K., Fish, T., & Moller, C. (2007). Teaching anxiety and teaching methods of university professors: A correlational analysis. *American Association of Behavioral and Social Sciences Journal, 11,* 78–90.

Gardner, L., & Leak, G. (1994). Characteristics and correlates of teaching anxiety among college psychology teachers. *Teaching of Psychology, 21,* 28–32.

Goss Lucas, S., & Bernstein, D. (2005). *Teaching psychology: A step by step guide.* Mahwah, NJ: Lawrence Erlbaum.

Huston, T. (2009). *Teaching what you don't know.* Cambridge, MA: Harvard University Press.

Lucas, C., & Murry, J. (2002). *New faculty: A practical guide for academic beginners.* New York: Palgrave.

Nilson, L. (2010). *Teaching at its best: A research-based resource for college instructors* (3rd ed.). Boston, MA: Anker.

Nyquist, J., Manning, L., Wulff, D., Austin, A., Sprague, J., Fraser, P., et al. (1999). On the road to becoming a professor: The graduate student experience. *Change, 31*(3), 18–27.

Showalter, E. (2003). *Teaching literature.* Malden, MA: Blackwell.

Svinicki, M., & McKeachie, W. (2011). *McKeachie's teaching tips: Strategies, research, and theory for college and university teachers* (13th ed.). Belmont, CA: Wadsworth/Cengage Learning.

Thomas, B. (2006). *Composition studies and teaching anxiety: A pilot study of teaching groups and discipline- and program-specific triggers* (Doctoral dissertation, Bowling Green State University). Retrieved from http://etd.ohiolink.edu/ send-pdf.cgi/Thomas%20Brennan%20M.pdf?bgsu1151207488

Chapter 4

Preparing for the Transition From Graduate School to the Academy

❖

An Exemplar From Psychology

Mark M. Silvestri, Brennan D. Cox, William Buskist,
and Jared W. Keeley

Many graduate students accept academic jobs after completing their doctoral degrees. For some of these new professors, the transition from one side of the lectern to the other may be a trying experience, as few new faculty feel fully prepared for college and university teaching (Golde & Dore, 2001). As a result, new professors may overextend themselves in preparing for teaching their courses, causing them to devote less time to developing their research (Boice, 2000).

Teaching loads for new professors vary depending on departmental needs and the nature of their institution. Research universities may ask their assistant professors to teach only one course per term for their first few years, whereas small colleges may ask their new professors to teach considerably more classes each term (Bernstein & Goss Lucas, 2004). Institutions also differ in their expectations of new professors. Some may place a greater emphasis on developing research programs. Others may emphasize developing teaching materials. Still others may emphasize both. On top of developing their research and teaching agendas, new faculty often perform service activities such as sitting on departmental committees and supervising student research.

Table 4.1   Exposure and Perceived Preparedness Rankings for 21 Teaching Content Areas

Content Area	Percentage Exposed (A)	Preparedness Rating[a] (B)	Gap Value (A–B)
Delivering lectures	86.5 (1.76)	5.94 (1.90)	0.14
Classroom management skills	78.4 (1.25)	5.25 (0.52)	0.73
Encouraging student participation	78.4 (1.25)	5.28 (0.58)	0.67
Asking/answering questions	73.0 (0.90)	5.50 (1.02)	0.12
First day of class	73.0 (0.90)	5.36 (0.74)	0.16
Ethical situations in teaching	70.3 (0.73)	4.97 (−0.04)	0.77
In-class group activities	70.3 (0.73)	4.92 (−0.14)	0.87
Leading group discussion	70.3 (0.73)	5.39 (0.80)	0.07
Organization of class time	64.9 (0.39)	5.22 (0.46)	0.07
Academic honesty	62.2 (0.22)	4.58 (−0.82)	1.04
Grading tests/quizzes/ papers	62.2 (0.22)	5.50 (1.02)	0.80
Teaching critical thinking skills	56.8 (−0.13)	5.00 (0.02)	0.15
College/university academic policies	54.1 (−0.30)	3.94 (−2.10)	1.80
Construction of test items	51.4 (−0.47)	5.06 (0.14)	0.61
Social skills for classroom teaching	45.9 (−0.82)	5.00 (0.02)	0.84
Ethnic, minority, or gender issues	43.2 (−1.00)	3.92 (−2.14)	1.14
Holding office hours	43.2 (−1.00)	5.17 (0.36)	1.36

Preparing handouts	40.5 (–1.17)	4.83 (–0.32)	0.85
Accommodating special needs	40.5 (–1.17)	4.25 (–1.48)	0.31
Using audiovisual equipment	35.1 (–1.51)	5.03 (0.08)	1.59
Using electronic technologies	35.1 (–1.51)	4.64 (–0.70)	0.81

[a]Respondents rated preparedness on a scale of 1 = "not at all prepared" to 7 = "very much prepared."

Given the responsibilities associated with transitioning from graduate student to assistant professor, and the perceived lack of preparation among new professors, it is beneficial for graduate students to receive preparation for teaching as a part of their academic training. Boice's (2000) research underscores this point. He examined differences in classroom environments between beginning professors who received individual coaching (10 sessions for 10 minutes each) on their teaching and those who did not. Individuals who received the coaching had greater student note taking, involvement, and comprehension—and higher classroom ratings. Thus, even brief preparation for teaching may enhance beginning teachers' overall teaching success and help prepare graduate students for the transition from being a graduate student to becoming an assistant professor.

Fortunately, many doctoral programs offer guidance for teaching in the form of workshops or semester-long courses. For example, many psychology graduate programs offer some form of a graduate teaching assistantship (Howard, Buskist, & Stowell, 2007; Wimer, Prieto, & Myers, 2004). As Prentice-Dunn (2006) noted, such a course on teaching can have a positive impact on shaping graduate students' disposition toward teaching. Although there are currently no established guidelines for what essentials to include in preparing graduate students to make a smooth transition from graduate school to the professoriate, Buskist, Tears, Davis, and Rodrigue's (2002) study produced a list of 21 content areas that appear in many graduate-level teaching courses (see Table 4.1).

Of course, mere coverage of these content areas does not guarantee adequate preparation of future professors. In this chapter, we report the results of a survey of newly minted assistant professors in psychology with respect to specific aspects of their preparation, including which content areas served them well and which areas they considered insufficient or irrelevant to their later teaching experience. Although this study involved assistant professors in psychology, its findings will likely be useful in help-ing graduate students prepare for teaching in other disciplines, too.

Some Data on Teacher Preparation

We e-mailed a cover letter, information letter, and 29-item survey to 106 assistant professors in psychology and received 45 replies (42% response rate). The sample consisted of graduate students who recently received their PhDs from Auburn University and a nationwide random sample of assistant professors. Of the 45 replies, 37 were from faculty who had participated in some form of a teaching course as graduate students. Participants were primarily male (57%) and Caucasian (97%) and represented academic institutions of all levels (21.6% baccalaureate, 48.6% master's, 29.7% doctoral). The remaining eight respondents either had no preparation for teaching or had participated only in teacher orientation experiences, such as pre-semester workshops.

The survey inquired about the teacher preparation experiences that assistant professors underwent as graduate students and how these experi-ences prepared them for their current teaching duties. Specifically, we asked (a) whether respondents participated in a teaching preparation course and, if so, for how many terms; (b) whether their preparation addressed the 21 content areas provided by Buskist et al. (2002); (c) if they had not taken a teaching preparation course, what was the nature of their teaching preparation as graduate students; and (d) to what extent they believed their training in these areas prepared them for teaching (respondents used a rat-ing scale of 1 = "not at all prepared" to 7 = "very much prepared"). We also included an open-ended item that requested respondents' recommendations for topics to include in a teaching preparation course based on their teach-ing experiences as assistant professors.

We performed three different analyses to answer questions related to the prevalence and effectiveness of teacher preparation training in the 21 content areas. The first analysis compared the percentage of respondents who received training in each content area to their perceived preparedness level in each area. The second analysis compared respondents' preparedness level based on whether they had received content-specific training in each area. The third analysis compared respondents' preparedness level based on whether they received a single semester or multiple semesters of a teaching preparation course.

Table 4.1 shows the percentage of respondents who received prepara-tion in each of the 21 content areas in their teaching preparation courses as graduate students (Column 1) and the mean perceived preparedness ratings for each content area (Column 2). Results in the final column in Table 4.1 represent the difference (gap) between the z-scores of the values in the first two columns. We converted the two variables to z-scores because both variables were in different metrics (percentages and a 1-to-7 scale), and z-scores are a standard, comparable metric, where the average is zero. Positive scores represent those above the mean, and negative scores represent those below. We subtracted these z-scores to create a measure of relative distance between respondents' exposure and perceived preparedness. We presented the gap values as an absolute value because of the nature of some z-scores being positive and others negative—simple subtraction would be misleading (i.e., is the value negative because participants feel less prepared than would be expected or because it was below the mean value to begin with?). Larger gap values indicate larger discrepancies between exposure and preparedness rankings.

We found considerable variation in the percentage of respondents who received preparation across the 21 content areas, ranging from 86.5% for lecture delivery to 35.1% for electronic technologies. Similarly, we found considerable differences in the mean preparedness ratings assigned to each content area. Respondents reported being most prepared to handle issues related to delivering lectures ($M = 5.94$) and least prepared to handle ethnic, minority, or gender issues ($M = 3.92$). Examining the gap scores suggests that content areas commonly covered in teaching preparation courses were not necessarily those that respondents felt well prepared to handle. At least 50% of respondents received preparation regarding ethical situations, in-class group activities, academic dishonesty, and academic policies. Nevertheless, many participants responded that they were unprepared in these areas. In contrast, respondents reported that they were better prepared for the cut-and-dried aspects of teaching, such as using audiovisual and electronic equipment, holding office hours, preparing handouts, and grading, even though they received relatively less exposure to these topics.

Table 4.2 presents a comparison of individuals who received training in an area to those who did not regarding their perceived preparedness for that area. We included participants who did not take a teaching preparation course in these analyses as part of the "did not receive training" group. For all 21 content areas, respondents who had content-specific teaching preparation training gave higher preparedness ratings compared to respondents who did not receive training in those areas. Taken as a whole, it is extremely unlikely that all 21 means would be higher (sign test $p < .000001$), thus indicating that those who received teaching training perceived themselves as more prepared.

Table 4.2   Differences in Perceived Preparedness Between Assistant Professors Who Had Content-Specific Training and Assistant Professors Who Did Not

Content Area	Trained in Area?	Mean (SD)	t-value
Delivering lectures	Yes = 32 No = 12	6.06 (1.19) 4.92 (1.08)	2.91**
Classroom management skills	Yes = 29 No = 15	5.28 (1.39) 4.33 (1.45)	2.11*
Encouraging student participation	Yes = 29 No = 15	5.34 (1.70) 4.53 (1.41)	1.59
Asking/answering questions	Yes = 27 No = 16	5.56 (0.97) 5.13 (1.31)	1.23
First day of class	Yes = 28 No = 16	5.57 (1.55) 4.44 (1.46)	2.38*
Ethical situations in teaching	Yes = 26 No = 18	5.35 (1.20) 4.11 (1.57)	2.96**
In-class group activities	Yes = 26 No = 18	5.15 (1.43) 4.17 (1.72)	2.08*
Leading group discussion	Yes = 26 No = 18	5.73 (1.00) 4.17 (1.65)	3.91***
Organization of class time	Yes = 24 No = 20	5.33 (1.49) 4.50 (1.57)	1.80
Academic honesty	Yes = 23 No = 21	4.83 (1.53) 4.52 (1.57)	0.65
Grading tests/ quizzes/papers	Yes = 23 No = 21	5.70 (1.29) 5.00 (1.18)	1.86
Teaching critical thinking skills	Yes = 21 No = 23	5.76 (1.22) 3.91 (1.50)	4.45***
College/university academic policies	Yes = 20 No = 24	4.50 (1.10) 3.33 (1.24)	3.27***
Construction of test items	Yes = 19 No = 24	5.47 (1.58) 4.54 (1.47)	2.00
Social skills for classroom teaching	Yes = 17 No = 27	5.65 (1.69) 4.37 (1.62)	2.50*
Ethnic, minority, or gender issues	Yes = 16 No = 28	4.63 (1.31) 3.57 (1.45)	2.40*

Holding office hours	Yes = 15	6.00 (1.69)	2.44*
	No = 28	4.64 (1.77)	
Preparing handouts	Yes = 15	5.47 (1.36)	2.70*
	No = 29	4.21 (1.52)	
Accommodating special needs	Yes = 15	4.73 (1.28)	2.01
	No = 29	3.86 (1.41)	
Using audiovisual equipment	Yes = 13	5.69 (1.44)	1.86
	No = 31	4.65 (1.80)	
Using electronic technologies	Yes = 13	5.31 (1.25)	1.76
	No = 31	4.29 (1.92)	

$*p < .05; **p < .01$; after Bonferroni correction, $***p < .002$.

We also examined the degree of difference in each individual area using a series of t-tests. A significant t-test indicates that the amount of difference between those who received training and those who did not is greater than would be expected by chance fluctuation. For 12 of the 21 content areas, the difference was statistically significant. However, because so many tests were conducted, some of the significant results could have been due to chance, and thus we performed an additional statistical test to correct for using multiple t-tests (Bonferroni correction). We found that only three of these areas (critical thinking, leading group discussion, and familiarity with academic policies) remained statistically significant. Thus, for these areas, having content-specific training in the teaching preparation course made a significant difference in enhancing respondents' perceived preparedness for their new teaching duties. Nonetheless, given that (a) preparedness ratings of all respondents who had received teaching training where higher than those of all respondents who had not received teaching training and (b) the Bonferroni is an extremely conservative statistic, we conclude that teaching training positively affects how prepared new assistant professors perceived themselves to be for teaching at the college and university level.

Table 4.3 presents means comparing content-specific preparedness ratings between respondents who participated in a single-term versus multiple-term teaching course (we excluded respondents who did not participate in such a course from these analyses). For 19 of 21 content areas, respondents who participated in a multiple-term teaching preparation course gave higher preparedness ratings in those areas compared to respondents who participated in a single-term teaching preparation course. Looking at the average preparedness ratings across all areas reveals that those who took multiple semesters of a teaching course ($M = 5.43$) perceived themselves to be more prepared than those who took only a single semester ($M = 4.64$; $F(1,33) = 6.07$, $p = .019$). We utilized the same analysis strategy as earlier to examine differences in individual areas. Only three of these nine areas did not overlap with the previous analysis (see Table 4.2). However, only the difference for encouraging student participation remained significant after a Bonferroni correction for multiple tests, although again, given (a) the positive direction of the data shown in Table 4.3 and (b) the ultra-conservative nature of the Bonferroni test, we conclude that graduate students who receive multiple semesters of teaching training perceive themselves to be more prepared for college and university teaching than those graduate students who received only a single semester of teaching training.

Table 4.3   Differences in Perceived Preparedness Between Assistant Professors Who Had a Single- Versus Multiple-Term TOP Course

Content Area	Single-Term Mean (SD) n = 20	Multiple-Term Mean (SD) n = 15	t-value
Delivering lectures	5.55 (1.39)	6.44 (0.89)	2.21*
Classroom management skills	4.80 (1.20)	5.81 (1.28)	2.45*
Encouraging student participation	4.55 (1.79)	6.19 (0.91)	3.32***
Asking/answering questions	5.30 (1.17)	5.75 (1.00)	1.22
First day of class	4.85 (1.90)	6.00 (0.82)	2.26*
Ethical situations in teaching	4.40 (1.50)	5.69 (1.08)	2.88**
In-class group activities	4.35 (1.60)	5.63 (1.26)	2.61*
Leading group discussion	4.90 (1.45)	6.00 (0.97)	2.61*
Organization of class time	4.90 (1.41)	5.63 (1.50)	1.49
Academic honesty	4.35 (1.46)	4.88 (1.50)	1.06
Grading tests/ quizzes/papers	5.10 (1.33)	6.00 (1.10)	2.17*

Teaching critical thinking skills	4.55 (1.88)	5.56 (1.09)	1.91
College/university academic policies	3.95 (1.43)	3.94 (1.44)	0.03
Construction of test items	4.50 (1.61)	5.75 (1.39)	2.46*
Social skills for classroom teaching	4.70 (2.00)	5.38 (1.54)	1.11
Ethnic, minority, or gender issues	3.65 (1.63)	4.25 (1.34)	1.18
Holding office hours	4.75 (2.05)	5.73 (1.71)	1.51
Preparing handouts	4.45 (1.36)	5.31 (1.70)	1.69
Accommodating special needs	4.10 (1.52)	4.44 (1.26)	0.71
Using audiovisual equipment	5.10 (1.80)	4.94 (1.73)	−0.27
Using electronic technologies	4.55 (1.76)	4.75 (1.88)	0.33

$*p < .05$; $**p < .01$; after Bonferroni correction, $***p < .002$.

We also asked participants to list the topics they would include in a teaching preparation course. Although participants reinforced the need for these types of courses to cover the 21 areas included in our survey, they suggested the following additional topics: incorporating outside resources for classroom teaching; preparing for job interviews, job talks, and job negotiations; managing teaching of multiple sections of courses; supervising and mentoring undergraduates; dealing with difficult students; choosing a textbook; academic advising; developing a teaching philosophy; establishing and maintaining academic standards; writing and managing grants; and preparing for service activities, politicking, and how to interact with faculty as a new professor.

Implications for Preparing Graduate Students to Teach

Based on these results, we offer several recommendations to faculty who supervise and train graduate students in college teaching and to graduate students who seek academic careers. First, because a course on teaching benefits graduate students who become assistant professors in terms of perceived preparedness, all graduate programs involved in training graduate students for the academy should incorporate a teaching course in that training. Second, because new faculty reported being the least prepared in issues related to social and cultural aspects of teaching, teaching courses should cover these dimensions of teaching in addition to covering teaching techniques. Davis (2009), Goss Lucas and Bernstein (2005), and Svinicki and McKeachie (2011) offer excellent suggestions along these lines. Third, to ensure that the teaching course remains current and effective at preparing new faculty for teaching, teachers of the course should occasionally survey graduates of their programs to learn what pressing problems confront new faculty and then incorporate these issues into future offerings of the course. Finally, considerations should be made for preparing graduate students to deal with professorial duties that exist outside the classroom, such as grant writing and supervision duties.

Conclusions

The benefits of preparing graduate students and new faculty to teach well are numerous. Obviously, new teachers benefit by learning how to (a) create a supportive learning environment, (b) design and implement effective lesson plans and assessment activities, and (c) help students become more successful learners. We speculate that an important and tangible benefit for new faculty is that receiving training for teaching in graduate school may reduce the time needed to prepare for teaching, thereby leaving more time to establish a productive research program at the outset of one's academic career, reinforcing Boice's (2000) argument on this issue. For the college or university, the benefits are equally obvious: Undergraduates are likely to benefit educationally from teachers who are well prepared to be in the classroom, a benefit that could translate into better retention of students. Well-prepared GTAs and new teachers will not only help students learn more, but also help them *enjoy* the process of learning more, which may set them on a path toward lifelong learning.

References

Bernstein, D. A., & Goss Lucas, S. G. (2004). Tips for effective teaching. In J. M. Darley, M. P. Zanna, & H. L. Roediger III (Eds.), *The compleat academic: A career guide* (2nd ed., pp. 79–115). Washington, DC: American Psychological Association.

Boice, R. (2000). *Advice for new faculty members: Nihil nimus*. Needham Heights, MA: Allyn & Bacon.

Buskist, W., Tears, R., Davis, S. F., & Rodrigue, K. M. (2002). The teaching of psychology course: Prevalence and content. *Teaching of Psychology, 29,* 140–142.

Davis, B. G. (2009). *Tools for teaching* (2nd ed.). San Francisco: Jossey-Bass.

Golde, C. M., & Dore, T. M. (2001). *At cross purposes: What the experiences of today's doctoral students reveal about doctoral education.* Retrieved from http://www.ssc.wisc.edu/~oliver/sociology/PhDEducationreport.pdf

Goss Lucas, S., & Bernstein, D. A. (2005). *Teaching psychology: A step by step guide.* Mahwah, NJ: Lawrence Erlbaum.

Howard, C., Buskist, W., & Stowell, J. (2007). *The STP guide to graduate student training in the teaching of psychology, 2007.* Retrieved from http://teachpsych.org/resources/e-books/gst2007/gst07.php

Prentice-Dunn, S. (2006). Supervision of new instructors: Promoting a rewarding first experience in teaching. *Teaching of Psychology, 33,* 45–47.

Svinicki, M., & McKeachie, W. J. (2011). *McKeachie's teaching tips: Strategies, research, and theory for college and university teachers* (13th ed.). Belmont, CA: Wadsworth.

Wimer, D. J., Prieto, L. R., & Meyers, S. A. (2004). To train or not to train, that is the question. In W. Buskist, B. Beins, & V. Hevern (Eds.), *Preparing the new psychology professoriate: Helping graduate students become competent teachers.* Retrieved from http://teachpsych.org/resources/e-books/pnpp/index_pnpp.php

Chapter 5

Teaching in the Context of Professional Development and Work–Private Life Balance ❖

Steven Prentice-Dunn

New graduate student:	It is way harder than undergrad, but if I shift all my research, coursework, and TA duties to Monday to Friday 10 to 5, I still have plenty of time for other life activities! I can do this!
Advanced graduate student:	It is not easy, but if I work hard on research, teaching, and writing my dissertation, I can still take one day off per week for other life activities. Unless no writing gets done . . . stupid dissertation!
Assistant professor:	Balance-schmalance, I'll worry about balance later. If I work really hard on my research, teaching, advising, writing, and service activities every day, 7 days a week, I can still get 5 to 6 hours of sleep a night! (Quinn, 2010, p. 15)

Author's Note: I would like to thank the following individuals who provided input on the recommendations contained in the chapter: Stanley Brodsky, Carl Clements, Lindsey Jacobs, Hannah Prentice-Dunn, and Alan Kinlaw.

Graduate students and new faculty members will knowingly chuckle at Quinn's (2010) exaggerated description of our professional experiences. If we have not personally lived through prolonged periods of such frantic activity, we know many colleagues who have. Tales of constant busyness are a strong and widespread source of camaraderie; yet we also know at least a few individuals who are productive in such environments and even maintain a rich personal life.

Juggling the multiple roles of a graduate student or new professor has always been challenging and, by all indications, the expectations are rising. With state legislatures and private donors providing lower levels of funding for higher education, universities have turned to increased enrollment to make up the difference. One result has been larger classes that bring the challenge of maintaining interactive teaching while also dealing with a greater number of student management issues (e.g., illness, disability accommodations, problematic conduct). Another result has been larger teaching loads and spending more time documenting activities through learning goals and outcomes assessment.

In disciplines whose scholarship is driven by external funding, new professors and graduate students are being asked to write grant proposals as never before. In addition, the push for universities to be more fully integrated into the surrounding towns and cities has produced a greater emphasis on service learning in classes and expectations for community service among graduate students and faculty.

Although a job in an academic setting has a number of positive features, including variety, flexibility, and considerable freedom (Prentice-Dunn, 2006b), the number and magnitude of time demands appear to be at an all-time high. This situation occurs at a time when, in unprecedented numbers, graduate students and new professors are seeking employment that still preserves personal and family time. In a recent survey of over 8,000 doctoral students, Mason, Goulden, and Frasch (2009) found that 84% of women and 74% of men were concerned about the family-friendliness of their career choice. In that regard, tenure-track positions at research-intensive universities were seen as appreciably less family friendly than were teaching-intensive colleges, policy or managerial careers, and research careers outside academia. The concerns were of sufficient magnitude that a substantial proportion of students (especially in the sciences) were redirecting their career goals once in graduate school.

To increase the retention of promising scholars, some universities have begun to address workload issues through innovative practices such as lengthening the tenure clock and placing a greater emphasis on research quality rather than quantity. As such efforts take hold, it remains important for graduate students and new faculty members to take individual actions to make their work efficient, enjoyable, and enriching. The goal of this chapter is to provide guidelines to help students and professors stay productive while recognizing the importance of issues outside the workplace.

Working Smart

Graduate students have substantial demands on their time. However, these responsibilities are usually divided into compartments (e.g., assistantship, one's own courses). In comparison, new faculty members have much less structure imposed from without (Huss, 2006; McClain, 2003). Whereas students receive frequent feedback through evaluations and grades, new professors must rely on self-assessment to supplement the infrequent formal feedback that they receive. Nonetheless, the considerable overlap in duties means that general advice for one group is likely to apply to the other. Royse (2001) calls such recommendations "working smart."

Permission to Be Less Than Perfect

Graduate programs are full of intelligent students with a strong desire to perform well. However, such high achievement motivation often becomes stressful when students confront the multiple demands of graduate school. Clearly, understanding that one cannot maintain impossibly high standards for every new task or responsibility is crucial. In fact, carefully targeting some work components for excellent performance and others for good (or even adequate) performance can be liberating, reducing one's overall stress level so that all tasks are done better than they otherwise would be.

Find Out What Is Valued

Royse (2001) suggested that faculty ask questions of those in a position to be helpful to them. For graduate students, that may mean going beyond departmental orientation programs to befriending successful advanced students about beneficial courses, training experiences, and tips on applying for positions. New faculty members will benefit from asking about available formal and informal mentoring programs as well as operational expectations for tenure and promotion. Once the criteria for success are known, they must become the lens through which one sees virtually all work activities.

Time Management

Zinn (2004) noted that it is all too easy to stay busy with unimportant activities. Thus, knowing how to spend one's day is crucial to meeting one's professional goals. Logging the actual time spent on various tasks over a few weeks is an effective way to identify "time robbers" (Royse, 2001) that can be curtailed to address career goals more directly (Myers, 2005).

Breaking large-scale tasks into smaller, more manageable units can provide a needed sense of accomplishment and movement toward completing goals. Maintaining a task list is a useful way of keeping up with such activities and serves to de-clutter one's mind. Periodically reordering the list to fit emerging priorities keeps it useful (McClain, 2003).

Immediate demands on our daily time tend to get addressed first. Thus, important tasks for career advancement such as writing and conducting research are often delayed (McClain, 2003). To overcome this tendency, proactively schedule the time to devote to such activities. Schedule blocks of time away from daily distractions to work on your writing projects; find a different location if your office is not conducive to concentrated work. One of my colleagues, a prolific writer, notes that starting a writing session with a defined ending time results in more a more focused effort (S. Brodsky, personal communication, September 9, 2010).

Teaching

Having taught a course on college teaching for the past two decades, I have had the opportunity to observe many students who thrived first in graduate school and then as assistant professors. They are skilled, enthusiastic presenters who build a supportive environment in the classroom (Polick, Cullen, & Buskist, 2010; Prentice-Dunn, 2006a). As graduate students, they are eager to master a variety of instructional methods such as participatory lectures, active learning, multimedia, and in-class writing. Through considerable effort, they develop a large repertoire of techniques for effective teaching. When they become faculty members, they are flexible enough to adjust how they teach to free time to devote to additional aspects of being a professor, such as teaching multiple courses, advising, service, mentoring, and establishing a program of scholarship.

"Canny" Preparation

I am not advocating mediocre teaching. However, I am suggesting what McClain (2003) called "canny" preparation. Instead of using an hour to locate that perfect alternative video clip or develop another demonstration, it is wise periodically to forgo that level of preparation to carve out time for another aspect of one's job (Hackney, 2004). When a batch of papers is to be submitted, plan a guest speaker or another low-preparation topic for the following class session (McClain, 2003). During a semester in which several writing projects are due, consider teaching multiple sections of the same course to save on prep time.

Bunching Courses

Some instructors, me included, find that teaching is both rewarding and draining. It takes time for us to gear up for the classroom and then wind down from it. I gradually recognized that on such days, I got little else accomplished. Taking Myers's (2005) advice, I now group my courses so that I have days that are primarily devoted to teaching and others that are devoted to writing and service. My teaching days include classroom instruction, office hours, grading assignments, class preparation, and the like. With such an arrangement, my teaching days are more enjoyable and my other days are more productive.

Staying Motivated

To remain a good instructor, one must stay energized. One of the best ways to remain excited and also learn new techniques is to be around others who share an interest in teaching. Attending regional and national teaching conferences is an ideal way to do that (Bernstein, 2005). I always return from such meetings armed with new methods to try, new colleagues to serve as resources, and a rekindled enthusiasm about what I am doing.

In addition to attending conferences that energize one's teaching, Bernstein (2005) suggested that it is okay to be a bit selfish. In other words, try to keep teaching enjoyable not just for your students, but also for yourself. For example, using a variety of approaches in class to communicate course content often leads not only to better learning outcomes, but also to more satisfaction. Such variety will help sustain you over the long run.

Research

Graduate students must produce a dissertation to obtain a degree and often considerably more scholarship to be hired as a faculty member. Research expectations for new professors will of course vary according to the amount of teaching one must do; however, few contemporary positions come without some research expectations for career advancement. Thus, students and faculty alike need to find ways to produce scholarly works.

Team Up

Perhaps the most effective way to produce a great deal of research is to collaborate with others. I stumbled upon this technique by accident in graduate school when colleagues and I met regularly to discuss common interests. After brainstorming multiple studies that we would like to conduct, we divided them among ourselves, with each person taking the lead role on one or two projects while maintaining a secondary role on additional studies. The result was many more publications (some first-authored) than any of us could have produced working solo. Of course, one's collaborators can be at other institutions as well. Connections made at conferences can increase the number of locations where data can be collected simultaneously.

Dual Goals

Graduate students should take advantage of the assignments in the courses that they are taking. For example, for a required literature review, select a topic that has received insufficient attention, thereby making the paper publishable with little additional work when the course is over. Courses may involve a project such as developing an educational or psychological measure; careful choice of the topic may lead to a publication. Some courses taught by graduate students and new professors may be appropriate for a group or individual research project that can lead to a publication coauthored by the student(s) and instructor. Finally, aspects of innovative teaching (e.g., multimedia, in-class exercises, student journals) may provide the opportunity to collect data on effectiveness that can then be submitted to a teaching-related journal in one's discipline.

Readily Accessible Data

Huss (2006) advised students to design their theses and dissertations with multiple publications as a desired goal. For example, a literature review or proposed theory may be published as a paper separate from an empirical study on the same topic. In addition, collecting data for two studies simultaneously is often an efficient use of the researcher's time and target population. Finally, students and faculty alike should also stay alert to the availability of large data sets collected by others. Investigators and agencies that control such resources often seek assistance and welcome an offer to take the lead role in studying a portion of the data set.

Service

Service entails a variety of possible domains, including department and institution, profession, and community. Graduate students rarely receive preparation in this area and are often surprised as new professors when they encounter appreciable service time demands. To contribute is expected and laudable; however, one must keep in mind that service activities are rarely regarded as highly as teaching and scholarship. Therefore, one must choose wisely and learn how to politely say "no." In deciding whether to volunteer, Royse (2001) suggested considering (a) the amount of your time a committee will need, (b) the relative risk to you if the topic is politically charged, (c) the visibility it will give you, and (d) whether you can make use of your expertise. In general, one should take on service activities slowly so that one can do them well (and even enjoy them).

Balance in Work and Personal Life

Popular lore suggests that having a successful career and a gratifying personal life are often, even usually, incompatible. Yet growing evidence suggests that each aspect can exert a positive influence on the other (Smith, 2002). For example, men who have a satisfying life at home experience less stress when problems arise at work (Barnett & Hyde, 2001). Being involved in child care is associated with a husband's psychological well-being and a wife's higher rating of their relationship. Based on such evidence, Grzywacz and Marks (2000) suggested that work and private life are more appropriately regarded as domains that can potentially affect each other in positive ways rather than automatically being in conflict.

Making Personal Care "Your Job"

Although most graduate students and new professors enjoy many aspects of their careers, the number and nature of new work requirements can be daunting. In the press of daily tasks, the first things to be delayed are exercise, personal reflection, and time with friends and family. However, there is now abundant evidence that neglecting such activities leads not only to reduced immune system functioning but to decreased work quality. To avoid these negative impacts, exercise and other personal activities must become as high a priority as one's career. Although this reorientation is substantial and difficult for almost all of us, it pays off in terms of better physical and psychological health and lower likelihood of career burnout in the long run. This action remains primarily an individual decision, although it is becoming increasingly easier to find training programs and work settings that value such balance.

Practical Steps

Scheduling exercise and other forms of "down time" is crucial to this reorientation. For example, exercising or meditating prior to going to the office is a practical method to ensure that such activity gets done instead of waiting until later in the day when unforeseen events can derail one's plans. Following the "working smart" recommendations described earlier opens spots in one's week for such important events. They also enable one to plan for breaks such as hobbies or weekend travel with reduced guilt and without being swamped with work chores upon return.

Developing at least a few friendships outside of the work setting can give us time to appreciate our careers as well as learn new perspectives (Zinn, 2004). Setting reasonable boundaries between personal time and work is also important, but difficult to follow in the age of instant communication technology. For example, some of the most productive and happiest graduate students and faculty colleagues I know will not check e-mail or text messages after a certain time each day and on an entire day on most weekends.

Conclusions

The beginning of a career is a time of great excitement and some anxiety. Regardless of the setting or type of position, it takes a great deal of effort to establish oneself as a graduate student or faculty member. However, in each of the teaching, scholarship, and service domains, there are several strategies available that will enable you to work more efficiently. Using such techniques within the context of a rich personal life can enable you to meet professional goals as you enjoy what you do.

References

Barnett, R. C., & Hyde, J. S. (2001). Women, men, work, and family: An expansionist theory. *American Psychologist, 56,* 781–796.

Bernstein, D. A. (2005). Was it good for you, too? Keeping teaching exciting for us and for them. In B. Perlman, L. L. McCann, & W. Buskist (Eds.), *Voices of experience: Memorable talks from the National Institute on the Teaching of Psychology* (pp. 111–118). Washington, DC: American Psychological Society.

Grzywacz, J. G., & Marks, N. F. (2000). Reconceptualizing the work-family interface: An ecological perspective on the correlates of positive and negative spillover between work and family. *Journal of Occupational Health Psychology, 5*, 111–126.

Hackney, A. (2004). Making the transition from graduate student to assistant professor. In W. Buskist, B. C. Beins, & V. W. Hevern (Eds.), *Preparing the new psychology professoriate: Helping graduate students become competent teachers* (pp. 144–147). Syracuse, NY: Society for the Teaching of Psychology. Retrieved from http://www.teachpsych.org/resources/e-books/pnpp/index_pnpp.php

Huss, M. T. (2006). Professional development through the integration of teaching, scholarship, and service: If it's not fun, I'm not doing it. In W. Buskist & S. F. Davis (Eds.), *Handbook of the teaching of psychology* (pp. 324–327). Malden, MA: Blackwell.

Mason, M. A., Goulden, M., & Frasch, K. (2009, January–February). Why graduate students reject the fast track. *Academe Online*. Retrieved from http://www.aaup.org/AAUP/pubsres/academe/2009/JF/Feat/maso.ht

McClain, L. T. (2003, December 16). Lessons in time management. *Chronicle of Higher Education*. Retrieved from http://chronicle.com/article/Lessons-in-Time-Management/45291/

Myers, D. G. (2005). Professing psychology with a passion: Lessons I have learned. In B. Perlman, L. L. McCann, & W. Buskist (Eds.), *Voices of experience: Memorable talks from the National Institute on the Teaching of Psychology* (pp. 155–163). Washington, DC: American Psychological Society.

Polick, A. S., Cullen, K. L., & Buskist, W. (2010, September). How teaching makes a difference in students' lives. *APS Observer, 23*, 31–33.

Prentice-Dunn, S. (2006a). Supervision of new instructors: Promoting a rewarding first experience in teaching. *Teaching of Psychology, 33*, 45–47.

Prentice-Dunn, S. (2006b). Variety and flexibility as a faculty member. In G. D. Oster (Ed.), *Life as a psychologist* (pp. 61–62). Westport, CT: Praeger.

Quinn, D. M. (2010). Stages of work-life balance. *Dialogue, 25*, 15.

Royse, D. (2001). *Teaching tips for college and university instructors: A practical guide*. Boston, MA: Allyn & Bacon.

Smith, D. (2002). Making work your family's ally. *Monitor on Psychology, 33*, 58.

Zinn, T. E. (2004). Moving on: Making the transition from graduate student to faculty member. In W. Buskist, B. C. Beins, & V. W. Hevern (Eds.), *Preparing the new psychology professoriate: Helping graduate students become competent teachers* (pp. 157–161). Syracuse, NY: Society for the Teaching of Psychology. Retrieved from http://www.teachpsych.org/resources/e-books/pnpp/index_pnpp.php

Chapter 6

The Science of Learning and Its Applications

❖

Mark A. McDaniel and Cynthia Wooldridge

In this chapter, we appeal to basic findings in cognitive psychology and theoretical advances in learning sciences to provide guidelines for organizing instruction to improve student learning. Our development of the foundations will not be extensive (see also McDaniel & Callender, 2008; Sawyer, 2006). Our objective is to highlight instructional techniques that are grounded in basic principles and to support these techniques with brief summaries of the pertinent studies conducted with authentic educational materials and in authentic educational contexts (e.g., classrooms). We have chosen to focus on techniques that are either not currently widespread in standard practice or are generally accepted but perhaps not instantiated optimally.

Test-Enhanced Learning

We begin with a cornerstone of educational practice, *testing*, that is significantly underappreciated as an effective learning tool, and is certainly underutilized in higher education as a technique to promote learning. Testing is typically used by educators to evaluate students and assign grades. Yet testing is not neutral; it also modifies learning. Accordingly, we suggest that low- or no-stakes quizzing (i.e., retrieval of target content) can be a key component for assisting students in learning target content.

Quizzing (with feedback) mobilizes at least three direct benefits for learning. First, quizzing promotes active retrieval of information from memory. A body of basic experimental evidence has established that active retrieval produces a powerful positive effect on later retention (Roediger & Karpicke, 2006) and transfer (Butler, 2010; McDaniel, Howard, & Einstein, 2009). Second, feedback that is provided after quizzing may be especially potent for stimulating learning. Memory research suggests that failing to answer a test question can potentiate learning for the correct answer when it is later provided (Kornell, Hays, & Bjork, 2009). When students answer a question incorrectly but with high confidence, the test-potentiated learning is especially great (Butterfield & Metcalfe, 2001). Experiments conducted with educationally relevant material consistently confirm that feedback (providing the correct answer) produces significant learning gains (Butler & Roediger, 2008). A third key outcome of quizzing is improvement in metacognition. Basic research suggests that learners generally cannot judge how well they will remember previously studied information (Dunlosky & Nelson, 1994). These poor metacognitive judgments in turn negatively affect the efficacy of student-directed study activities. Theoretically, then, interventions that improve metacognition should result in more effective student-directed studying. Quizzing also has a number of positive indirect effects. These include encouraging students to keep up with material (Leeming, 2002), possibly lowering test anxiety, and alerting students to adopt self-quizzing as a learning tool (Karpicke, 2009).

Evidence

Studies conducted in college courses (Daniel & Broida, 2004; Lyle & Crawford, 2011) and medical schools (Larsen, Butler, & Roediger, 2009) have demonstrated that low- or no-stakes quizzing improves performance on subsequent class examinations. One potential criticism of relying on quizzing to assist learning is that it is only useful for learning "inert" facts that will not transfer to other uses. Recent laboratory evidence disfavors this hypothesis. Active processing via retrieval creates knowledge that can also be retrieved in other contexts (see, e.g., Butler, 2010; McDaniel et al., 2009). However, the evidence just cited relied on initial tests (quizzes) that required recall; in contrast, most of the published experiments in authentic classrooms have relied on multiple-choice quizzes, which tend to require recognition rather than recall processes.

In the classroom context, initial findings with multiple-choice quizzes are mixed, with one experimental study finding that multiple-choice quizzing limited the potency of the quizzing benefits (McDaniel et al., 2009).

In contrast, in a web-based college brain and behavior course, taking a no-stakes online multiple-choice quiz repeatedly (four times) produced benefits on exam questions that were related (not identical) to quizzed content, benefits that were as robust as those produced by repeated short-answer quizzing (McDaniel, Wildman, & Anderson, 2010). Also, in a college educational psychology course, multiple-choice quiz questions followed by class discussion about the reasoning supporting the answers significantly improved course exam performances (which had both similar and dissimilar questions to those given on the quiz) relative to no quizzing or to a condition in which the multiple-choice quizzes were not accompanied by class discussion (Mayer et al., 2009). On balance, the available experimental evidence suggests that even multiple-choice quizzing, if administered with appropriate parameters (e.g., perhaps repetition of quizzes, discussion of quiz answers) can stimulate learning that leads to flexible use of target material.

Spacing

In education, target information may often be presented several times. Also, homework and workbooks often mass practice on one particular kind of item, instead of spacing. To the extent that repeated presentation of material can be spaced rather than massed, much laboratory work indicates that learning should be more efficient and retention should be improved with spaced presentation (Cepeda, Pashler, Vul, Wixted, & Rohrer, 2006). The idea is that repetition of target content and practice of cognitive skills is more effective when repetition is spaced rather than massed. Unfortunately, in college instruction, key concepts covered in one massed lesson are often not considered again during the course. Spacing the coverage of these key concepts throughout the course would be expected to significantly improve retention of course material. Several studies conducted in college classrooms support the idea that spacing produces better retention of educational content than massed repetition (Rohrer & Taylor, 2006).

Desirable Difficulties

A common assumption is that instruction that enhances performance during *learning* also produces superior long-term retention and transfer. However, performance during learning can be a poor indicator of whether that knowledge or skill will be accessible (or available) in the future (Bjork, 1994).

The counterintuitive idea that has emerged from basic memory and skill learning literatures is that introducing difficulties and challenges during learning has desirable outcomes, such as promoting retention and transfer of learned material and more accurate metacognition regarding the degree of learning (Bjork, 1994; McDaniel & Butler, in press). These challenges might include interleaving of content rather than blocking content (e.g., Kornell & Bjork, 2008), spacing of content rather than massing it, and generation of content rather than reception of content (e.g., McDaniel, Waddill, & Einstein, 1988).

Evidence

There is a body of basic research supporting the idea that introducing difficulties during learning can increase long-term retention and transfer (Bjork, 1994; McDaniel & Butler, in press). Additionally, difficulties that create disfluency (e.g., presenting target materials in a font that is difficult to read) have been shown to prompt individuals to engage more controlled problem-solving strategies and to think more abstractly (Alter & Oppenheimer, 2008). For instance, when people were presented with math problems for which a reflexive answer is incorrect, presentation in disfluent type fonts produced more correct answers (Alter, Oppenheimer, Epley, & Eyre, 2007). However, only a handful of research-based efforts have been directed at developing and evaluating educationally relevant desirable difficulties.

Rohrer and Taylor (2007) found that interleaving instruction and subsequent practice on different types of mathematics problems (computing volumes of different solids) produced better application (retention) of the solution procedures to new problems than did blocking the problems, even though initial performance on the practice problems was superior when the practice was blocked relative to interleaving (see Kornell & Bjork, 2008, for parallel effects with learning about artists' painting styles). Note that the standard practice for arranging practice problems in textbooks is to block practice problems by topic. More desirable from the perspective of promoting retention would be to mix and distribute practice problems from different procedures.

Regarding authentic classroom contexts, in an experiment using passages from an introductory psychology text, key terminology was remembered better when college students were required to generate the terms in the context of the assigned reading (from word fragments) relative to when students read the terms (DeWinstanley & Bjork, 2004). Once students had experienced better memory performance after generating than reading, on subsequent paragraphs these students remembered read terms as well as they remembered generated terms. This result may suggest that students acquire better strategies for encoding material once they have been forced to generate.

In science classes, students can be required to generate predicted outcomes prior to classroom demonstrations, rather than being told about the expected result. In the domain of physics, research has established that demonstrations typically do not enhance learning (Crouch, Fagen, Callan, & Mazur, 2004). To investigate the benefits of generating predictions, Crouch et al. conducted an experiment in a college physics class that contrasted end-of-semester exam performances relating to demonstrations for which students generated predictions relative to exam performances after standard demonstrations (no predictions were required). Confirming previous findings, relative to a no-demonstration condition, observation of the demonstration promoted no significant improvement in students' ability to explain the outcome of related (to the demonstration) physical situations on a test at the end of the semester. When students were required to generate predictions prior to the demonstrations, their exam performances improved significantly. Interestingly, a third condition in which students were required to discuss and evaluate the generated predictions after the demonstrations did not produce significant increases in exam performances relative to the generate-only condition. This pattern suggests that generation of predictions may be sufficient to stimulate students to ponder and evaluate the demonstration with regard to the targeted conceptual information.

Several prominent challenges exist for effectively implementing desirable difficulties in the classroom. One challenge is to identify presentation formats or tasks that are tractable and acceptable in school settings, but that nevertheless create some difficulty for the student in initial processing or learning of the target material. Another challenge is that the desirability of any particular difficulty will depend on a number of factors that vary in the educational environment (see McDaniel & Butler, in press). For instance, difficulty will not be desirable when the summative assessments are not sensitive to the processing stimulated by difficulty (Thomas & McDaniel, 2007) or when the learners' cognitive skills (and prior knowledge) are overly challenged by the difficulty (McDaniel, Hines, & Guynn, 2002). Accordingly, successful implementation of desirable difficulties may depend in part on instructors' sensitivities to whether students' skills are sufficient to accommodate difficulties that are introduced and whether the summative assessments reflect the learning that is enhanced by a particular difficulty.

Interleave Example Solutions and Problem-Solving Exercises

Typically, in mathematics and science courses, instructors present a slew of example problems, and then students are required to solve a set of related problems. Yet, experimental evidence shows that student learning is markedly enhanced when worked example solutions are alternated with problems that the student is asked to solve. For example, Sweller and Cooper (1985) found that eighth- and ninth-grade students who solved eight algebra problems (as students might have to do in a homework assignment) took more time to complete the problems and performed worse on a post-test than students who were given pairs of a solution example followed by a problem. Note that this interleaved condition required less generation of solutions or active solving of solutions than did the condition in which students solved eight problems, but the worked example–problem pairing nevertheless led to superior performance (see also Cooper & Sweller, 1987; Renkl, 2002).

The implication of this research is that the standard practice of a teacher presenting a set of solved problems followed by homework assignments on a set of problems could be improved. Instead, teachers might present one worked example and then have students (either in small groups or as individuals) solve a problem on their own. Then the teacher could orient the class to another worked example and give the students a second problem to solve.

Forge Understanding

Understanding is the foundation for assimilating new information, remembering that information, and applying it. Next, we mention several techniques that evidence shows will assist in stimulating greater understanding.

Ask Deep-Level Questions

Encouraging students to engage in self-explanation, often by posing "why" questions, promotes deep understanding (see, e.g., McDaniel & Donnelly, 1996). Once students have acquired basic knowledge about a topic of study, deeper explanations and understanding of the key concepts can be facilitated by questions that prompt deep explanations of the target concepts. These questions often involve asking "what if" and "how does X compare to Y"; they are intended to prompt "deep" explanations that relate causes and consequences, motivation of people (e.g., involved in historical events), and scientific evidence for particular theories. The questions and explanations can occur in the context of classroom instruction, discussion, and independent study.

Use Graphics With Verbal Descriptions

Augmenting text and verbal descriptions with relevant graphical presentations that illustrate key processes and concepts facilitates student understanding. For instance, scientific processes and how things work (such as disk brakes, volcanic eruptions, bicycle pumps) can be visually illustrated through diagrams and schematics. Experimental studies demonstrate that such schematics improve learning, including problem solving and application of target constructs (Mayer, 2009). These visual representations may help students construct a mental model that effectively supports deep understanding of the content. It is worth noting that the available evidence suggests that pictures or series of pictures can be as effective in promoting learning as animated narratives.

Abstract and Concrete Representations of Concepts

In introducing students to a concept, teachers can focus on concrete realizations of the concept or can render a more abstract representation of the concept. Researchers suggest limitations of relying exclusively on either approach. Learning with concrete objects facilitates initial understanding but does not necessarily foster transfer to related contexts (Resnick & Omanson, 1987), whereas introducing the concept at an abstract level may slow students' mastery, though application to novel contexts may be facilitated. Current approaches suggest incorporating both concrete and abstract representations of target concepts during instruction. One critical feature of this approach is that teachers guide students toward the relevant and shared components of the concrete and abstract representations. Another particular approach is that of "concreteness fading," wherein initial learning is supported with a concrete representation that is gradually replaced with a more abstract representation.

Analogy

A key component of understanding is activating and focusing relevant prior knowledge on new material. Theorists have suggested that use of analogy to activate familiar concepts (prior knowledge) in the service of understanding new concepts may facilitate classroom learning (e.g., Halpern, 1987). For instance, if students are taught that "memory operates like a library," then the aspects of a library that are familiar to students can be activated to understand that organization of memory is essential for efficiency of memory, and that locating information in memory may be a process of restricting search to a general topic (e.g., a floor within a library) and then individuating particular information within that topic (a particular book or set of books on that floor). Using educationally relevant content, laboratory experiments with college students have shown benefits of analogy for learning astrophysics concepts, especially when summative tests focus on inference-level responses (Donnelly & McDaniel, 1993).

Appropriate Summative Testing

The benefits of the instructional techniques outlined in the previous paragraphs (or for that matter any instructional technique) will hinge in part on the nature of the exams that are constructed to evaluate students' mastery of the material. In the basic memory literature, a well-established principle is that particular encoding (study) activities effectively enhance memory performance to the extent that the criterial task depends on the information/processing engaged during encoding (e.g., McDaniel, Friedman, & Bourne, 1978). For instance, a generation task that focuses the learner on interrelations among the target concepts in a text will produce benefits on a test of relational information but not on a test of details (relative to a no-generation control); by contrast, a generation task that focuses the learner on the details in a text will benefit the detail test but not the relational test (Thomas & McDaniel, 2007).

The implications for educational practice are straightforward: Exams need to be constructed to reflect the kind of skill and knowledge that are targeted in the instructional goals and activities. In practice, however, this transfer-appropriate principle is often not appreciated. Teachers may design study activities that engage their students in analysis and synthesis of the core materials but then unwittingly undermine the effectiveness of these activities by giving exams that focus on individual details (see McDaniel, 2007, for an authentic example). In a related vein, in science and math domains, in many cases exams focus on students recording correct answers (i.e., a student's score depends on how many correct answers were provided). More effective for evaluating understanding and transfer of knowledge is to also focus on the thinking processes and approach that students use in arriving at their answers. The idea is to have students "show their work" (externalize thinking processes) and to give them feedback on the validity of the approach, not just on their final answer.

Another important consideration in effective use of exams is whether to include cumulative testing. Theoretically, cumulative testing is beneficial because it produces spacing of the material and it provides additional opportunities for active retrieval of target material (relative to giving a single unit exam on target content), both of which should contribute to long-term retention of key material. Some researchers have noted that when students are only given unit exams, students often comment after an exam that they no longer have to worry about that material. In some sense, the material may be treated like that in laboratory experiments in which subjects are directed to forget some studied items, which results in poorer retention for those items (e.g., Szpunar, McDermott, & Roediger, 2007).

Conclusions

Research in psychology and education has pointed to many different means of designing courses to maximize student learning. There is not sufficient evidence at this time to claim that a particular instructional technique is "best," and so the challenge is for instructors to choose from among these many techniques. Some of the earlier recommendations require small changes to existing courses. Some researchers have added small changes such as generating predictions prior to demonstrations (Crouch et al., 2004) or various hands-on activities (Cobern et al., 2010) and found that such modest changes may be sufficient to significantly increase learning and transfer. Accordingly, we believe that it may be possible for instructors to foster significant gains in student learning without dramatic changes in their current teaching methods. Incorporating the relatively modest kinds of changes like those suggested in this chapter may be sufficient to stimulate and enhance student learning.

References

Alter, A. L., & Oppenheimer, D. M. (2008). Effects of fluency on psychological distance and mental construal (or why New York is a large city, but New York is a civilized jungle). *Psychological Science, 19*, 161–167.

Alter, A. L., Oppenheimer, D. M., Epley, N., & Eyre, R. N. (2007). Overcoming intuition: Metacognitive difficulty activates analytic reasoning. *Journal of Experimental Psychology: General, 136*, 569–576.

Bjork, R. A. (1994). Memory and metamemory considerations in the training of human beings. In J. Metcalfe & A. Shimamura (Eds.), *Metacognition: Knowing about knowing* (pp. 185–205). Cambridge, MA: MIT Press.

Butler, A. C. (2010). Repeated testing produces improved transfer of learning relative to repeated studying. *Journal of Experimental Psychology: Learning, Memory, and Cognition, 36*, 1118–1133.

Butler, A. C., & Roediger, H. L. (2008). Feedback enhances the positive effects and reduces the negative effects of multiple-choice testing. *Memory & Cognition, 36*, 604–616.

Butterfield, B., & Metcalfe, J. (2001). Errors made with high confidence are hypercorrected. *Journal of Experimental Psychology: Learning, Memory, and Cognition, 27*, 1491–1494.

Cepeda, N. J., Pashler, H., Vul, E., Wixted, J. T., & Rohrer, D. (2006). Distributed practice in verbal recall tasks: A review and quantitative synthesis. *Psychological Bulletin, 132*, 354–380.

Cobern, W. W., Schuster, D., Adams, B., Applegate, B., Skjold, B., Undreiu, A., et al. (2010). Experimental comparison of inquiry and direct instruction in science. *Research in Science & Technological Education, 28*(1), 81–96.

Cooper, G., & Sweller, J. (1987). The effects of schema acquisition and rule automation on mathematical problem-solving transfer. *Journal of Educational Psychology, 79*, 347–362.

Crouch, C. H., Fagen, A. P., Callan, J. P., & Mazur, E. (2004). Classroom demonstrations: Learning tools or entertainment? *American Journal of Physics, 72*, 835–838.

Daniel, D. B., & Broida, J. (2004). Using web-based quizzing to improve exam performance: Lessons learned. *Teaching of Psychology, 31*, 207–208.

DeWinstanley, P. A., & Bjork, R. (2004). Processing strategies and the generation effect: Implications for making a better reader. *Memory and Cognition, 32*, 945–955.

Donnelly, C. M., & McDaniel, M. A. (1993). Use of analogy in learning scientific concepts. *Journal of Experimental Psychology: Learning, Memory, and Cognition, 19*, 975–987.

Dunlosky, J., & Nelson, T. O. (1994). Does the sensitivity of judgments of learning (JOLs) to the effects of various study activities depend on when the JOLs occur? *Journal of Memory and Language, 33*, 545–565.

Halpern, D. F. (1987). Analogies as a critical thinking skill. In D. E. Berger, K. Bezdek, & W. P. Banks (Eds.), *Applications of cognitive psychology: Problem solving, education, and computing* (pp. 75–86). Hillsdale, NJ: Lawrence Erlbaum.

Karpicke, J. D. (2009). Metacognitive control and strategy selection: Deciding to practice retrieval during learning. *Journal of Experimental Psychology: General, 138*, 469–486.

Kornell, N., & Bjork, R. A. (2008). Learning concepts and categories: Is spacing the "enemy of induction"? *Psychological Science, 19*, 585–592.

Kornell, N., Hays, M. J., & Bjork, R. A. (2009). Unsuccessful retrieval attempts enhance subsequent learning. *Journal of Experimental Psychology: Learning, Memory, and Cognition, 35*, 989–998.

Larsen, D. P., Butler, A. C., & Roediger, H. L. (2009). Repeated testing improves long-term retention relative to repeated study: A randomized controlled trial. *Medical Education, 43*, 1174–1181.

Leeming, F. C. (2002). The exam-a-day procedure improves performance in psychology classes. *Teaching of Psychology, 29,* 210–212.

Lyle, K. B., & Crawford, N. A. (2011). Retrieving essential material at the end of the lecture improves performance on statistics exams. *Teaching of Psychology, 38,* 94–97.

Mayer, R. E. (2009). *Multimedia learning.* (2nd ed.) New York: Cambridge University Press.

Mayer, R. E., Stull, A., DeLeeuw, K., Almeroth, K., Bimber, B., Chun, D., et al. (2009). Clickers in college classrooms: Fostering learning with questioning methods in large lecture classes. *Contemporary Educational Psychology, 34,* 51–57.

McDaniel, M. A. (2007). Rediscovering transfer as a central concept. In H. L. Roediger, Y. Dudai, & S. Fitzpatrick (Eds.), *Science of memory: Concepts* (pp. 267–270). New York: Oxford University Press.

McDaniel, M. A., & Butler, A. C. (in press). A contextual framework for understanding when difficulties are desirable. In A. Benjamin (Ed.), *Successful remembering and successful forgetting: A festschrift in honor of Robert A. Bjork.* New York: Taylor & Francis.

McDaniel, M. A., & Callender, A. A. (2008). Cognition, memory, and education. In J. Byrne (Ed.), *Learning and memory: A comprehensive reference* (pp. 819–844). Oxford, UK: Elsevier.

McDaniel, M. A., & Donnelly, C. M. (1996). Learning with analogy and elaborative interrogation. *Journal of Educational Psychology, 88,* 508–519.

McDaniel, M. A., Friedman, A., & Bourne, L. E., Jr. (1978). Remembering the levels of information in words. *Memory & Cognition, 6,* 156–164.

McDaniel, M. A., Hines, R. J., & Guynn, M. J. (2002). When text difficulty benefits less-skilled readers. *Journal of Memory and Language, 46,* 544–561.

McDaniel, M. A., Howard, D. C., & Einstein, G. O. (2009). The read-recite-review study strategy: Effective and portable. *Psychological Science, 20,* 516–522.

McDaniel, M. A., Waddill, P. J., & Einstein, G. O. (1988). A contextual account of the generation effect: A three-factor theory. *Journal of Memory and Language, 27,* 521–536.

McDaniel, M. A., Wildman, K. M., & Anderson, J. L. (2010). *Using quizzes to enhance summative-assessment performance in a web-based class: An experimental study.* Manuscript under review.

Renkl, A. (2002). Worked-out examples: Instructional explanations support learning by self-explanations. *Learning and Instruction, 12,* 529–556.

Resnick, L. B., & Omanson, S. F. (1987). Learning to understand arithmetic. In R. Glaser (Ed.). *Advances in instructional psychology* (Vol. 3, pp. 41–95). Hillsdale, NJ: Lawrence Erlbaum.

Roediger, H. L., & Karpicke, J. D. (2006). Test-enhanced learning. *Psychological Science, 17,* 249–255.

Rohrer, D., & Taylor, K. (2006). The effects of overlearning and distributed practice on the retention of mathematics knowledge. *Applied Cognitive Psychology, 20,* 1209–1224.

Rohrer, D., & Taylor, K. (2007). The shuffling of mathematics problems improves learning. *Instructional Science, 35*, 481–498.

Sawyer, R. K. (Ed.). (2006). *Cambridge handbook of the learning sciences.* New York: Cambridge University Press.

Sweller, J., & Cooper, G. A. (1985). The use of worked examples as a substitute for problem solving in learning algebra. *Cognition and Instruction, 2*, 59–89.

Szpunar, K. K., McDermott, K. B., & Roediger, H. L. (2007). Expectation of a final cumulative test enhances long-term retention. *Memory & Cognition, 35*, 1007–1013.

Thomas, A. K., & McDaniel, M. A. (2007). Metacomprehension for educationally relevant materials: Dramatic effects of encoding-retrieval interactions. *Psychonomic Bulletin & Review, 14*, 212–218.

Chapter 7

Course Design

Victor A. Benassi and Gary S. Goldstein

Once upon a time, a graduate student was preparing for the beginning of the second year in his doctoral program when the chair of his department said she wanted to talk with him. The chair said, "I have some good news and some bad news. The good news is that your advisor and I have decided that you are ready to teach a course in the department because of your good work to date. Congratulations. The bad news is that the course begins in 3 weeks. So, now you have to leave because you have a lot to do before classes begin. Good luck." That was it. No advice, no instructions on what to do next, no information on how to order a textbook, no context for the place of the course in the department's curriculum. Over the following weeks and throughout the semester, the graduate student did the best he could to prepare and offer a good course. He was fortunate to receive guidance and advice from his advisor. However, preparing for and teaching that course was a challenging and a stressful experience for him.

In fact, a situation similar to this one is what one of us (VAB) experienced as a graduate student many years ago. Fortunately, many—although far too few—graduate programs now include preparation for graduate students prior to beginning their first teaching experience, as well as, often, concurrent supervision during that first course. Our aim in this chapter is to provide faculty who teach a course on college teaching an approach to help their soon-to-be graduate student teachers design a solid academic course in the department's curriculum. In addition, this chapter should be useful to graduate students to use on their own.

Although there are more design issues than considered here, we focus on the following topics: setting and following a timeline for preparing a course offering; situating the course in the curriculum; aligning learning outcomes, content, and assessment of student learning; selecting course content, assignments, and academic material; developing assessment and grading practices; preparing teaching units; and putting everything together in a course syllabus.

The Timeline

In their book, Svinicki and McKeachie (2011) presented a "Countdown for Course Preparation" (p. 10). Starting about 3 months before the first class meeting, they recommend that teachers begin to prepare their teaching goals and student learning outcomes (SLOs) for their course (see Bubb's Chapter 13). There are many issues to consider as one prepares such a list. Most college and university courses are part of a formal curriculum in a major, interdisciplinary program, or general education sequence. Thus, objectives and SLOs for a course already may be stipulated. However, there are usually degrees of freedom for a teacher to focus more on some objectives and outcomes than on others. We recommend that teachers, especially beginning teachers, begin to consider these choices sooner rather than later. In our work with graduate student teachers, we ask them to complete the Teaching Goals Inventory (TGI; Angelo & Cross, 1993a, 1993b). The TGI may be completed online, and the respondent receives a report of the results (Teaching Goals Inventory, University of Iowa; http://fm.iowa.uiowa.edu/fmi/xsl/tgi/data_entry.xsl?-db=tgi_data&-lay=Layout01&-view). Results from the TGI can help teachers clarify their goals for a course—for example, whether they would like students to improve their writing, reading, or problem-solving skills; whether they want them to develop an informed historical perspective concerning the subject of the course; whether they want them to be able to distinguish between facts and opinions; and so on. In addition to completing and considering the results of the TGI, we urge all graduate student teachers to begin to develop a teaching philosophy statement (see Korn's Chapter 8).

Selecting textbooks, readings, lab supplies, and other resources that students will need to complete the work of the course can be a time-consuming and daunting process. The resources one selects will need to match course goals, course structure, student skill levels, and so on. There are many general (e.g., Davis, 2009) and discipline-specific (e.g., Griggs, 2006) references designed to help teachers in the selection process.

Two Months Before the Start of Course

One way to work on course design is to prepare a draft syllabus. There are many issues to consider when preparing a course syllabus. What will transpire during class time? Will the class meet face-to-face, online, or both? What assignments will be given to students? What will be the average hours of work expected per week outside of class in order for students to perform well in the course? Will there be quizzes, exams (unit and comprehensive), papers, projects (individual, group)?

A well-prepared syllabus is a key component of any well-designed course. The syllabus should be presented at the first class to help shape the students' understanding of their responsibilities in the course, the breadth and depth of the course topics, and how the teacher will foster their learning within and across topics. Most important, students should leave the first class with some understanding of the skills that will be fostered by the teacher (e.g., writing, debating, lab skills) and of the overall SLOs that have been set for the course.

There is no one model for what should be included in a course syllabus. However, at a minimum, syllabi should include information about

- the teacher (name, office location, office hours, phone number, e-mail address),
- the course (course description, ideally from the institution's undergraduate or graduate catalog),
- required and optional resources for the course (texts, readers, primary sources),
- assignments for the course (readings, attendance at outside activities such as plays, court deliberations, etc.),
- important dates in the course (test dates, paper submission due dates),
- the sequence of topics to be covered in the course (ideally in the form of a course calendar with dates topics are to be covered, along with assigned work for those dates),
- assessment of student learning (information on testing, use of rubrics to assess written or oral work, grading practices; see Bubb's Chapter 13), and
- civil behavior (in class, online, during office hour meetings; see Silvestri & Buskist's Chapter 15).

There are many resources available that teachers can refer to when they are designing a course syllabus—some general (e.g., Altman & Cashin, 1992; Svinicki & McKeachie, 2011) and some related to specific disciplines (e.g., Society for the Teaching of Psychology's Office of Teaching Resources in Psychology, n.d.).

One Month Before Start of Course

Svinicki and McKeachie (2011) recommended that teachers begin preparing lesson plans (what we call teaching units) for new course offerings about a month before the start of the course. We recommend that graduate students complete three to five teaching units before the start of the course, mainly so they are not overwhelmed during the first few weeks of the term with preparing their teaching units. Teaching units should include the content of a unit of study, how the unit is taught (e.g., lecture, discussion, group work, in class and out of class), whether/how technology is used during the unit, and the out-of-class work students are expected to complete.

In the next few paragraphs, we describe an approach to teaching unit preparation that we have used with psychology PhD students at the University of New Hampshire for 30 years (Benassi, Jordan, & Harrison, 1994). For the past decade, we also have used the approach with graduate students who have completed an online course on course design that we have offered to students from across the United States and from nearly a dozen other countries (University of New Hampshire, n.d.).

SLOs for the Unit

The SLOs for a unit address material from the textbook(s), other reading assignments, other out-of-class assignments, and material covered during class time. Teachers provide the foundation for the preparation of the remainder of the teaching unit by stating clearly, for example, what they want students to know, to be able to discuss, and to be able to apply. It is important to consider how the outcomes for a given unit relate to the overall SLOs for the course (as spelled out in the course syllabus). Teachers should make their expected SLOs for each teaching unit available to students in writing prior to the start of that unit.

General Outline

This brief outline cross-references each topic included in a unit of study in the course with one or more SLOs. For example, if a learning outcome for the unit is that students will be able to discuss the merits of a theory covered in the unit, there should be instruction and/or an assignment that will allow students to achieve this outcome. Similarly, if a teacher wants students to be able to compare and contrast two competing theories, there should be opportunities provided in the unit to facilitate the development of this skill.

Detailed Outline

This section of a teaching unit should include detailed information on what the teacher will be doing in the unit (e.g., discussion formats, lecture notes, information on demonstrations, questions to be asked of students, descriptions of group activities). Chapters 6, 10, 11, 12, 13, and 17 in this book contain much useful information and many excellent suggestions on methods that may promote students' performance in academic courses. When considering the instructional approaches that will be used during a unit, teachers should also consider whether they will use any technological aids and, if so, how they will be used (see Howard's Chapter 18; Mayer, 2009). The key requirement for this section of a teaching unit is that teachers provide sufficient information that will allow them to implement the unit of study effectively and efficiently.

Table of Specifications

The table of specifications (Mehrens & Lehmann, 1984; Special Connections, University of Kansas, n.d.) should relate evaluation items (e.g., items on an exam) to the SLOs for the unit. Overall, this table should document that the teacher assesses SLOs in a balanced way. Assessment should reflect the SLOs for the unit and, thus, the material that was taught during the unit. The practice that some teachers use of randomly selecting items for an exam from a preexisting test bank is, in our view, indefensible. Assessments should assess what a teacher has previously determined to be a major outcome for a unit, and the table of specifications provides a mechanism to ensure that this process occurs. It is beyond our scope to provide a detailed description of how a table of specifications can be developed and used. We refer you to Jacobs (2004) for an example of a discussion of a table of specifications for a unit on oxygen in a chemistry course.

Evaluation of Student Work

There are many ways to assess the various aspects of student learning, including application and generalization of learning, problem solving, and critical thinking. The table of specifications informs the type of assessment that should be applied by a teacher. For example, if there are SLOs for a unit that focus on students being able to compare and contrast several viewpoints on a topic, then an assessment (e.g., an exam) should potentially include an item that asks students to do just that. There are numerous sources available on the assessment of student learning in college and university courses. We recommend Bubb (Chapter 13 in this book), Svinicki and McKeachie (2011), and Davis (1999b). Also, there are dozens of websites that contain excellent information and suggestions on the assessment of course-related SLOs and related issues (e.g., Office of Academic Assessment at Northern Arizona University, n.d.).

Two Weeks Before the Start of the Course

As the start date of a course approaches, it is important to ensure that everything is ready. Teachers should take care to confirm that texts and other resources are available to students, that any equipment needed for a course is in fact set to be in class or otherwise available to students, that there are enough seats in a scheduled classroom for the number of students enrolled in the course, that scheduled guests for class have been reminded about their visit, and so on.

Selecting Course Content

Even when the topics to be covered in a course are firmly established by policy or practice, teachers typically still have a good deal of choice in selecting specific content. For example, in our own discipline, the introductory psychology survey course at our university requires coverage of nine fields that represent some of the major areas in psychology (e.g., behavioral neuroscience, cognition, development, learning, psychopathology). However, within each of these topical areas, there are numerous choices that can be made regarding the specific content that will be covered. It is important for beginning teachers to determine early on how much individual control they have over the subject matter that they will cover in their courses. Senior faculty in the area of the course, the chair of the department curriculum committee, and the department chair will be able to provide guidance. Specific suggestions for selecting course content can be found at many college/university websites (e.g., Office of Graduate Studies, University of Nebraska, n.d.). In making decisions about what will be covered in a course, we urge teachers to do so taking into account their SLOs and outcomes for the course as well as the results from the Teaching Goals Inventory. In this way, SLOs and content will be integrated seamlessly into the course.

Conclusions

There are many factors to consider, much planning to do, and multiple tasks to complete before the first day of a new course. Even after the first class, there is much to be done beyond a teacher's direct interactions with students. We have provided a basic framework of the issues that teachers—especially novice teachers—should consider before teaching a course for the first time. Ideally, all novice graduate student teachers would receive direct assistance, support, and supervision from their advisor, a teacher of a course on college teaching, and/or a staff person from a teaching and learning center on their campus. Similarly, faculty and other professional staff ideally would be knowledgeable about course design issues considered here. Neither scenario is as common as we think it should be in higher education. Graduate students are far too often left to their own devices to prepare and deliver college- and university-level courses. Our hope is that this chapter offers information and suggestions that will be helpful to both novice teachers and to senior colleagues who have a major responsibility to assist them.

Recommended Additional Resources

We recommend the work of Chickering and Gamson (1987) and Fink (1999, 2005) to faculty who have responsibility for helping graduate students design and deliver college or university courses as well as to graduate students who wish to delve more deeply into issues related to course design. For an excellent and in-depth resource on course design, including an online course design tutorial, we recommend Tewksbury and Macdonald (2005). This resource contains a wealth of information that will be helpful to faculty who work with graduate student teachers. In addition, the online tutorial will provide new graduate student teachers with step-by-step guidance on designing a course offering, including information on setting course goals, constructing a syllabus, assessing student learning, and much more.

References

Altman, H. B., & Cashin, W. E. (1992). *Writing a syllabus: Integrated course design.* The Idea Center. Idea Paper No. 42. Retrieved from http://www.theideacenter.org/sites/default/files/Idea_Paper_27.pdf

Angelo, T. A., & Cross, K. P. (1993a). *Classroom assessment techniques: A handbook for college teachers* (2nd ed.). San Francisco, CA: Jossey-Bass.

Angelo, T. A., & Cross, K. P. (1993b). *Classroom assessment techniques: A handbook for college teachers* (Teaching Goals Inventory). Retrieved from http://fm.iowa.uiowa.edu/fmi/xsl/tgi/data_entry.xsl?-db=tgi_data&-lay=Layout01&-view

Benassi, V. A., Jordan, E. A., & Harrison, L. M. (1994). Using teaching modules to train and supervise graduate TAs. In K. G. Lewis (Ed.), *The TA experience: Preparing for multiple roles* (pp. 183–188). Stillwater, OK: New Forums Press.

Chickering, A. W., & Gamson, Z. F. (1987). Seven principles for good practice in undergraduate education. *American Association of Higher Education Bulletin, 39*(7), 3–7. Retrieved from http://www.aahea.org/bulletins/bulletins.htm

Davis, B. G. (1999a). *Tools for teaching* (Preparing or revising a course). San Francisco, CA: Jossey-Bass. Retrieved from http://honolulu.hawaii.edu/intranet/committees/FacDevCom/guidebk/teachtip/prepcors.htm

Davis, B. G. (1999b). *Tools for teaching* (Quizzes, tests, and exams). San Francisco, CA: Jossey-Bass. Retrieved from http://honolulu.hawaii.edu/intranet/committees/FacDevCom/guidebk/teachtip/quizzes.htm

Davis, B. G. (2009). *Tools for teaching* (Selecting textbooks, readings, and course materials) (2nd ed.). San Francisco, CA: Jossey-Bass. Retrieved from http://teaching.berkeley.edu/textbooks/docs/textbookselection.pdf

Fink, L. D. (1999). *Five principles of good course design.* Retrieved from http://honolulu.hawaii.edu/intranet/committees/FacDevCom/guidebk/teachtip/finks5.htm

Fink, L. D. (2005). *Integrated course design.* The Idea Center. Idea Paper #42. Retrieved from http://www.theideacenter.org/sites/default/files/Idea_Paper_42.pdf

Griggs, R. A. (2006). Selecting an introductory textbook: They are not "all the same." In D. Dunn & S. L. Chew (Eds.), *Best practices in teaching introductory psychology* (pp. 11–23). Mahwah, NJ: Lawrence Erlbaum.

Jacobs, L. C. (2004). *How to write better tests: A handbook for improving test construction skills.* Indiana University Bloomington Evaluation Services & Testing. Retrieved from http://www.indiana.edu/~best/write_better_tests.shtml

Mayer, R. E. (2009). *Multimedia learning* (2nd ed.). New York: Cambridge University Press.

Mehrens, W. A., & Lehmann, I. J. (1984). *Measurement and evaluation in education and psychology* (3rd ed.). New York, NY: Holt, Rinehart, and Winston.

Office of Academic Assessment at Northern Arizona University. (n.d.). Enabling Learner-Centered Education Through Student Learning Assessment. Retrieved from https://www4.nau.edu/assessment/assessment/course/lce.htm

Office of Graduate Studies, University of Nebraska, Lincoln. (n.d.). *Step by step: Planning a college course* (Select course content; arrange course content). Retrieved from http://www.unl.edu/gradstudies/current/dev/teachingtools/planning.shtml#Step3

Society for the Teaching of Psychology's Office of Teaching Resources in Psychology. (n.d.). *Project syllabus.* Retrieved from http://teachpsych.org/otrp/syllabi/index.php

Special Connections, University of Kansas. (n.d.) *Table of specifications.* Retrieved from http://www.specialconnections.ku.edu/cgi-bin/cgiwrap/specconn/main.php?cat=assessment&section=main&subsection=qualitytest/table

Svinicki, M., & McKeachie, W. J. (2011). *McKeachie's teaching tips: Strategies, research, and theory for college and university teachers* (13th ed.). Belmont, CA: Wadsworth.

Tewksbury, B. J., & Macdonald, R. H. (2005). *Course design tutorial.* Cutting Edge, Carleton College. Retrieved from http://serc.carleton.edu/NAGTWorkshops/coursedesign/tutorial/index.html

University of New Hampshire, Center for Excellence in Teaching and Learning. (n.d.). *Online course: GRAD 980 preparing to teach a psychology course.* Retrieved from http://www.unh.edu/teaching-excellence/GRAD980/Index.htm

Chapter 8

Writing and Developing Your Philosophy of Teaching

❖

James H. Korn

"There is nothing so practical as a good theory." This quotation is closely associated with the renowned social psychologist Kurt Lewin, who also believed that good theories are shaped by practical experiences. Your teaching philosophy is the theory that guides what you do as a teacher and that is shaped by your experiences. For graduate students and other beginning teachers, writing this statement reveals the choices you must make in developing your teaching style. For those teachers with more experience, writing a philosophy can be a form of renewal. There also are practical reasons for having a well-developed statement. When you apply for an academic position, most universities expect it, especially those institutions where teaching is the primary mission. Later you may need your statement for promotion and tenure purposes.

In the years that I taught teachers in classes and workshops, we followed this model:

$$\text{Philosophy} \rightarrow \text{Objectives} \rightarrow \text{Methods} \rightarrow \text{Learning}$$
$$\rightarrow \text{Evaluation} \rightarrow \text{Reflection}$$

Your philosophy (explicit or implicit) of teaching and learning determines the objectives you choose for your courses. These objectives lead to decisions about the most appropriate teaching methods and ways of assessing student learning. All of these decisions are evaluated and modified based on the data you obtain, and after you take time to think about it. Your reflection may lead you to revise your philosophy, and the cycle repeats.

Writing Your Philosophy Statement

You can find a lot of advice on the Internet about how to write a philosophy statement, some of which I will describe later in this chapter. Most of these sources tell you to do specific things concerning content, form, and style. My approach to this task is simply to ask you to write your philosophy of teaching, with no other directions. (See Korn & Sikorski, 2010, Unit 2, for a more detailed description of this approach, including learning activities.)

Given that direct, open-ended instruction, most graduate students are dismayed and have questions. What should I write? How long should it be? The primary reason for asking you to write without preparation and suggestions is that this statement should be *your* philosophy, not that of some expert. It should be yours in form as well as content. You are not starting from a blank slate, but from years of experience as a student and perhaps with a little or a lot of teaching experience. The only requirements that I make are that you write in the first person (this is *your* philosophy) and use nontechnical language because others will read it eventually. I provide these instructions for getting started:

Find a quiet place where you won't be disturbed. Think for a while about teaching and whatever that brings to mind, perhaps occasionally jotting a note. Then do some free writing, where you write continuously without taking your pen from the page. Next, reflect on what you have written, and finally, rewrite it, doing a little organizing in preparation for showing this first draft to someone else.

Our experience provides the basis for much of what we write in a teaching philosophy. We think of good and bad teachers we have had, in and outside of the classroom. We recall reading things about teaching that struck us as profound or useful. Our view of human nature and the meaning of life come into play.

Below are some potentially useful questions to stimulate your thinking about your teaching philosophy:

1. Who was the best teacher you ever had? Who was the worst? (Or think of a composite of these good and bad teachers.) List their characteristics.

2. If you were to overhear students talking about you and your teaching, what would you want them to be saying? Why is that important to you?

3. Does (or would) your teaching vary depending on the course you are teaching and the kind of students you have? Are there essential principles in your philosophy that would *not* depend on the situation?

4. Think of a metaphor for your teaching. Why is your teaching like this metaphor, and in what ways is it not like your chosen metaphor?

After thinking about these questions, revise your draft.

You might be tempted to view this task as an exercise in the creation of socially acceptable clichés. Avoid this temptation and instead show your commitment to teaching and to students. Developing a philosophy of teaching is a good test of the scientist-practitioner model of graduate education because it allows us to apply our knowledge of learning, memory, and human relationships to teaching. When you have written a draft of your philosophy, put it aside while you plan your course and do your teaching. After a few weeks, return to what you wrote and see whether your teaching practices follow your beliefs. If not, one or the other should be changed.

There may be some clichés in what we write, but mostly our ideas are deeply felt. Writing that is deeply felt may not, however, be writing that is clear, and that is why having someone else read your essay can be helpful. Find another person who also is developing a teaching philosophy and exchange your essays. I follow this practice face-to-face in workshops, but you could do it by e-mail or use regular mail and the telephone. For most of us, showing our writing to another person is threatening, especially when it is an early draft. Realize that you both are in the same boat, that yes, it is rough, and you do have some grammatical and spelling errors, and you really can say it better. After getting over your reluctance for self-revelation, use these questions to guide your critique of each other's essay:

• What are the main points?
• What is the strongest part?
• What is the weakest part?
• What additional questions do you have and what other subtopics would you like to read about in this essay?

Write your responses to these questions about your partner's philosophy statement, then communicate with that person and discuss what each of you wrote. One of the best methods for developing as a teacher is talking with others about what we do and think. Now, with feedback from another person in hand and your conversation in mind, make some notes for yourself about how you may want to revise your philosophy.

Teaching Style

Your philosophy may include a description of what you are or will be like as a teacher—your classroom performance and how you relate to students. Your style is related to your personality, which is partly determined by heredity, but much of your teaching style is learned and can be changed.

Jay Parini (1997) said that teachers "need to invent and cultivate a voice that serves their personal needs, their students, and the material at hand," and this "self-presentation involves the donning of a mask," our teaching persona (p. A92). I agree with Parini that you "learn to teach by listening closely to your own teachers, by taking on their voices, imitating them, digesting them so that they become part of your own voice" (p. A92). These characteristics are blended with our own qualities, and over time we discover what works well so that a more authentic persona develops.

Typologies of teaching styles have been developed to describe ways of relating to students, but the categories almost always are incomplete and overlapping. However, Anthony Grasha (1996) has developed a typology that is useful as an exercise to understand your teaching style. His book *Teaching With Style* includes an inventory (pp. 159–164) that will give you a score for each of these five teaching styles (adapted from Grasha, p. 154):

Expert. Possesses knowledge and expertise that students need. Maintains status by displaying detailed knowledge and challenging students to enhance their competence. Concerned with transmitting information and ensuring that students are well prepared.

Formal Authority. Status comes from knowledge and role as a faculty member. Concerned with giving positive and negative feedback, establishing learning goals, expectations, and rules of conduct. Provides students with the structure they need to learn.

Personal Model. Teaches by personal example and models how to think and behave. Oversees, guides, and directs by showing how to do things and encouraging students to observe and emulate the model.

Facilitator. Emphasizes the personal nature of student-teacher interactions. Guides students by asking questions, suggesting alternatives, and encouraging students to make informed choices. Overall goal is to develop the capacity for independent action and responsibility.

Delegator. Concerned with developing the capacity to function in an autonomous fashion. Students work independently or in teams with the teacher as a resource person.

The instructions for this inventory ask respondents to keep a specific course in mind when completing the inventory, thus recognizing that teaching style may vary depending on the situation. Grasha (1996) has done extensive research with the inventory and reports clusters of styles that go together. For example, he found that the most common cluster (38% of faculty) has a combination of expert and formal authority as the primary teaching style. You can take this survey by going to http://www.longleaf.net/teachingstyle.html

When you complete this survey, compare the results to your teaching philosophy. If there are differences, will you change your philosophy? You may find that your style is different depending on the course you are considering, for example, a seminar in your specialty area and a beginning methods course, which shows that style and philosophy are not the same. Style may be related to the situation, while your philosophy represents your basic values and beliefs about teaching.

Other Resources

A major objective of this chapter is to help you develop your teaching philosophy. To increase the likelihood that it really is yours, I have provided minimal direction on the content and style of your statement. However, there are sources you can use that give more specific directions about how to write a philosophy of teaching.

Two documents (American Chemical Society [ACS], 2000; Chism, 1997–1998) provide particularly useful suggestions. Internet addresses to access these sources are in the reference section at the end of this chapter. I agree with Nancy Van Note Chism's suggestion that the philosophy statement should be individual, reflective, and personal, creating "a vivid portrait of a person who is intentional about teaching practices and committed to a career" (p. 32). The ACS brochure is more directive but has a lot of good specific advice with a section on documentation and reflection.

The staff of the teaching and learning center at the University of Michigan conducted a survey of faculty search committee chairs at large universities (Kaplan, Meizlish, O'Neal, & Wright, 2007) and asked, "What makes a teaching statement successful?" The responses were sorted into these five categories (p. 248):

- Offers evidence of practice. Statements provided specific examples linking their philosophy to what they actually did as teachers.
- Is student-centered and uses active learning.
- Demonstrates reflectiveness showing how the author has made changes in the classroom.
- Conveys enthusiasm for teaching and a vision.
- Is well written, clear, and readable.

On the negative side, unsuccessful statements were "generic, full of boilerplate language, [and did] not appear to be taken seriously" (Kaplan et al., 2007, p. 249).

The report of this research includes a rubric used in the Michigan teaching center to evaluate philosophy statements. This rubric and examples of teaching statements can be found at http://www.crlt.umich.edu/tstrategies/tstpts.php. You may find this resource helpful, but as I said before, the philosophy statement should be *your* statement.

Audience

The documents referred to in the last section tell you to be aware of the audience for your statement, which is absolutely essential. As the ACS brochure says, "The most important audience . . . is yourself" (p. 7). For that audience, you are least constrained by style, length, and other details. Eventually you may have a file with notes, drafts of early versions, and reflections on your development. These materials form the practical theory you use to implement your teaching style.

However, there will be other important audiences. When you search for an academic position, many places will ask specifically for your teaching philosophy, and will expect to see it in a more concise form than you have written for yourself. If you are successful in your job search—or already have that academic position—you will be evaluated for salary increments, promotion, and tenure. Then deans and committees will want to know how you view teaching. Be informed about your audience. Your core values should not change, but you can use different examples and emphasize certain elements of your philosophy for these different audiences.

There is one other version of your philosophy you probably will need if you interview for a job, the "sound bite." A busy dean will have glanced at your materials but not have had time to read them carefully. The dean says, "Tell me about this teaching philosophy of yours." You have about 2 minutes. What will you say? Develop your sound bite and present it to a friend.

Developing Your Teaching Philosophy

Reading and Reflection

We are not the first people to have thought about a philosophy of teaching or, more generally, of education. Real philosophers like Aristotle, Kant, and Dewey have written with great wisdom on this topic (Frankena,

1965). One of the characteristics of good teachers is that they are scholars of teaching, which means that they read extensively to discover what others think and do, and keep up with the research on teaching, both in general and in their discipline. It is not enough to base your ideas about teaching only on personal experience. We would not want our students to do that in their coursework, but we do want them to become educated by reading and thinking critically. Among the books that helped me develop my philosophy of teaching are two that are practical (Brookfield, 1995; Svinicki, 2004) and two that are inspirational (Palmer, 1998; Tompkins, 1996).

Talking With Colleagues

Earlier, I suggested that when writing your philosophy statement you should ask others to read it. Comparing your ideas with those of other teachers, including those in other disciplines, is an excellent way to develop your philosophy. These discussions may force you to justify and clarify your ideas and change the way you think about teaching. I have had vigorous discussions about things like frequency of testing and class attendance policies where my position grew out of my teaching philosophy. These discussions happen at lunch, in the local pub, or in more professional settings. I strongly recommend attending sessions on teaching at regional or national meetings in your field. You also should search for interdisciplinary teaching conferences such as those sponsored by the Lilly Foundation.

Your Teaching Experience

What you actually do as a teacher is the ultimate challenge to your philosophy. Each version of my own philosophy mentioned the importance of students' active learning, especially through discussion. Yet at the end of many semesters, I would reflect on what had happened and wonder why I had talked so much in class. If my lectures were accomplishing important objectives better than some student activity, I should find out why that is so and include that in my philosophy. By the way, this "finding out" process is what is called the Scholarship of Teaching (Halpern et al., 1998; Kreber, 2001).

Doing careful course evaluation at the end of each semester may reveal areas where you can develop your philosophy (see Korn & Sikorski, 2010, Unit 8, and Chapter 19, this volume). For example, many students did not share my belief in the benefits of active learning. Was this discrepancy a matter of individual student differences or an indication I should design better activities? On the other hand, perhaps I could do a better job of explaining my philosophy to students. Here was something else I had to find out.

Reflection for Renewal

A philosophy statement can continue to be a medium for developing your teaching even later in your career. A time may come when you think about issues bigger than your attendance policy, and question the value of what you are doing and of your commitment to teaching. Promotion and tenure no longer are issues; now it is a matter of being honest with yourself. Do you really believe and do what is in your teaching philosophy?

I had this time of doubt when I was less than 10 years from retirement. My philosophy said that I had a passion for teaching, but passion was not what I felt. That was someone else's word. A colleague helped me rethink my philosophy and I realized that my discomfort was due to wanting what we will never quite achieve in any of the classes we teach. I knew I could do better, but rather than see that as a shortcoming, the desire for excellence became my guiding principle:

> It shows itself in teaching most often in the daily work we do . . . not in prizes for excellence that some of us receive. I want to be a good teacher at the mundane level of class preparation, teaching methods, and relationships with students. . . . *That* is the excellence of desire. (Korn, 2002, p. 208)

Final Thoughts: Looking Ahead

In the previous chapter, you read about basic course design. Course design is where you put your teaching philosophy to work. As you write your teaching philosophy statement, you probably will think about teaching experiences you have had or expect to have. Using your imagination is a good way to develop your philosophy. You may have visualized yourself standing in the front of an auditorium full of students, speaking eloquently, and seeing the students being fascinated and inspired. Yet in your philosophy you may have stated the importance of active learning and frequent assessment. Planning a course will force you to make choices about objectives, methods, assessments, and how they all fit with each other and with your philosophy.

References

American Chemical Society. (2000). *How to write a teaching philosophy for academic employment*. Washington, DC: ACS Department of Career Services. Retrieved from portal.acs.org/portal/PublicWebSite/careers/advice/CTP_005351

Brookfield, S. D. (1995). *Becoming a critically reflective teacher.* San Francisco, CA: Jossey-Bass.

Chism, N. V. N. (1997–1998). Developing a philosophy of teaching statement. *Essays on Teaching Excellence: Toward the Best in the Academy, 9,* 3. Retrieved from http://www.podnetwork.org/publications/teachingexcellence/97-98/V9, %20N3%20Chism.pdf

Frankena, W. K. (1965). *Three historical philosophies of education: Aristotle, Kant, Dewey.* Glenview, IL: Scott, Foresman and Company.

Grasha, A. F. (1996). *Teaching with style.* Pittsburgh, PA: Alliance.

Halpern, D. F., Smothergill, D. W., Allen, M., Baker, S., Baum, C., Best, D., Ferrari, J., . . . & Weaver, K. A. (1998). Scholarship in psychology: A paradigm for the twenty-first century. *American Psychologist, 53,* 1292–1297.

Kaplan, M., Meizlish, D. S., O'Neal, C., & Wright, M. C. (2007). A research-based rubric for developing statements of teaching philosophy. In D. R. Robertson & L. B. Nilson (Eds.), *To improve the academy: Vol. 26. Resources for faculty, instructional and organizational development* (pp. 242–262). San Francisco, CA: Jossey-Bass.

Korn, J. H. (2002). Beyond tenure: The teaching portfolio for reflection and change. In S. F. Davis & W. Buskist (Eds.), *The teaching of psychology: Essays in honor of Wilbert J. McKeachie and Charles L. Brewer* (pp. 203–213). Mahwah, NJ: Lawrence Erlbaum.

Korn, J. H., & Sikorski, J. (2010). *A guide for beginning teachers of psychology.* Retrieved from the Society for the Teaching of Psychology website: http://teachpsych.org/resources/e-books/guide2010/index.php

Kreber. C. (Ed.). (2001). *Scholarship revisited: Perspectives on the scholarship of teaching.* New Directions for Teaching and Learning, No. 86. San Francisco, CA: Jossey-Bass.

Palmer, P. J. (1998). *The courage to teach.* San Francisco, CA: Jossey-Bass.

Parini, J. (1997, September 5). Cultivating a teaching persona. *Chronicle of Higher Education,* p. A92.

Svinicki, M. D. (2004). *Learning and motivation in the postsecondary classroom.* Bolton, MA: Anker.

Tompkins, J. (1996). *A life in school: What the teacher learned.* Reading, MA: Perseus Books.

Chapter 9

Developing Student-Teacher Rapport in the Undergraduate Classroom

❖

Janie H. Wilson and Rebecca G. Ryan

As a teacher, your good fortune brings you to the undergraduate classroom, where you get to share a wealth of information and your passion for teaching with students. At this point, you hold the key to learning in your hand. Knowledge exudes from your pores, and you stand ready to impart wisdom to anyone who will listen. But how do you get students to listen? How do you make them care? Dangling grades in front of them certainly helps, but an entire literature points to another—often overlooked—method of motivating students, enhancing their attitudes, and even improving their grades. In this chapter, we discuss rapport, including evidence of its importance, how teachers foster rapport with their students, and why rapport is crucial to teaching. We discuss how student-teacher rapport offers benefits to both students and teachers and conclude the chapter with suggestions about how teachers can develop rapport with their students.

Building Rapport

Numerous ways to build rapport exist, including specific positive teacher behaviors in the classroom, general positive teacher attitudes conveyed to students, availability outside of the classroom, and even seemingly trivial practices, such as dressing informally and using slang. Rapport supports useful student outcomes such as class attendance and participation as well as increased student motivation; more positive student attitudes toward the course, teacher, and learning; and better grades. Such positive outcomes should lead us to build rapport as quickly as possible, highlighting the importance of the teacher's first contact with students.

Teacher Behaviors and Attitudes

Teacher immediacy traditionally defines a key aspect of rapport. Immediacy behaviors communicate to students that their teacher is available and willing to help them succeed (Andersen, 1979). The immediacy literature traces back several decades, and a plethora of research lists the importance of specific teacher verbal and nonverbal behaviors, including calling students by name and praising students' work, actions, and comments (Gorham, 1988); looking at the class while talking; moving around the room while lecturing; and gesturing appropriately during lecture (Richmond, Gorham, & McCroskey, 1987). Both verbal and nonverbal behaviors relate to student motivation, projected course grades, evaluations of the course, and evaluations of the instructor (Wilson & Locker, 2008). In a large meta-analysis, Witt, Wheeless, and Allen (2004) found consistently positive evaluations of the course and professor with higher levels of immediacy. Perhaps more important, teacher immediacy behaviors related positively with student learning.

Although Gorham and Christophel's (1990) list of 23 teacher behaviors offers a useful beginning point for thinking about specific rapport-building actions, Wilson (2006) argued that such a list might stifle creativity as teachers work to foster rapport through their own genuine behaviors. Rapport represents a more general construct than immediacy and includes students' general impressions of their teachers. Benson, Cohen, and Buskist (2005) asked students to provide examples of professor behaviors that led to rapport. From most to least commonly mentioned, students responded with "encouraging, open-mindedness, creative, interesting, accessible, happy, having a 'good' personality, promoting class discussions, approachability, concern for students, and fairness" (p. 238).

Benson and colleagues (2005) also found that students who perceived rapport with their instructors engaged in numerous pro-academic behaviors compared with those instructors without rapport. Students first read two definitions of rapport, and then considered classes in which they perceived rapport with the instructor versus classes in which they did not perceive rapport. They then rated the likelihood of engaging in specific behaviors—attend class, pay attention, study for class, enjoy the subject and professor, attend office hours, e-mail the professor, and take another class with the professor. Students reported that the likelihood of engaging in these behaviors was much higher if they perceived rapport with their teachers than if they perceived little or no rapport with their teachers.

Frisby and Martin (2010) measured student-teacher rapport with an 11-item scale adapted from an employee-satisfaction instrument. Participants rated how strongly they agreed with statements pertaining to their relationship with their instructor, such as perceived warmth, comfort, caring, and harmony. Rapport significantly predicted cognitive learning, affective learning, and student participation in class. Wilson, Ryan, and Pugh (2010) created a student-teacher rapport scale to offer a more general measure of the rapport construct based on students' impressions of their teacher, regardless of the teacher's method of creating rapport. Based on this scale, rapport predicted attitudes toward the instructor, attitudes toward the course, motivation, perceptions of learning, and self-reported grades. Thus, general perceptions of rapport as well as specific in-class immediacy behaviors relate with positive student outcomes.

Out-of-Class Communication

In addition to in-class behaviors, teachers build rapport by interacting with students outside of the classroom, or what is termed out-of-class communication (OCC). For example, Dobransky and Frymier (2004) found that students reported more intimacy when teachers engaged in OCC. Similarly, frequency as well as length of students' office visits related positively to student ratings of teacher verbal immediacy and student motivation (Jaasma & Koper, 1999).

OCC includes traditional office hours, but technology also allows for communication via e-mail and Facebook, to name two opportunities. Legg and Wilson (2009) sent a welcoming e-mail to students 1 week prior to the first day of class. Students who received the e-mail reported more motivation and more positive attitudes toward the instructor and the course on the first day of class (and, for females, throughout the semester) than students who did not receive an e-mail. As an added bonus, retention remained higher in the e-mail group. Based on this simple manipulation, we envision a wealth of opportunities to bond with students via e-mail—even before meeting students face-to-face. When teachers use e-mail to communicate with students during the term, student ratings of interpersonal relationships and instructor evaluations become more positive (Sheer & Fung, 2007). Specifically, professor e-mail frequency, reply promptness, and helpfulness predicted student ratings of trust, equality, closeness, and satisfaction.

Facebook offers another option to interact with students. Mazer, Murphy, and Simonds (2007) reported that high professor self-disclosure on Facebook correlated with students' anticipated motivation as well as positive affect toward the course material and the classroom climate. Although students responded favorably to teachers' Facebook pages, the authors cautioned that professors' use of Facebook may not be universally well received because some students may see it as an infringement on their social space. However, based on informal discussions with our students, we believe that new teachers' lifelong use of Facebook would make such connections with students acceptable and perhaps even valued.

Teacher Similarities to Undergraduates

Graduate student assistant teachers (GTAs) and new teachers have the unique opportunity to bond with undergraduates due to similarities, including age, style of dress, and use of slang, to name a few. Research in social psychology shows that people like individuals similar to them, which enhances one's ability to build rapport. Teachers can capitalize on age similarity by dressing informally. For example, Morris, Gorham, Cohen, and Huffman (1996) asked GTAs to wear either casual (faded jeans, a T-shirt, and a plaid flannel shirt worn open), casual-professional (tan slacks or skirt and a button-down shirt or sweater), or formal-professional (business suit) attire to lectures. Student participants rated GTAs in casual clothing as more social, extroverted, and presenting more interesting material than GTAs wearing less casual styles of dress. However, immediacy behaviors far overshadowed effects of instructor dress when examining positive student outcomes (Gorham, Cohen, & Morris, 1997).

Another way to enhance similarity involves using slang. Mazer and Hunt (2008) conducted a qualitative analysis of students' perceptions of a lecturer who used slang such as "cool," "awesome, "rocks," "sweet," and "let's get fired up!" (p. 23) throughout a presentation. Students reported that slang made the lecturer seem more casual, approachable, and easy to talk to. They also felt that the lecturer worked to relate to them and create a comfortable learning environment.

Of course, teachers should not use slang such as profanity in class or wear inappropriately revealing clothing—these sorts of behaviors are not likely to enhance rapport; in fact, engaging in these actions may likely reduce it. Even if new teachers prefer to hide their age, dress formally, or not use slang, lack of teaching experience creates certain expectations in students, and violating students' expectations might compromise rapport unless teachers take special care to show students they genuinely care about them and want to help them succeed.

Regardless of a teacher's approach to building rapport, it is crucial to create positive relationships with students as soon as possible. First impressions create powerful expectations and rarely change once formed (e.g., Sunnafrank & Ramirez, 2004), and the classroom is no exception to this rule. Students who watched only a 30-second video clip of a lecture maintained their impressions of the teacher throughout the entire semester (Ambady & Rosenthal, 1993). Wilson and Wilson (2007) reported enhanced student motivation and even higher final-exam grades for students with a positive first day (e.g., the professor covering the syllabus in a friendly manner and releasing class early) versus a neutral first day (e.g., the professor covering the syllabus in a straightforward manner, lecturing, using the full class period, and assigning homework).

Maintaining Rapport

New teachers often readily adopt best practices for teaching, which of course includes building rapport. Unfortunately, rapport is quickly destroyed when teachers engage in certain teacher misbehaviors. To maintain rapport with students, teachers must diligently focus on exhibiting positive behaviors and attitudes.

For example, Thweatt and McCroskey (1998) asked students to read descriptions of teachers either high or low in immediacy and with or without teacher misbehaviors. Misbehavior included actions such as being unprepared, offering confusing information, overloading students with work, not adhering to the syllabus, and abruptly canceling class. In the low-immediacy conditions, student ratings of teacher caring remained low regardless of teacher misbehaviors. However, across the high-immediacy conditions, teacher misbehaviors significantly compromised students' perceptions of caring, suggesting that rapport declines when teachers misbehave.

In a related study, Banfield, Richmond, and McCroskey (2006) asked students to read descriptions of teachers supposedly written by other students. Participants who read about a teacher who behaved unfairly toward students, insulted students, came late to class, provided useless or no feedback on assignments, assigned an inappropriate amount of work, and revealed a lack of knowledge rated the teacher as less caring than students who read about a teacher with no misbehaviors.

Beyond simple descriptions of teachers, researchers have examined student reports of teachers with whom they took courses. Plax, Kearney, McCroskey, and Richmond (1986) investigated the impact of negative behaviors such as teachers emphasizing their authority over students (e.g., not allowing students to question the teacher) and using punishment (e.g., threatening students with failing grades). These techniques inversely correlated with student ratings of immediacy. Plax and colleagues concluded that employing negative teaching techniques destroys immediacy and compromises students' affective learning. Similarly, Rocca and McCroskey (1999) reported that teacher verbal aggressiveness (being confrontational, disrespectful, and critical of students; belittling students) toward students correlated negatively with student ratings of teacher immediacy.

Thus, maintaining rapport requires teachers to be competent as well as kind. The foundation of rapport on which we build classes begins to crumble when we engage in negative teaching behaviors. Unfortunately, subsequent negative feedback from students often creates a cycle of dissatisfaction by both students and teachers, leading some teachers to dislike students.

Teachers should avoid complaining about students or listening to others doing so. Teachers who make a habit of discussing students' negative qualities find themselves more prone to teacher burnout (Bakker & Schaufeli, 2000). Conversely, colleagues who seldom discuss student problems report less emotional stress, perhaps because they avoid dwelling on negative views of others. GTAs and new teachers need to recognize that one or two troublesome students do not define the entire class. Students need to know that their teachers support them and plan to help them through the learning process. A consistently positive attitude goes a long way toward maintaining student-teacher rapport.

Conclusions

In this chapter, we have outlined empirical research to support the importance of developing rapport with students. Positive student-teacher interactions enhance student learning and student enjoyment of the learning process. GTAs and new teachers can develop rapport with their students by

- engaging in verbal and nonverbal immediacy behaviors;
- treating students respectfully;
- offering out-of-class communications such as holding office hours, using e-mail, and using Facebook;
- welcoming students to the class via e-mail before the term begins;
- wearing casual clothing and using appropriate slang, if they are comfortable with these behaviors;
- being kind and positive on the first day of class to set up positive student expectations;

- being competent and conscientious;
- avoiding emphasizing power over students;
- avoiding threatening students (e.g., with poor grades); and
- not making a habit of discussing student problems with others.

Although these suggestions emerge from empirical research, individual teachers may find that some of them work better than others given their unique teaching styles and personalities. In the end, all teachers must decide which attitudes and behaviors are the most genuine in their approach to teaching.

Perhaps Ken Bain (2004) said it best:

> I cannot stress enough the simple yet powerful notion that the key to understanding the best teaching can be found not in particular practices or rules but in the attitudes of the teachers, in their faith in their students' abilities to achieve, in their willingness to take their students seriously and to let them assume control of their own education, and in their commitment to let all policies and practices flow from central learning objectives and from a mutual respect and agreement between students and teachers. (p. 78)

References

Andersen, J. F. (1979). Teacher immediacy as a predictor of teaching effectiveness. In D. Nimmo (Ed.), *Communication yearbook 3* (pp. 543–559). New Brunswick, NJ: Transaction Books.

Ambady, N., & Rosenthal, R. (1993). Half a minute: Predicting teacher evaluations from thin slices of nonverbal behavior and physical attractiveness. *Journal of Personality and Social Psychology, 64,* 431–441.

Bain, K. (2004). *What the best college teachers do.* Cambridge, MA: Harvard University Press.

Bakker, A. B., & Schaufeli, W. B. (2000). Burnout contagion processes among teachers. *Journal of Applied Social Psychology, 30,* 2289–2308.

Banfield, S. R., Richmond, V. P., & McCroskey, J. C. (2006). The effect of teacher misbehaviors on teacher credibility and affect for the teacher. *Communication Education, 55,* 63–72.

Benson, T. A., Cohen, A. L., & Buskist, W. (2005). Rapport: Its relation to student attitudes and behaviors toward teachers and classes. *Teaching of Psychology, 32,* 237–239.

Dobransky, N. D., & Frymier, A. B. (2004). Developing teacher-student relationships through out of class communication. *Communication Quarterly, 52,* 211–223.

Frisby, B. N., & Martin, M. M. (2010). Instructor-student and student-student rapport in the classroom. *Communication Education, 59,* 146–164.

Gorham, J. (1988). The relationship between verbal teacher immediacy behaviors and student learning. *Communication Education, 37,* 40–53.

Gorham, J., & Christophel, D. M. (1990). The relationship of teachers' use of humor in the classroom to immediacy and student learning. *Communication Education, 39,* 46–62.

Gorham, J., Cohen, S. H., & Morris, T. L. (1997). Fashion in the classroom II: Instructor immediacy and attire. *Communication Research Reports, 14,* 11–23.

Jaasma, M. A., & Koper, R. J. (1999). The relationship of student-faculty out-of-class communication to instructor immediacy and trust to student motivation. *Communication Education, 48,* 41–47.

Legg, A. M., & Wilson, J. H. (2009). E-mail from professor enhances student motivation and attitudes. *Teaching of Psychology, 36,* 205–211.

Mazer, J. P., & Hunt, S. K. (2008). "Cool" communication in the classroom: A preliminary examination of student perceptions of instructor use of positive slang. *Qualitative Research Reports in Communication, 9,* 20–28.

Mazer, J. P., Murphy, R. E., & Simonds, C. J. (2007). The effects of teacher self-disclosure via Facebook on teacher credibility. *Learning, Media, & Technology, 34,* 175–183.

Morris, T. L., Gorham, J., Cohen, S. H., & Huffman, D. (1996). Fashion in the classroom: Effects of attire on student perceptions of instructors in college classes. *Communication Education, 45,* 135–148.

Plax, T. G., Kearney, P., McCroskey, J. C., & Richmond, V. P. (1986). Power in the classroom IV: Verbal control strategies, nonverbal immediacy, and affective learning. *Communication Education, 35,* 43–55.

Richmond, V. P., Gorham, J. S., & McCroskey, J. C. (1987). The relationship between selected immediacy behaviors and cognitive learning. In M. McLaughlin (Ed.), *Communication yearbook 10* (pp. 574–590). Beverly Hills, CA: Sage.

Rocca, K. A., & McCroskey, J. C. (1999). The interrelationship of student ratings of instructor's immediacy, verbal aggressiveness, homophily, and interpersonal attraction. *Communication Education, 48,* 308–316.

Sheer, V. C., & Fung, T. K. (2007). Can e-mail communication enhance professor-student relationship and student evaluation of professor? Some empirical evidence. *Journal of Educational Computing Research, 37,* 289–306.

Sunnafrank, M., & Ramirez, A. (2004). At first sight: Persistent relational effects of get-acquainted conversations. *Journal of Social and Personal Relationships, 21,* 361–379.

Thweatt, K. S., & McCroskey, J. C. (1998). The impact of teacher immediacy and misbehaviors on teacher credibility. *Communication Education, 47,* 348–358.

Wilson, J. H. (2006). Predicting student attitudes and grades from perceptions of instructors' attitudes. *Teaching of Psychology, 33,* 91–95.

Wilson, J. H., & Locker, L. (2008). Immediacy scale represents four factors: Nonverbal and verbal components predict student outcomes. *Journal of Classroom Interaction, 42,* 4–10.

Wilson, J. H., Ryan, R. G., & Pugh, J. L. (2010). Professor-student rapport scale predicts student outcomes. *Teaching of Psychology, 37,* 246–251.

Wilson, J. H., & Wilson, S. B. (2007). The first day of class affects student motivation: An experimental study. *Teaching of Psychology, 34*, 226–230.

Witt, P. L., Wheeless, L. R., & Allen, M. (2004). A meta-analytical review of the relationship between teacher immediacy and student learning. *Communication Monographs, 71,* 184–207.

Chapter 10

Learning-Centered Lecturing ❖

David B. Daniel

It is quite fashionable to bash lecturing as an ineffective method employed by the lazy and/or misinformed to the ultimate misfortune of their students. Replete with zealous converts, this movement has deemed lecturing as outmoded and universally ineffective. They preach that lecturing should be abandoned for the newest craze in education. Innocent victims of the lecture, they claim, are rendered passive by the experience, with little ability to efficiently process information deep enough to encourage true learning. I learned all of this information, by the way, while being lectured to at teaching conferences.

It is essential to remember that classroom teaching is inherently a dynamic interaction of many variables (Daniel & Poole, 2009). Thus, it is not surprising that no single strategy works for every teacher in every situation (Halonen, 2002; Hardin, 2007). Lecturing is a deeply personal interaction among the teacher, material, student, and context. Like every good teacher, the lecturer must master this complex interaction to be effective. Regardless of one's ultimate style, however, one will not learn how to be a good lecturer from a book, chapter, or literature review. Such strategies are better for learning how to avoid mistakes. Although several important issues will be discussed in this chapter, keep in mind that *teaching is personally empirical*: A teacher has to figure out what tools work best through critically reflective trial and error. This chapter will revolve around a very simple premise: Good lecturers can be very effective teachers.

Lecturing Versus Presenting

Lecturing to undergraduates is a strategic endeavor that differs considerably from the mere presentation of information, which is an important distinction to consider. Like lecturing, a goal of presenting is effective communication. However, when we are presenting to interested peers, we can assume a modicum of prior knowledge and higher levels of motivation to engage in the material.

A lecture goes beyond presenting information: The goal of lecturing is teaching. Especially at the undergraduate level, a teacher cannot assume interest, prior knowledge, or a skilled learner. A good lecture is scaffolded, structured, and aligned with learning objectives. The goal of these strategies is to cultivate attention and motivation in learners while guiding them toward mastery of the subject matter. Good lecturers focus on, cultivate, and make efficient the work of learning as they deliver content (Svinicki & McKeachie, 2011). Thus, it is important that a good lecturer have a plan to incorporate content as well as knowledge of the learner and the learning process into a lecture.

Basics

Content Mastery: With Great Knowledge Comes Great Flexibility

In many ways, a teacher is a cognitive guide. A teacher who is very well versed on the material has a considerable advantage over those who are not. The first rule of lecturing as a teaching strategy is to know the content well enough to move beyond merely presenting information toward offering students a rich and informative learning experience. Content mastery allows a teacher to approach the topic from various angles, develop rich examples, and link the material to relevant experiences in students' lives. It is not enough to be one chapter ahead of the students. A teacher's charge is to connect the material to the learner in a way that promotes intellectual engagement. Successful execution of this task requires flexible knowledge of the material, depth, and creativity. A good lecturer has to know the terrain well enough to serve as a guide, be prepared for the unexpected, and be able to take advantage of teachable moments.

Enthusiasm

There are incredible individual differences among effective lecturers. Yet, there are also commonalities. For example, excellent teachers are often rated high on enthusiasm (Benjamin, 2002; Buskist, 2004; Murray, 1985; Svinicki & McKeachie, 2011). This does not mean that they are hyper. It means that the teacher exudes a commitment to the importance of the material that is obvious, even infectious, to the learner. Teachers are not always enthusiastic about the content they are teaching. In such circumstances, a "trick" teachers can use with some authenticity is to focus on getting enthusiastic about the *way* they teach a class, rather than about the material itself.

Style After Substance

We have all been witness to incredibly stimulating lectures as well as been victims of dull, pedantic, and nonsensical ones. Distinguishing a good lecturer from a poor one is a complicated matter. Like comedians, there are low-key lecturers, charismatic showmen, formal lecturers, casual lecturers, and everything in between. Some lecturers bounce around a room gesturing wildly while others stand nearly motionless behind a lectern. A teacher's style is an outward expression of his or her teaching philosophy, integrates personal characteristics, and incorporates effective pedagogical strategies. An accomplished lecturer cultivates a style and works within it to communicate effectively (Banner & Cannon, 1997; Benjamin, 2002).

An authentic style is much easier to teach within than adopting a teaching persona that is several steps away from who one really is. The more natural teachers are in the classroom, the more they can focus on the quality of their teaching. Most lecturers have a "stage personality" that exaggerates certain of their personal qualities to aid in effective communication. One way to glimpse the upper range of a potential teaching persona is to pay attention to the way people behave when debating a position to which they are personally committed. Are they calm and reasonable? Do they gesture wildly and take it a little over the top? Tapping into the way one behaves in situations in which one is passionate will help develop the boundaries of a persona and provide the freedom to authentically communicate enthusiasm, guide attention, and be comfortable in one's own classroom.

Ultimately, however, a teacher's persona will develop with experience. The singular best thing that a new teacher can do to become a better lecturer is to lecture. If not presently teaching a class, one may seek out opportunities for guest lectures. If enrolled in or teaching a class on teaching, consider implementing opportunities for several micro-lectures (e.g., 10 minutes or so) to experiment. It is like shopping for shoes: We all have our preferred style, but there are several versions of each style, and some fit better than others. The best way to figure out which is best is to try several of them on, even walk around in them. One does not want to be stuck in a painful pair of shoes when it's time to dance! To take the analogy a bit further, some people find a brand of shoes and stick with them forever, despite changes in their feet, their tasks, and the blisters they have learned to live with. It is important to periodically revisit a teaching persona, seek feedback on its effectiveness, and encourage it—and oneself as a teacher—to evolve.

Say It in Pictures: Using Metaphors for Individual Differences

While teaching to real or perceived learning styles has not been successfully demonstrated in the literature (Pashler, McDaniel, Rohrer, & Bjork, 2009), the concept of learning styles is very popular with teachers. Generally, learning styles theories claim that each student has a dominant style for information input or processing, based on sensory dominance (e.g., visual, kinesthetic, auditory) or other criteria (e.g., sequential/holistic, right brain/left brain). Thus, teaching can be more effective if we can identify the student's "dominant" input mode and provide the material to be learned in that modality. Lecturing has been criticized for favoring one of these styles (e.g., kinesthetic, sequential, left brained) and penalizing students with others—again, despite empirical evidence.

Many people erroneously believe that a lecture is simply an auditory experience. This simplistic view misses the point: The point is not how material is *delivered* by the teacher. The point is how the material is *processed* by the student. A student can process information in many ways if the material is delivered in a manner conducive to multiple representations. A rich learning experience with multiple avenues of cognitive access to the material can greatly increase learning. Being careful to avoid unnecessarily narrow or potentially exclusionary teaching methods will enable students to access the material with greater flexibility (Rose & Meyer, 2002). Thus, a lecture rich in visual references (even if spoken), appropriate physical gestures, movement, and variable pacing that also taps into the student's store of relevant experience is a powerful learning tool.

Attracting Attention: Humor and Seduction as Distractions

There are many speakers, articles, and chapters that promote the use of humor in the classroom. However, it is best to be authentic in one's teaching and to avoid contrived and/or desperate attempts to use humor to increase engagement: There is nothing sadder than a person failing in attempts to be funny.

Although humor may attract a bit of attention, it does not necessarily help students learn (Kaplan & Pascoe, 1977). A poor reason for humor is to make the students laugh. Yet, humor can be very satisfying to both teacher and student. Humor can establish and/or reinforce a connection that is valuable in human interactions. Remember, a teacher's job is to help students learn, and a good laugh about something unrelated to the material can divert attention, and memory, to the wrong things. To be an effective pedagogical tool, humor should effectively map onto the learning objectives and elucidate the primary point of focus, or serve one of several other strategic purposes. Humor can also be used to cleanse the palate between topics, to capture and redirect attention when students drift off a bit, or to reduce tension.

However, humor must match the style of the lecturer. Cultivating humor that is authentic and reinforces the learning objectives is often a very organic process. With experience, a teacher will find that certain comments or delivery methods receive a positive and constructive reaction from students. Humor interacts with personality, as well as delivery style, the material, and the context. Thus, humor is most effective when it fits a particular style and seems to flow naturally in the context of the lecture and is used to elucidate, not divert from, the learning objectives.

Cool Stories About Something Else: Seductive Details

Related to gratuitous attempts at humor is the concept of seductive details. Seductive details are interesting stories, tidbits, and asides that, while very interesting, subvert the learning process by offering a detour from the target material (Harp & Mayer, 1997, 1998). They are seductive for the teacher and the student in that they promote interest. Like humor, seductive details are often remembered better than the learning objectives (Garner, Gillingham, & White, 1989).

Cultivating attention for its own sake is not teaching. Teaching is directing attention. Attention directed toward an interesting distraction can backfire when it comes to learning. A good lecturer guides attention with very specific goals in mind, which is not to say that humor, stories, and interesting facts do not have their place in lecture. They certainly do if mapped onto learning objectives. Embellishments are potentially powerful tools that can both encourage and subvert the work of learning. They should be used strategically to focus attention on the learning objectives, develop metaphor, and reinforce memory.

Selecting and Structuring Lecture Content: Explanations Over Definitions

There are generally two basic structures for developing a lecture. The more traditional style is to begin with basic concepts and build toward greater complexity. This style tends to organize all information on a topic together; when finished with one topic, the teacher moves to the next topic. A common variation is a presentation style with which the teacher simply presents one topic or vocabulary word after another until all are covered (see Svinicki & McKeachie, 2011, for several other variations). Another structure for developing a lecture is to weave the main topics throughout the lecture, periodically revisiting them from different angles and over time. This method of spacing rather than massing content and encouraging the learner to make connections is sometimes referred to as "interleaving" and offers some advantages with respect to retention of learned material (Kornell & Bjork, 2008).

In an introductory-level survey course, a lecturer cannot a cover all of the material well (Hobbs, 2006). Attempts to do so lead to crowded presentations with verbatim definitions of concepts already covered in the text. To develop a rich learning experience, a lecturer must select the topics most conducive to the medium. Although definitions are an important first step for deeper learning (Willingham, 2009), a rich lecture can be a wonderful learning experience if done well. Choose a few core concepts, interesting ideas, topics that are likely to be confusing for students, or some combination of the three. Bring these topics to life. Explain how they work. Connect them to other concepts and connect them to the students' prior knowledge or experience. Do not feel bad for selecting material because you like it. One caution, though: Teachers sometimes have a difficult time teaching concepts with which they are very familiar to neophytes. Be careful to scaffold areas of interest at a level appropriate for the students.

Regardless of which structure is adopted, it is important to consider time as a variable. A rushed lecture is not an optimal learning experience. Students need time to process, consider, formulate questions, and modulate attention. A teacher needs time to monitor students for feedback. A rushed teacher creates a culture that discourages questions, deep processing, and sinking-in time. The primary way teachers endorse shallow processing to our students is through crowded PowerPoint slides and the ever-popular talking faster and faster to cover everything as the end of class draws near. If the primary goal is to cover all the material rather than teach it, one must assess one's priorities. If the teacher's goal is to encourage mastery of the content, then the teacher must allow students the time to do so. Leave time for learning, leave time for questions, and leave time to go deeper into a subject when the situation arises. Like a good conversation, lecturing requires participation from everyone involved.

Work the Room: Lecturing Is a Conversation

Delivering a lecture is often seen as a one-sided event: The sage speaks, the student listens (Bligh, 2000). However, the goal of a good lecture is to encourage students to actively process information. In this sense, the teacher is actually engaged in a reciprocal conversation with students. If teachers have achieved content mastery and have an authentic teaching style, they will be able to devote attention to active listening. They scan the room, not just the first few rows, to make sure students are comprehending the material. If students seem uninterested or confused, teachers back up and attack the content from a different angle. They encourage students to ask questions and facilitate teaching. They seek feedback at every step in this process, both verbal and nonverbal, and do not move on in the lecture until the students are ready. It is not uncommon for good teachers to be thoroughly exhausted at the end of a lecture due to such vigilance.

Conclusions

A great lecture is a truly memorable experience. It leaves the student informed, curious, and enthusiastic to engage in the material. Teachers working to improve their lecturing should allow themselves time to develop and space to experiment, and endeavor to avoid complacency by periodically revisiting their teaching persona. At all points in the development of this skill, cultivate opportunities to experiment while continually seeking feedback as to how these efforts impact learning, and do not fall into the trap of confusing entertainment with teaching. Last, teachers of all styles should experiment with a variety of teaching methods so they can match the method to their strengths as well as to course learning objectives.

References

Banner, J. M., & Cannon, H. C. (1997). *The elements of teaching*. New Haven, CT: Yale University Press.

Benjamin, L. T. (2002). Lecturing. In S. F. Davis & W. Buskist (Eds.), *The teaching of psychology: Essays in honor of Wilbert J. McKeachie and Charles L. Brewer* (pp. 57–67). Mahwah, NJ: Lawrence Erlbaum.

Bligh, D. A. (2000). *What's the use of lectures?* San Francisco, CA: Jossey-Bass.

Buskist, W. (2004). Ways of the master teacher. *APS Observer, 17*(9), 23–26.

Daniel, D. B., & Poole, D. A. (2009). The ecology of pedagogy: How collaborative research can prevent us from harming students. *Perspectives on Psychological Science, 4,* 91–96.

Garner, R., Gillingham, M. G., & White, C. S. (1989). Effects of "seductive details" on macroprocessing and microprocessing in adults and children. *Cognition and Instruction, 6,* 41–57.

Halonen, J. S. (2002). Classroom presence. In S. F. Davis & W. Buskist (Eds.), *The teaching of psychology: Essays in honor of Wilbert J. McKeachie and Charles L. Brewer* (pp. 57–67). Mahwah, NJ: Lawrence Erlbaum.

Hardin, E. (2007). Presentation software in the college classroom: Don't forget the instructor. *Teaching of Psychology, 34,* 53–57.

Harp, S. F., & Mayer, R. E. (1997). The role of interest in learning from scientific text and illustrations: On the distinction between emotional interest and cognitive interest. *Journal of Educational Psychology, 89,* 92–102.

Harp, S. F., & Mayer, R. E. (1998). How seductive details do their damage: A theory of cognitive interest in science learning. *Journal of Educational Psychology, 90,* 414–434.

Hobbs, S. H. (2006). The classroom lecture. In W. Buskist & S. F. Davis (Eds.), *Handbook of the teaching of psychology* (pp. 49–53). Malden, MA: Blackwell.

Kaplan, R. M., & Pascoe, G. C. (1977). Humorous lectures and humorous examples: Some effects upon comprehension and retention. *Journal of Educational Psychology, 69,* 61–66.

Kornell, N., & Bjork, R. A. (2008). Learning concepts and categories: Is spacing the "enemy of induction"? *Psychological Science, 19,* 585–592.

Murray, H. G. (1985). Classroom teaching behaviors related to college teaching effectiveness. In J. G. Donald & A. M. Sullivan (Eds.), *Using research to improve teaching*. New Directions for Teaching and Learning, No. 23 (pp. 21–34). San Francisco, CA: Jossey-Bass.

Pashler, H., McDaniel, M., Rohrer, D., & Bjork, R. (2009). Learning styles: Concepts and evidence. *Psychological Science in the Public Interest, 9,* 105–119.

Rose, D. H., & Meyer, A. (2002). *Teaching every student in the digital age: Universal design for learning*. Alexandria, VA: Association for Supervision and Curriculum Development.

Svinicki, M., & McKeachie, W. J. (2011). *McKeachie's teaching tips: Strategies, research, and theory for college and university teachers* (13th ed.). Belmont, CA: Wadsworth.

Willingham, D. T. (2009). *Why don't students like school?* San Francisco, CA: Jossey-Bass.

Chapter 11

Active Learning ❖

Elizabeth Yost Hammer and Peter J. Giordano

Think back to your undergraduate years and describe a specific class session that stands out in your memory—is there a specific lecture or class day that you can still recall vividly to this day? If you can, jot down a few notes about it. What exactly is it that you remember, and what made it memorable?

For Elizabeth, it was a day in Dr. Pamela Manners's Developmental Psychology course (circa 1987). Dr. Manners was covering the research on birth order and had the class discuss this research in groups based on our own birth order (e.g., firstborn). It was the first time Elizabeth was exposed to group work in class and it's the only vivid memory she has of that course. For Peter, it was working hard to understand the idea of inter-actions in factorial experimental designs in an advanced statistics course while an undergraduate (circa 1978). Instead of reading dry accounts of this concept in a textbook, the professor had students use "canned" data sets to get printouts of statistical analyses. Students had to interpret the results of analyses of variance and draw graphs of the main effects and interactions. For the first time, the lightbulb went on about what the term "interaction" meant. It was a huge boost to his sense of statistical self-efficacy!

What these examples have in common, and what they probably have in common with your response, is that they both include *active learning*. Something about those class sessions moved us beyond passively taking in information to engaging with it in much deeper ways.

Almost without exception, when faculty members recall specific memories from their undergraduate days, their recollections reflect some component of active learning. This observation should come as little surprise, however, based on what we now know about how people learn (Bransford, Brown, & Cocking, 1999). Although well-organized and stimulating lectures can enhance learning (Lowman, 1995; Svinicki & McKeachie, 2011), some form of active learning is typically needed for deeper, more persistent learning to take place (Halpern & Hakel, 2003). Significant learning experiences usually involve both powerful cognitive and emotional components (Owen-Smith, 2004, 2007). The stories that we shared at the outset of this chapter illustrate the interconnections between these dimensions of learning.

It this chapter, we will present two metaphors for teaching. We then discuss ways to incorporate active learning into any course and offer some tips for getting started on using active learning techniques in teaching.

Metaphors for Teaching

To fully embrace active learning as a teaching strategy, it needs to fit one's metaphors for teaching. Consider your own metaphor. Do you view the teacher as coach? Cheerleader? Judge? Jury? Each of us has a metaphor for teaching and learning (whether we can explicitly articulate it or not), and it drives our behavior in the classroom. All too often our metaphors come not from thoughtful reflection and scholarly inquiry, but from what was traditionally "done" to us by our teachers.

The traditional metaphor of teaching conjures the image of a fountain in the center of a courtyard (the teacher) spouting fresh water into surrounding empty buckets (students). This metaphor conveys a teacher-centered model in which all-knowing teachers pour their knowledge into the unfilled heads of their students. MacGregor (1990) noted that this model leads to passive learning in students. Students listen and take notes, both of which can be done with no real thinking at all. This model breeds a low expectation in students for class preparation because they view the teacher and assigned texts as the sole sources of knowledge.

We endorse more of a student-centered model of teaching and learning, in which teachers ignite student thought, reflection, application, and curiosity. Students are not merely passive listeners, but instead active problem solvers who begin to see themselves and their peers as sources of knowledge (MacGregor, 1990).

Transforming classrooms from passive to active environments requires a shift in our "mental models," or how we think about course objectives, assignments, and in-class teaching methods. It requires that students engage with the material—that they reflect on it, struggle with it, discuss it with peers, or otherwise *do* something with it. It requires that we implement active learning strategies.

Incorporating Active Learning Into Teaching

The benefits of active learning are numerous and well documented. Svinicki and McKeachie (2011) asserted that active learning helps eliminate the "illusion of understanding" (p. 190) by affording students opportunities to demonstrate their own level of understanding. Bain (2004) noted that the "best" college teachers are ones that create learning environments in which students confront real problems, struggle with ideas, and engage genuinely with important ideas.

Classroom Assessment Techniques

One of the easiest ways to get started with active learning is to incorporate classroom assessment techniques (CATs) into class sessions. CATs are brief, non-credit exercises intended to assess student understanding of the class material. They allow teachers to assess quickly what students do and do not understand and, as a result, adjust their teaching. Palomba and Banta (1999) argued that CATs should be used to assess course-related knowledge, to uncover students' attitudes and values, and to assess students' reactions to specific instruction. More to our purposes, CATs have the added benefit of incorporating an active learning component into the class. Thus, if used skillfully, CATs can shift a traditional lecture to a more interactive format.

Angelo and Cross's (1993) well-known book is the definitive source for CATs. It describes 50 CATs, including examples, detailed instructions for implementation, and ideas for adapting each technique. In the following paragraphs, we describe a few of the most widely applicable CATs.

Think-Pair-Share

Using this technique, the teacher poses a question or dilemma for the students, gives them time to think about it, and asks them to share their thoughts with a partner. The teacher can then ask if there were any issues, concerns, or questions that arose, or randomly call on a few pairs to share their thoughts. This process takes a relatively short time to implement and provides a valuable opportunity to break up a lecture with an engaging activity that can bring to light any student confusion or misunderstandings.

Think-pair-shares are useful because one can use almost anything as the stem for students to consider. We have observed mathematics courses in which instructors will pose a challenging multiple-choice question that requires calculations, have students work them individually and compare answers with their partner, and then take questions from the class. Likewise, in an introductory sociology course, a teacher could ask students to explain a specific phenomenon using contemporary sociological perspectives. Once students have their individual examples, they can compare those examples to those of their partners, and then class discussion ensues. The questions teachers might pose to begin the process are limitless and can range from strictly objective to totally opinion based, depending on the nature of the material. The bottom line is that this CAT engages students by making them struggle with the material rather than passively receiving it.

Tell Your Partner

Another quick and easy CAT is Tell Your Partner. This technique is especially useful when covering complicated, detailed, or technical information. In this technique, the teacher arranges students in pairs and asks the partner on the left to explain concept X while the partner on the right explains concept Y. For instance, in a biology course, the partner on the left might explain in his or her own words the process of neural transmission to the partner on the right. Later in the class, the partner on the right might explain nerve impulses to the partner on the left. The assignments teachers can provide students using this CAT are limitless and can be modified to fit any specific course objective. Like other CATs, this one allows teachers to identify sources of misunderstanding, but it has the added benefit of encouraging students to see themselves and their peers as sources of knowledge.

Directed Paraphrasing

Another way to get students to think more deeply about course content is to ask them to paraphrase concepts for a specific audience. This technique, called Directed Paraphrasing, requires that students understand material at a level that allows them to communicate it to different audiences. For instance, one might ask students to explain John Calvin's understanding of the Eucharist to their 7-year-old nephew. Or, we might ask students to explain to their grandmother who has never been to college how one arrives at a research hypothesis. This exercise, besides being fun and adding an unexpected twist to the class, forces students to wrestle with their own level of understanding of the concepts.

Getting Started With CATs

Angelo and Cross (1993) offered several suggestions for integrating CATs into any course. First, if a technique is not appealing, do not use it. Teaching methods must match one's teaching style, academic discipline, and course objectives, and be suitable for one's students. If a teacher forces a method that does not feel right, then it will come across as awkward and unauthentic. Second, start small. Teachers should incorporate one or two CATs into their courses and see how well they work, especially if those courses have been primarily lecture oriented. Third, socialize students. Teachers should explain to their students why they are integrating these techniques into the classroom and what they hope to accomplish with them. Finally, because CATs often increase class discussion, teachers should be sure to build in some extra time for interacting with their students. CATs often bring to light issues that need clarification, and as a result, students can learn a lot from these activities and from each other. As active learning implies, teachers do not have to be the only person sharing with students what they know. Do not think that because a teacher is lecturing less that students are learning less. In fact, they are learning more (Nelson, 1989).

Group-Based Learning

Group-based learning (also called collaborative or cooperative learning) has been used in many ways in higher education. There are traditional out-of-class group projects, in-class group presentations, and study groups. There are specific group-based approaches to teaching and learning, such as Just-in-Time Teaching (Novak, in press), Problem-Based Learning (Rhem, 1998), and Interteaching (Saville & Zinn, in press). However, in this section we will focus on using in-class groups to foster active learning.

In-class group work provides an excellent venue for incorporating active learning into class sessions. Svinicki and McKeachie (2011) noted that collaborative learning encourages mutual peer support; provides opportunities for students to explain, summarize, and argue key issues; and produces better cognitive outcomes. Students also are more likely to talk in small groups, which encourages engagement and involvement.

Creating Effective In-Class Group Tasks and Experiences

The teacher's role in collaborative learning is to create a meaningful group task with clear objectives. Setting up meaningful and clear tasks is key to the success of group-based work. The group tasks should also be unmistakably tied to assessment strategies in the course. For example, if a teacher utilizes group activities that require students to work with broad issues, but then tests students on factual minutiae in multiple-choice tests, students will soon perceive the group work as meaningless.

Giordano and Hammer (1999) offered the following guidelines for maximizing success for using in-class group tasks.

- Discuss successful group work with students. Explain the characteristics of successful group process and let students share their ideas about it. Consider involving the class in developing guidelines for effective group work.
- Promote collaborative learning norms on the first day of class. This tactic emphasizes that group work is an integral part of the course. In fact, we form groups on the first day of class and have group members read the syllabus and together develop questions about the syllabus.
- Assign students to in-class groups and change groups periodically to ensure that students will interact with more peers than just the ones with whom they are already familiar. This also allows for more diverse groups in terms of student backgrounds. Changing groups periodically (e.g., after each exam) ensures that students do not get "stuck" in one group and allows more of the class to interact.
- Create a clear division of labor by assigning individual tasks within the group and change these roles regularly to decrease instances of social loafing and to avoid group dominators. Table 11.1 lists typical in-class group roles.
- Stay in contact with the groups. Avoid the temptation to hover over groups, which may cause students to struggle with the material, but float around the classroom and check in on groups to ensure that they are on task. Have "filler tasks" ready, in case one group finishes their task well before the others. For example, if a group is working on characteristics of sensory memory, you might ask them to begin thinking about working memory if they finish the task early.

Table 11.1   Typical Roles and Responsibilities for In-Class Groups

Role	Responsibilities
Group leader	Keeps the group focused on the task at hand
Recorder	Takes notes on the group's discussion (teacher can copy these notes and distribute to group members)
Devil's advocate	Challenges the group's thinking
Timekeeper	Monitors the time spent on task to ensure that the group finishes
Group spokesperson	Shares major points of the group's discussion with the whole class

Common Student Complaints About Group Work

If you make the shift to using in-class group activities, it is wise to anticipate student complaints. Here are three of the most common complaints we have experienced over the years.

- "I came to learn from YOU, the expert, not my peers." When we hear this complaint about group work, we take it as an invitation to talk to students about our teaching philosophies and the relevance of active learning. Explaining our rationale goes a long way toward encouraging student buy-in. We also point out that in the "real world," developing teamwork skills and working collaboratively is highly important.

- "I don't like my group." When we hear this complaint, we assure students that they will get to change groups periodically. More often than not, however, students are happy with their groups. In some classes, we have used semester-long groups. In this case, we take a proactive approach in dealing with interpersonal issues to prevent them from becoming a problem. One strategy is to have anonymous peer evaluations completed periodically by each group member. Keep in mind that teachers should evaluate the quality of the peer evaluation, otherwise students may not take it seriously. To evaluate the quality of peer evaluations, we have developed clear criteria for what we expect in such evaluations, which we share with students.

- "I don't get good notes from group work." Students want clean, neat notes that lead them directly to what will be on the test. Group work is inherently messy, so we have had to work on helping students develop their note-taking skills in these activities. We often suggest that a group appoint a note taker for the entire group (see Table 11.1). The group can review the notes together to make sure they are adequate. We have also offered to make copies of the notes (one page maximum) for each member of the group. Again, explaining the rationale and the objectives behind each task helps students see clearly those tasks on which they should be focusing their energies and how the task fits into the course material.

Conclusions

At the beginning of this chapter, we asked you to reflect on a specific classroom experience from your college years. If what you recalled had an active learning component like our recollections did, then you know well the power of active learning in creating memorable learning experiences. This type of vivid recollection—this type of impact—is exactly what teachers hope for in their students. Interspersing CATs or in-class group work throughout a lecture can achieve this type of student engagement, as can planning an entire course on a single active learning strategy.

References

Angelo, T. A., & Cross, K. P. (1993). *Classroom assessment techniques: A handbook for college teachers* (2nd ed.). San Francisco, CA: Jossey-Bass.

Bain, K. (2004). *What the best college teachers do.* Cambridge, MA: Harvard University Press.

Bransford, J. D., Brown, A. L., & Cocking, R. R. (Eds.). (1999). *How people learn: Brain, mind, experience, and school.* Washington, DC: National Academy Press.

Giordano, P. J., & Hammer E. Y. (1999). In-class collaborative learning: Practical suggestions from the teaching trenches. *Teaching of Psychology, 26,* 42–44.

Halpern, D. F., & Hakel, M. D. (2003). Applying the science of learning to the university and beyond. *Change, 35,* 36–41.

Lowman, J. (1995). *Mastering the techniques of teaching* (2nd ed.). San Francisco, CA: Jossey-Bass.

MacGregor, J. (1990). Collaborative learning: Shared inquiry as a process of reform. In M. D. Svinicki (Ed.), *The changing face of college teaching.* New Directions for Teaching and Learning, No. 42 (pp. 19–30). San Francisco, CA: Jossey-Bass.

Nelson, C. E. (1989). Skewered on the unicorn's horn: The illusion of tragic tradeoff between content and critical thinking in the teaching of science. In L. Crow (Ed.), *Enhancing critical thinking in the sciences* (pp. 17–27). Washington, DC: Society for College Science Teachers.

Novak, G. (in press). Just-in-time-teaching. In W. Buskist & J. E. Groccia (Eds.), *Evidence-based teaching.* New Directions in Teaching and Learning. San Francisco, CA: Jossey-Bass.

Owen-Smith, P. (2004). What is cognitive-affective learning (CAL)? *Journal of Cognitive Affective Learning, 1,* 11.

Owen-Smith, P. (2007, March). *Rescuing the affective in teaching and learning.* Paper presented at the 19th Southeastern Conference on the Teaching of Psychology, Kennesaw State University, Marietta, GA.

Palomba, C., & Banta, T. (1999). *Assessment essentials: Planning, implementing, and improving assessment in higher education.* San Francisco, CA: Jossey-Bass.

Rhem, J. (1998). Problem-based learning: An introduction. *The National Teaching and Learning Forum, 8,* 1–4.

Saville, B. K., & Zinn, T. E. (in press). Interteaching. In W. Buskist & J. E. Groccia (Eds.), *Evidence-based teaching.* New Directions for Teaching and Learning. San Francisco, CA: Jossey-Bass.

Svinicki, M., & McKeachie, W. J. (2011). *McKeachie's teaching tips: Strategies, research, and theory for college and university teachers* (13th ed.). Belmont, CA: Wadsworth.

Chapter 12

Leading Discussions

❖

Bryan K. Saville, Tracy E. Zinn, and Krisztina Varga Jakobsen

As any teacher can tell you, teaching is hard work—it can be demanding, challenging, even frustrating. This statement may be especially true for graduate students and new assistant professors, who often have little, if any, teaching experience. Thrust into the teaching spotlight for the first time and not knowing exactly what to expect, new college teachers often resort to tactics their teachers used. But as many new teachers soon discover, what works effectively for some teachers may not work so well for others. In reality, effective teaching likely entails an interaction among the characteristics of the teacher, the material being taught, the students, and other factors present in the classroom.

Nevertheless, research on human learning suggests that some teaching practices are likely to be more effective than others, regardless of who happens to be using them or the context in which they are used. For instance, although most college teachers use lecture-based teaching methods (Benjamin, 2002), a sizeable body of research shows that traditional lectures tend to be less effective than alternative teaching methods at promoting student learning (e.g., Benedict & Anderton, 2004; Kulik, Kulik, & Cohen, 1979; Saville, Zinn, Neef, Norman, & Ferreri, 2006). Why might this be? For one, lectures tend to promote student passivity. Traditional lectures also fail to capitalize on much of what researchers know about human learning (Halpern & Hakel, 2002; McDaniel & Wooldridge, Chapter 6). In contrast, teaching methods that promote active involvement tend to produce greater amounts of student learning and enjoyment (Mathie et al., 1993). Thus, taking steps to increase students' involvement is likely to be a boon for teachers who want to improve their classes. In the following paragraphs, we will discuss one way teachers can increase active learning in their classrooms: by incorporating more discussion. Specifically, we will discuss what teachers can do both before and during class to improve the chances that their students will have a good discussion.

Preparing for Class Discussion

As many teachers will attest, engaging students in a class discussion can be a lot like pulling teeth. Excited about the material and assuming that students will be as well, teachers ask questions expecting hands to shoot up all over the classroom. Instead, the question is followed by deafening silence. Although the silence really only lasts a few seconds, to many teachers, especially those who are new to the classroom, it seems to last forever.

Why is it that so many students fail to participate in class discussions? There are likely a number of reasons: Some fail to read the material before class and do not want to appear unprepared; some read but fail to understand the material and do not want to appear ignorant; and to some, it might simply be a matter of habit—they do not have to talk in their other classes, so why start now?

Certainly, each of the preceding assumptions might be correct. Another possibility, however, is that some students, even if they have read, have understood, and are willing to discuss the material, may not be prepared to discuss it on such short notice. Although spontaneous discussions have their place in the classroom, preparation for discussion on the part of both students and teachers is likely to produce better results.

Of course, encouraging students to read before class is vital for having effective discussions. There are some ways that teachers can make pre-class reading more likely. For example, reading quizzes that students take online or at the beginning of class tend to increase class preparation (Kouyoumdjian, 2004) and may even help students notice the link between reading and class performance (Sappington, Kinsey, & Munsayac, 2002). As most teachers and students will acknowledge, though, effectively preparing for discussion often entails more than just getting students to read.

Teachers need to ponder their reasons for wanting to conduct a class discussion. Whether teachers want to help students articulate their thoughts or better understand course material, they should always attempt to connect the discussion to the student learning objectives for the unit or course. It is also important that students understand the reasons for the discussion. Some students erroneously believe that teaching involves only lecturing and that, without lecture, teachers are not actually doing their job (Boyce & Hineline, 2002). Explaining to students that discussion is important to their learning may go a long way in heading off these arguments.

Once teachers have identified reasons for incorporating discussions into their courses, they should consider what material might lend itself nicely to discussion (Hansen, 1983). Topics that are controversial or those about which one can take a side on an issue may be ideal. Teachers also should identify what they hope to accomplish in terms of knowledge complexity (Zinn, Reis-Bergan, & Baker, 2010). For example, in an upper-level capstone experience, teachers might expect the discussions to focus on synthesizing information across courses, whereas in a sophomore-level survey course, discussion might focus more on defining concepts and giving real-world examples. Teachers should establish expectations at the beginning of the course and repeatedly communicate those expectations to students throughout the semester.

Prior to the discussions, guidelines should be set. The guidelines should include ground rules that provide a safe environment in which students can share their ideas. Teachers can provide a confidentiality statement that highlights the importance of not sharing other students' personal information outside of class. Such a statement can promote an environment in which students feel comfortable discussing their ideas, especially in courses that cover sensitive topics. The guidelines should include expectations for behavior during the discussion (e.g., respecting others, raising one's hand to speak, not interrupting). Although teachers should ultimately decide which guidelines will be in place, they should consider involving students in the process. As research on procedural justice shows, people are more likely to view a process as fair if they are involved in its development (Greenberg & Folger, 1983). Thus, when students are involved in the process, they may be more likely to follow the guidelines and may even be more comfortable sharing their ideas during the discussions (Fassinger, 1995; Yoakley, 1975). In addition, teachers should model the type of behavior they want their students to display (Svinicki & McKeachie, 2011).

Course Design

Teachers affect the quality of class discussions by the way they design their courses. One way to facilitate class discussions is by using specific teaching tools or teaching methods that facilitate class discussion. Some examples include (a) Questions, Quotations, and Talking Points (QQTPs); (b) Just-in-Time-Teaching (JiTT); and (c) various types of collaborative learning.

QQTPs are daily or weekly response papers that students submit before class. The QQTPs include questions about the material, a quotation that is particularly interesting or controversial, and a list of talking points to which students can refer when participating in the discussion (Connor-Greene, 2005). Depending on the course, teachers may require that questions focus on analysis, evaluation, or synthesis of the material. Teachers can ask students to share their questions before class (e.g., via *Blackboard*©) or simply bring them to class. Either way, by preparing QQTPs beforehand, students will have thought about the material and may thus be more likely to contribute something to the discussion. Students have rated the use of QQTPs positively and report that the structure enhances preparation for class discussion (Connor-Greene, 2005).

JiTT is a web-based teaching method that allows students to share what they know about the course material before class (Novak, in press). Specifically, JiTT entails the teacher preparing several short-answer or multiple-choice questions (called pre-class questions, or PCQs) that students answer online before coming to class. By reviewing students' answers before class and identifying common mistakes, the teacher can better understand the difficulties students are having with the material. The teacher can then discuss specific material with the class. The teacher selects several representative responses to the PCQs (correct, partially correct, and incorrect) and discusses those answers with the students, in whatever form the teacher chooses (e.g., whole class, small groups). At the end of the discussion, the teacher then presents correct answers to the PCQs in order to reinforce the concepts. Because students attempted to answer the PCQs before class, they are better prepared to engage in discussion about the PCQs and related material, as well as share their understanding (or lack thereof) of the material.

Finally, collaborative-learning methods are also useful for stimulating student discussion. Examples include team-based learning (Michaelsen, Knight, & Fink, 2004; Michaelsen & Sweet, in press), peer tutoring (Annis, 1983), peer instruction (Crouch & Mazur, 2001), and interteaching (Boyce & Hineline, 2002; Saville & Zinn, in press). With each of these methods, students discuss the material with each other and can practice elaborating, listening, and explaining.

Although QQTPs, JiTT, and collaborative-learning methods help facilitate discussion, teachers do not necessarily need to use specific teaching methods in order to encourage students to prepare for class discussion. Several less formulaic approaches can serve the same function. For example, teachers can require students to answer a set of questions before class or have students construct their own questions about the material. Teachers can further refine these approaches by requiring students to answer both fact-based questions, such as providing the definition of a particular concept, and more complex questions, for example, applying the concept to a real-life situation or discussing it in the context of a research study. In addition, teachers can incorporate asynchronous discussion boards on which students post questions before class in order to prepare for class discussion (see Suler, 2004).

Facilitating Discussion

Preparing for class discussion takes time and effort, not only with regard to student preparation but also with regard to deciding what the actual class discussion should look like. In this section, we describe ways in which teachers can structure the discussion and keep it moving forward.

Getting Discussion Started

Teachers can structure discussions in a number of ways. For instance, before moving to a whole-group discussion, teachers might ask students to take a few minutes to think about the discussion topic and jot down their ideas. This strategy may be particularly useful in classes where the students are not particularly talkative.

Teachers could also begin with small-group discussions. This strategy is beneficial for a number of reasons. First, students can share their ideas with members of their group and receive feedback from their peers before sharing their ideas with the entire class. Another advantage of this strategy is that students who are quiet may be more likely to speak in a small group than in front of the whole class. Depending on how the small-group discussions are going, teachers might have individual students voice their ideas to the larger group, or they may turn to intergroup discussions where students take sides on an issue, for example, and then discuss their reasons for choosing one side or the other.

Keeping Discussion Going

What should teachers do if students are not participating in the discussions? In cases in which a teacher has chosen to begin with small-group discussions, the teacher might use a strategy in which numbers are assigned to each group and to each student within a group. The teacher (or a student) can then select numbers at random to decide which student from which group will speak. Assuming that the teacher has given the groups adequate time to think about a question or topic, everyone should have prepared something to say. In addition, because the group members have talked among themselves, they may be more likely to support each other when one of their group members speaks out individually. This method also reduces, if not completely eliminates, the likelihood that any one student will dominate the discussion. It is important, however, to let students know that they will be called on randomly. All students thus have to pay attention during the discussion because they do not know if or when the teacher might select their name. If teachers decide to use this strategy in their course, they should let students know at the beginning of the semester that students should be prepared for each discussion as they may be called on, even if they do not volunteer to speak. Several studies have found that calling on students who do not volunteer actually helps to encourage class participation (Auster & MacRone, 1994; Dallimore, Hertenstein, & Platt, 2004). In addition, teachers should encourage students who may be anxious about speaking in front of the class to meet with them so that they can devise a plan to help the student succeed in the course.

It is also important for teachers to know ahead of time what they are going to do if the discussion strays. Teachers can try to avoid off-track discussions by providing students with very specific questions that are important to address during the discussion. If the discussion does, indeed, go off track, it is the teacher's responsibility to steer students back in the right direction. Ultimately, teachers should have a plan about where a discussion should go, but they should also be flexible in the event the discussion takes a turn that improves students' understanding of the material.

Giving Students a Voice

As students share their ideas, it is particularly important to keep in mind that students may sometimes not hear what others have said. Teachers should restate students' comments so the rest of the class can be involved in the discussion. In addition, if teachers elaborate at all when restating students' comments, they should be sure to delineate what information was theirs and what information was the student's. In this way, students realize that their ideas are important and ultimately drive the discussion.

Conclusions

Incorporating discussion in the classroom capitalizes on much of what we know about human learning. Regardless of the techniques teachers use, effective discussions are more likely to occur if both teacher and students are prepared. New teachers should also remember that incorporating class discussion changes their role from "sage on the stage" to "guide on the side" (King, 1993). Facilitating good discussions takes practice, preparation, and patience, especially when teachers are used to dominating the conversation.

References

Annis, L. F. (1983). The processes and effects of peer tutoring. *Human Learning, 2*, 39–47.

Auster, C. J., & MacRone, M. (1994). The classroom as a negotiated social setting: An empirical study of the effects of faculty members' behavior on students' participation. *Teaching Sociology, 22*, 289–300.

Benedict, J. O., & Anderton, J. B. (2004). Applying the Just-in-Time Teaching approach to teaching statistics. *Teaching of Psychology, 31*, 197–199.

Benjamin, L. T., Jr. (2002). Lecturing. In S. F. Davis & W. Buskist (Eds.). *The teaching of psychology: Essays in honor of Wilbert J. McKeachie and Charles L. Brewer* (pp. 57–67). Mahwah, NJ: Lawrence Erlbaum.

Boyce, T. E., & Hineline, P. N. (2002). Interteaching: A strategy for enhancing the user-friendliness of behavioral arrangements in the college classroom. *The Behavior Analyst, 25*, 215–226.

Connor-Greene, P. A. (2005). Fostering meaningful classroom discussions: Student-generated questions, quotations, and talking points. *Teaching of Psychology, 32*, 173–175.

Crouch, C. H., & Mazur, E. (2001). Peer instruction: Ten years of experience and results. *American Journal of Physics, 69*, 970–977.

Dallimore, E. J., Hertenstein, J. H., & Platt, M. B. (2004). Classroom participation and discussion effectiveness: Student-generated strategies. *Communication Education 53*, 103–115.

Fassinger, P. A. (1995). Understanding classroom interaction: Students' and professors' contributions to students' silence. *Journal of Higher Education, 66*, 82–96.

Greenberg, J., & Folger, R. (1983). Procedural justice, participation, and the fair process effect in groups and organizations. In P. Paulus (Ed.), *Basic group processes* (pp. 235–256). New York, NY: Springer Verlag.

Halpern, D. F., & Hakel, M. D. (Eds.). (2002). *Applying the science of learning to the university and beyond*. San Francisco, CA: Jossey-Bass.

Hansen, W. L. (1983). Improving classroom discussion in economics courses. *Journal of Economic Education, 14*, 40–49.

King, A. (1993). From sage on the stage to guide on the side. *College Teaching, 41*, 30–35.

Kouyoumdjian, H. (2004). Influence of unannounced quizzes and cumulative exam on attendance and study behavior. *Teaching of Psychology, 31*, 110–111.

Kulik, J. A., Kulik, C. C., & Cohen, P. A. (1979). A meta-analysis of outcome studies of Keller's personalized system of instruction. *American Psychologist, 34*, 307–318.

Mathie, V. A., Beins, B., Benjamin, L. T., Jr., Ewing, M. M., Hall, C. C., Henderson, B., McAdam, D. W., Smith, R. A. (1993). Promoting active learning in psychology courses. In T. V. McGovern (Ed.), *Handbook for enhancing undergraduate education in psychology* (pp. 183–214). Washington, DC: American Psychological Association.

Michaelsen, L. K., Knight, A. B., & Fink, L. D. (Eds.). (2004). *Team-based learning: A transformative use of small groups in college teaching*. Sterling, VA: Stylus.

Michaelsen, L. K., & Sweet, M. (in press). Team-based learning. In W. Buskist & J. E. Groccia (Eds.), *Evidence-based teaching*. New Directions in Teaching and Learning. San Francisco, CA: Jossey-Bass.

Novak, G. M. (in press). Just-in-Time Teaching. In W. Buskist & J. E. Groccia (Eds.), *Evidence-based teaching*. New Directions in Teaching and Learning. San Francisco, CA: Jossey-Bass.

Sappington, J., Kinsey, K., & Munsayac, K. (2002). Two studies on reading compliance among college students. *Teaching of Psychology, 29*, 272–274.

Saville, B. K., & Zinn, T. E. (in press). Interteaching. In W. Buskist & J. E. Groccia (Eds.), *Evidence-based teaching*. New Directions in Teaching and Learning. San Francisco, CA: Jossey-Bass.

Saville, B. K., Zinn, T. E., Neef, N. A., Norman, R. V., & Ferreri, S. J. (2006). A comparison of interteaching and lecture in the college classroom. *Journal of Applied Behavior Analysis, 39*, 49–61.

Suler, J. (2004). The online disinhibition effect. *CyberPsychology and Behavior, 7*, 321–326.

Svinicki, M., & McKeachie, W. J. (2011). *McKeachie's teaching tips: Strategies, research, and theory for college and university teachers* (13th ed.). Belmont, CA: Wadsworth.

Yoakley, D. H. (1975). A study of student participation in classroom management to effect an increase in appropriate behavior. *Journal of Educational Research, 69*, 31–35.

Zinn, T. E., Reis-Bergan, M. J., & Baker, S. C. (2010). Ten things I hate about my capstone course—and a few ways to fix them. In D. S. Dunn, B. C. Beins, M. A. McCarthy, & G. W. Hill, IV (Eds.), *Best practices for teaching beginnings and endings in the psychology major: Research, cases, and recommendations* (pp. 237–251). New York, NY: Oxford University Press.

Chapter 13

Assessing Student Learning

❖

Robert Bubb

Whatever exists at all exists in some amount. To know it thoroughly involves knowing its quantity as well as its quality.
—E. L. Thorndike (1918, p. 16)

The assessment of learning involves the measurement of newly acquired information, skills, attitudes, behavior, and values. Learning involves a change in some aspect of the learner, yet that change often occurs beyond direct observation (Thorndike, 1918). Precisely when that change occurs is just as ambiguous. Learning can occur between the beginning and end of a semester, within a class period, during an exam, while reading, during a peer conversation, or while viewing popular media. Learning can occur multiple times and in a multitude of contexts over the course of a semester. To be sure, the process of learning is complex. However, assessment of learning does not need to be. This chapter will describe the elements of learning in terms of specific student learning objectives (SLOs), the methods for measuring SLOs, and the general grading procedures related to those assessment methods.

In short, evidence of learning comes from the methods of assessment that teachers use to measure the extent to which students successfully achieve SLOs. Figure 13.1 summarizes the basic approach to assessing learning outlined in this chapter. Teachers derive SLOs from course-specific goals and measure them by various assessment methods such as exams and

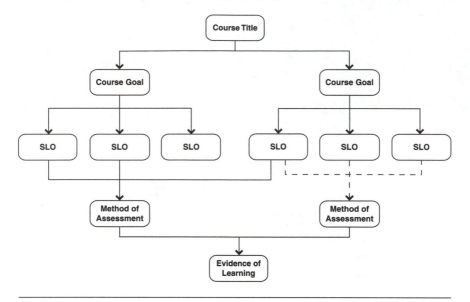

Figure 13.1   The Basic Process of Assessing Student Learning

written assignments. Proper assessment methods provide evidence of the extent that students have met SLOs and learned the subject matter.

Student Learning Objectives and Learning

A teacher's preparation for any course begins well before the start of the semester by carefully crafting specific course goals that will specify students' behavior, dispositions, and ways of thinking that will lead to the achievement of significant learning outcomes (Maki, 2004). However, goals are not merely restricted to having students learn content-related facts. Rather, goals also establish specific outcomes related to lifelong learning, critical thinking, and values that are meaningful now and in the future (Svinicki & McKeachie, 2011). For example, interpersonal, problem-solving, and communication skills are highly valued by employers, and pro-social behavior and ethical decision-making skills are valued by society (Davis, 2009; Suskie, 2009). Setting and helping students achieve meaningful goals contribute to students' successes in their citizenship and social roles as well as in their current courses, future courses, and careers.

To select appropriate goals, teachers should first read the official course description and consider the role of the course within the curriculum (e.g., an introductory course is usually intended to familiarize students with the discipline). In many instances, a curriculum committee has already designated basic learning criteria important for student development. Teachers should then choose as many goals as they can realistically expect to accomplish, and, of course, these goals will determine course planning decisions such as choice of textbook, teaching technique, course design, and SLOs.

Once course goals have been established, teachers should identify specific SLOs for each aspect of the subject matter that they will address over the semester (see Figure 13.1). SLOs typically consist of three parts: the learner as the subject, an action verb, and the subject matter content. The action verb describes the learner's behavior relative to the subject matter content, and generally represents a cognitive dimension of Bloom's taxonomy of learning (Krathwohl, 2002). Bloom's taxonomy is a loose hierarchy of simple-to-complex thinking skills taught by the teacher and employed by the learner throughout a course. The simplest cognitive dimension is *remember,* followed by *understand, apply, analyze, evaluate,* and *create* as the highest cognitive dimension (Krathwohl, 2002). Examples of SLOs that tap into specific elements of Bloom's taxonomy might be that students will

- remember the dates of major events in American history,
- analyze the prevailing motivational theories of human behavior, or
- apply poetic elements such as prosody and dictation in their writing assignments.

There can be hundreds of SLOs related to a given subject matter, and, of course, there is not enough time in an academic term for students to understand everything there is to know about a particular topic (Davis, 2009). That is why selection of SLOs for any given course is critical both to how teachers approach teaching course content and to students learning it. Once teachers have selected SLOs, they can then start to tailor class presentations, projects, in-class activities, exams, and other assessments that address those SLOs.

Assessment Methods for Measuring Learning

Once key SLOs have been established, teachers next need to develop appropriate measures of student learning (see Figure 13.1). Quizzes, exams, and written assignments are the most common methods of assessment, but there are many less common and creative methods available, too (see Buskist & Davis, 2006; Davis, 2009; Svinicki & McKeachie, 2011). Depending on the SLO, some assessment methods may be more appropriate than others. For example, multiple-choice exams typically assess simple cognitive skills such as remembering and understanding, while terminal papers assess more complex cognitive skills such as analyzing and evaluating.

Additionally, not all SLOs that teachers develop need to be assessed. In fact, it might be impossible for some teachers to assess every SLO in their courses, especially if the primary goal of a course is only to convey the facts and figures of the subject matter. In such cases, the teacher needs simply to sample the content domain as an appropriate assessment of learning. However, teachers should assess students' achievement of highly important SLOs using multiple methods (e.g., an in-class activity, quiz, *and* exam). Indeed, testing different SLOs using a variety of measures will increase the reliability of the overall assessment of student learning (Bachiochi & Weiner, 2004). Remember, too, that not all methods of assessment need to be graded or count toward a grade.

Classroom Assessment Techniques (CATs)

CATs are exercises designed to measure student understanding of material presented in the classroom course (Angelo & Cross, 1993). For example, a teacher might use the CAT known as the "muddiest point." Prior to ending class, the teacher asks students to write anonymously on a blank sheet of paper the concept that they found was the most difficult to understand during class. The muddiest point, as with most CATs, helps teachers identify student misunderstanding of class material, provides teachers the opportunity to develop materials for subsequent classes that will clarify difficult concepts, and helps students improve their learning of the subject matter because they can review the material an additional time before moving to new course material.

There are a variety of CATs that can be used to assess a range of cognitive skills. The "one-sentence summary" challenges students to synthesize several points into one long sentence describing who does what to whom, where, when, how, and why. Another CAT known as "analytic memos" requires students to write a one- to two-page analysis to a hypothetical decision maker and apply course concepts to solve a "real-world" problem. For more details about CATs, see Angelo and Cross (1993).

Quizzes and Examinations

Quizzes and examinations are the most common methods of assessing student learning. Quizzes are usually short, non-cumulative, and frequent assessments, whereas examinations tend to be long, cumulative, and infrequent. Both typically consist of multiple-choice, short-answer, and essay questions. Teachers interested in assessing a wide range of SLOs usually create quizzes and examinations that integrate all of these types of questions.

Multiple-choice questions typically assess lower-level cognitive dimensions of learning and are the easiest to grade because of their objective nature. However, writing a good multiple-choice question—one that is unambiguous—is not an easy task. Each multiple-choice question contains an item stem and a set of possible answers. The item stem is the question or a description of the problem to be solved. The set of possible answers includes a correct answer and several distracters—answers similar to the correct answer, but that are incorrect. When writing multiple-choice questions, teachers should seek to make item stems clear and offer distractors that are plausible. Teachers should avoid using negative phrasing (e.g., words like "is not" or "never") in the stem because such wording tends to confuse students or may give away the correct answer. The correct answer should be obvious to students who have studied the material.

Textbook publishers often provide test banks that reduce the amount of time teachers spend on generating multiple-choice and other types of questions. However, test bank questions sometimes are poorly constructed or require teachers to edit some of the questions in order to match their SLOs. Also, test bank questions reflect only the material covered in the text; they do not address new material that teachers present in class. Thus, teachers often supplement test bank questions with questions they write based on their class presentations.

In contrast to multiple-choice and other forms of objective questions, short-answer questions require students to generate written responses. Open-ended responses assess student understanding of the subject matter more effectively than objective questions by reducing the possibility of students guessing correctly. Short-answer questions are easier to develop than multiple-choice questions because there are no distractors to generate, but the downside is that grading requires more time. Of course, open-ended questions result in a wide range of responses, which is why it is often helpful for teachers to create a rubric—an outline or summary of the "perfect" answer to each question—when grading short-answer questions.

Like short-answer questions, essay questions are relatively easy to develop but often difficult to grade. A good essay question requires students to generate original answers by using higher-order cognitive skills to integrate and organize course concepts or solve problems. Good essay questions will clearly and precisely explain the required task. Juve (2006, p. 252) provided an example of a problematic and improved essay question:

Problematic: "Describe the normal distribution."

Improved: "Briefly describe how the standard normal distribution serves as a statistical model for estimation and hypothesis testing."

Depending on the question, the responses can be lengthy. Students who are unsure of the answer will often respond using the shotgun approach: They will write everything they think is even tangentially related to the question. Unfortunately, the grader is left with the unenviable task of sifting through the response to determine if the student actually knows the answer to the question. Here are a couple of tips that can help in these types of grading situations. First, prior to grading any questions, teachers should create a rubric. Second, the teacher should select and read a random sample of four or five questions to determine if the rubric is as finely tuned as it should be. The resulting rubric will focus the teacher to look for the key points and increase the reliability of the assessment across all students' essay responses.

Worksheets

Worksheets are assessment methods that contain several questions or problems and are used to measure how well students remember, understand, apply, or evaluate various aspects of the subject matter. Worksheet questions can be multiple choice, true-false, fill-in-the-blank, and short answer and may present problems to analyze, questions to solve, and the like. Worksheets can serve as gradable and genuine learning activities for students. After all, presenting information in class and then asking students to apply that knowledge to solve a worksheet problem provides students with opportunities to integrate and synthesize information in new and creative ways.

There are many ways to grade worksheets. If the SLOs for one's course require lower-level cognitive skills, then grading does not have to be precise and time-consuming. Teachers can adopt a check-plus, check, or check-minus grading system. Teachers may even provide students with an answer key and ask students to assess their own work. Self-assessment is a lifelong skill that is useful when instructors are no longer around to provide feedback (Mentkowski & Loacker, 1985).

If the SLOs for one's course require higher-level cognitive skills such as application, integration, and synthesis of information, then more precision and time may be necessary for grading. Rubrics can help increase grading accuracy and decrease the amount of grading time.

Low-Stakes Written Assignments

Written assessments generally take two forms: low and high stakes. Low-stakes writing is typically informal, nongraded writing that allows students to become familiar with course concepts. High-stakes writing is formal writing and typically accounts for a significant portion of a student's grade. Teachers can use low- and high-stakes writing to assess all levels of Bloom's taxonomy.

Two examples of low-stakes writing are minute papers and journaling. A teacher may ask students to take a minute and summarize a concept that was discussed in class, apply a concept to their life, or briefly analyze competing concepts or theories discussed in a text (Wilson, 1986). Like the muddiest point, teachers may collect minute papers and check them for student understanding. Teachers may ask their students to write journal entries on a daily or weekly basis, or even after each class. Teachers often assign a small percentage of course credit for journaling. When grading journal entries, teachers must be careful in grading and in their comments because many journal entries are subjective and personal.

High-Stakes Written Assignments

High-stakes writing assignments, such as essays or research papers, require higher-level cognitive skills and are typically longer-term projects than low-stakes writing assignments. When assessing high-stakes writing assignments, many teachers develop and provide their students with a copy of the grading rubric. From the students' perspective, a rubric reduces the ambiguity in grading and increases the likelihood that they will understand their teacher's expectations in completing the assignment. Figure 13.2 provides an example of a basic rubric. Examples of discipline-specific rubrics can be found in Walvoord and Anderson (2010).

In addition to marking the paper according to the rubric, teachers often provide more detailed feedback in the form of marginal comments throughout the assignment. Students can then use this feedback to revise their writing on future drafts. Requiring students to submit drafts of each section of the assignment before submitting the entire paper often reduces students' tendency to procrastinate writing until just before the due date and improves the overall quality of the final draft. Well-written papers are easier and less time-consuming to grade than poorly written papers.

Group Work

Many kinds of learning exercises can be completed by students working in groups. When teachers choose to use group work as part of their assessment plan, they must consider two key questions—how will they divide students into groups and how will they assess group work? When teachers allow students to choose their own groups, many students choose to form groups with their friends in the class, which may interfere with students staying on task because discussion often gets sidetracked on outside-of-class events. If a course goal is to prepare students for team-building experiences, then forming groups based on random assignment or particular skill sets

	Unacceptable	Acceptable	Good	Excellent

Grading Criteria:

Subject Matter Content
Comments:

Organization of Writing
Comments:

Logical Conclusions
Comments:

Writing Quality
Comments:

Grammar and Spelling
Comments:

References and Citations
Comments:

Overall Grade: _____ / 100%

Figure 13.2   Example of a Grading Rubric for a High-Stakes Written Assignment

would provide a more beneficial learning experience. To be sure, an important aspect of learning to work with others is the ability to generate group cohesion and produce a quality product.

In addition to the overall quality of the product, assessment should include individual student contributions to the group assignment. Providing students with a rubric to assess each other anonymously on the key objectives for the group assignment will minimize the tendency of individual group members to exert less effort than when working alone. Teachers often include an open-ended question on the grading rubric to allow other group members to receive feedback on how they can improve their contributions to the group effort and outcome. Once students complete their assessment of their group's performance, the teacher collects the completed grading rubric and then offers an assessment, in writing, of the group's work before giving students their final grade on the team product.

Conclusions

There are many ways for teachers to assess their students' learning. Descriptions of the most common have been included in this chapter. However, it is important to note that new teachers have a unique perspective when it comes to assessment: They still remember being students. Now, as teachers, they can reflect back on their experiences as students and include assessments that they remember to be particularly effective, exclude or modify assessments that were ineffective, or create entirely new forms of assessment. Teachers should carefully articulate their course goals and SLOs to their students so that they understand what is expected of them throughout the course relative to how their course performance will be assessed. Careful development of an assessment strategy prior to the semester will increase the likelihood that one's assessment plan will accurately measure student learning.

References

Angelo, T. A., & Cross, K. P. (1993). *Classroom assessment techniques: A handbook for college teachers* (2nd ed.). San Francisco, CA: Jossey-Bass.

Bachiochi, P. D., & Weiner, S. P. (2004). Qualitative data collection and analysis. In S. G. Rogelberg (Ed.), *Handbook of research methods in industrial and organizational psychology* (pp. 161–183). Malden, MA: Blackwell.

Buskist, W., & Davis, S. F. (2006). *Handbook of the teaching of psychology.* Malden, MA: Blackwell.

Davis, B. G. (2009). *Tools for teaching* (2nd ed.). San Francisco, CA: Jossey-Bass.

Juve, J. A. (2006). Test construction. In W. Buskist & S. F. Davis (Eds.), *Handbook of the teaching of psychology* (pp. 247–253). Malden, MA: Blackwell.

Krathwohl, D. R. (2002). The revision of Bloom's taxonomy: An overview. *Theory Into Practice, 41*(4), 212–218.

Maki, P. L. (2004). *Assessing for learning: Building a sustainable commitment across the institution.* Sterling, VA: Stylus.

Mentkowski, M., & Loacker, G. (1985). Assessing and validating the outcomes of college. *New Directions for Institutional Research, 47,* 47–64.

Suskie, L. (2009). *Assessing student learning: A common sense guide.* San Francisco, CA: Jossey-Bass.

Svinicki, M., & McKeachie, W. J. (2011). *McKeachie's teaching tips: Strategies, research, and theory for college and university teachers* (13th ed.). Belmont, CA: Wadsworth.

Thorndike, E. L. (1918). The nature, purposes, and general methods of measurements of educational products. In G. M. Whipple (Ed.), *The seventeenth yearbook of the national society for the study of education.* Bloomington, IL: Public School Publishing Company.

Walvoord, B. E., & Anderson, V. J. (2010). *Effective grading: A tool for learning and assessment in college* (2nd ed.). San Francisco, CA: Jossey-Bass.

Wilson, R. C. (1986). Improving faculty teaching: Effective use of student evaluations and consultation. *Journal of Higher Education, 57,* 196–211.

Chapter 14

Becoming an Ethical Teacher ❖

G. William Hill IV and Dorothy D. Zinsmeister

As Uncle Ben told Peter Parker (Spider-Man), "With great power comes great responsibility." Like Spider-Man, graduate teaching assistants (GTAs) and new teachers are endowed with great power over students, and that power comes with great responsibility. A teacher's fundamental responsibilities include constructing courses and classroom environments that encourage learning, evaluating learning fairly, and treating students respectfully. Ethical teaching means engaging in behaviors that meet these responsibilities in ways expected by students, your institution, and your discipline (Keith-Spiegel, Whitley, Balogh, Perkins, & Wittig, 2002). Keith-Spiegel et al. argued that ethical teaching includes attention to avoiding actions or inactions that may cause students educational or emotional harm.

The responsibilities listed above form the foundational elements of ethical behavior in teaching and are embedded within ethical codes and principles for teachers. Unfortunately, like most ethical standards, these codes only provide general guidelines for ethical teaching. Our intent in this chapter is to provide an overview of key principles of ethical teaching, some suggestions to increase teachers' sensitivity and awareness about ethical pitfalls, and a few strategies for avoiding ethical dilemmas.

Challenges for Ethical Awareness for Beginning Teachers

GTAs and beginning teachers tend to focus on preparing for teaching basic content more than on ethical relationships with students (Keith-Spiegel et al., 2002). In fact, it appears that new teachers are poorly prepared to handle ethical dilemmas they might encounter (Branstetter & Handelsman, 2000; Handelsman, 1986; Keith-Spiegel, Wittig, Perkins, Balogh, & Whitley, 2001; Keith-Spiegel et al., 2002). Although GTAs and new teachers may be aware of the more obvious or illegal unethical situations (dating students, sexual harassment, confidentiality of grades), they appear to be less prepared for more subtle situations (Keith-Spiegel et al., 2002). Relatively few GTAs are aware of ethical principles or codes related to teaching, much less intentionally trained or mentored in identifying and resolving potential ethical dilemmas (Branstetter & Handelsman, 2000; Handelsman, 1986). GTAs differ from more experienced teachers in their perception of what constitutes ethical teaching behavior. Keith-Spiegel et al. (2001) found that GTAs rated potentially ethically questionable behaviors as less problematic than did more experienced teachers (e.g., accepting gifts from students, teaching class when unprepared).

Becoming and remaining an ethical teacher is not a simple task. Although there are aspirational principles and guidelines for ethical teaching, there are few absolute rules. Some ethical issues are codified legally (e.g., confidentiality, sexual harassment, discrimination) or are set by institutional policy (e.g., rules with respect to student-teacher dating, academic dishonesty). However, faculty often face many ethically ambiguous situations. Braxton and Bayer (1999) and Tabachnick, Keith-Spiegel, and Pope (1991) surveyed faculty asking them to rate whether a variety of different teaching-related behaviors were ethical. Both studies found a lack of consensus for most of the listed behaviors. For example, although most ethical codes include guidelines emphasizing subject matter competence, Tabachnick et al. reported almost 30% of respondents rated teaching material they haven't mastered as ethical. These results highlight the fact that perceptions of particular ethical (or unethical) behaviors vary widely among faculty. These results also suggest the importance of engaging GTAs and new teachers (and for that matter, experienced teachers) in discussions about ethical behavior, in both clear-cut and ambiguous situations. Whether discussions are included in courses on teaching for GTAs, mentoring, or programs offered by university teaching or ethics centers, sharing perspectives on what constitutes ethical behavior in teaching provides the opportunity to increase awareness of ethical challenges and thinking critically about them. It is a practice that should continue throughout a teacher's career.

Basic Ethical Principles for Teaching

In order to provide a starting point for thinking about ethical teaching behavior, we list and briefly describe some basic ethical principles for teachers and examples of how GTAs and new teachers might proactively think about situations related to each. Our list is based on our analysis of disciplinary and professional teaching organization ethical principles and codes for teachers (American Association of University Professors, 2001a, 2001b; American Chemical Society, 2011; American Historical Association, 2005; American Psychological Association, 2010; American Sociological Association, 1999; Murray, Gillese, Lennon, Mercer, & Robinson, 1996; National Education Association, 2002–2011).

Ethical Teachers Have Disciplinary Competence

When teaching any course, faculty must have the necessary content knowledge to provide their students with up-to-date information relevant to course objectives, which in some cases may be standardized by a department for core or required courses. In addition, including specific content will be an expectation when a course is a prerequisite for subsequent courses in the curriculum. Ethical concerns arise when teachers are asked to teach courses outside their area of expertise (which occurs frequently in smaller institutions with few faculty) or when they propose courses that reflect personal interests for which they have a limited background.

When teaching a course for the first time, teachers should investigate whether there are established departmental learning objectives and ensure they incorporate them into the teaching of that course. If an administrator asks a teacher to teach a course outside of her expertise because of a departmental need, she should make it a personal ethical responsibility to avail herself of educational resources to increase her content knowledge (e.g., reading journals or advanced texts, attending conference sessions on the content area, soliciting advice from others who teach the course).

Ethical Teachers Teach Effectively Through Effective Pedagogy

Although content knowledge is foundational, many ethical codes also emphasize that teachers are cognizant of effective pedagogical strategies. Research over the last 25 years has produced a plethora of data-based information about how students learn and the effectiveness of various pedagogical techniques (e.g., Davis, 2009; Donovan, Bransford, & Pellegrino, 2000; Walvoord & Anderson, 2009). Many disciplines publish journals devoted to pedagogical research on discipline-specific teaching in higher educational settings (see Pusateri, 2011, for an extensive listing of disciplinary pedagogical journals). Ethical teachers use these resources to implement teaching practices that enable them to enhance student learning. Ethical teachers also evaluate their effectiveness through midcourse and end-of-course student evaluations or peer review of their teaching, and based on this feedback, make adjustments necessary to improve their teaching effectiveness.

Ethical Teachers Provide Balanced Content and Free Inquiry

Faculty must provide students with a representative balance of mainstream theoretical perspectives and current knowledge that encourages students to think critically about different points of view. Our duty as teachers is to present information and guide students in making informed and objective conclusions based on data, and not to coerce, indoctrinate, or intimidate students to adopt a particular perspective, especially one that reflects our personal biases. Ethical teachers encourage open discussion of alternative theoretical positions and focus on content explicitly related to the course objectives.

Ethical Teachers Respect Students

Students must be treated as individuals who may bring strongly held perspectives on the course content as well as personal issues that affect their ability to meet course requirements. Thus, teachers must continually be sensitive to (a) inadvertent behaviors that might embarrass or disparage student comments and (b) course content that is potentially discomforting to some students. Of course, teachers should never omit or avoid controversial or sensitive content that is integral to meeting course objectives. However, teachers have a responsibility to forewarn students about course content that may be potentially discomforting (e.g., sexually explicit content, material that includes explicit language, racist or sexist readings). When content may be sensitive, teachers should also explain its relevance so that students understand why it is included as part of the course content.

Discussion of sensitive material requires teachers to establish a classroom atmosphere that is open, respectful, and encouraging of discussions of sensitive topics and that does not disparage or discriminate against individual student perspectives. Before responding to student comments that are potentially discriminatory or based on personal anecdotal beliefs, teachers should take a moment and carefully construct a response that avoids embarrassing the student or discouraging future student participation.

Despite our desire that students make our classes their primary priority, students have lives that interfere with course participation, just as our personal and professional lives sometimes interfere with meeting our teaching responsibilities. Thus, teachers should avoid make-up policies that are unfair or insensitive to unavoidable student conflicts. For example, is it fair to allow no make-up exams or establish attendance policies that fail to take into account students who must be absent because of illness, legal obligations, taking care of a sick child, or unavoidable work situations?

Ethical Teachers Foster Academic Integrity

Teachers have a core responsibility to encourage academic integrity and honesty. Student academic dishonesty undermines student learning and its objective assessment. Ethical teachers establish, communicate, and assist students in understanding disciplinary and institutional expectations concerning academic integrity. In addition, they communicate and apply clearly stated consequences for academic dishonesty that incorporate course-specific consequences (e.g., the specific impact of a violation on a student's grade, a zero on an assignment versus a failing grade in the course) as well as institutional policies concerning academic integrity violations. Ethical teachers include a description of the consequences of academic dishonesty as part of the stated grading policy in their syllabi and consistently apply those consequences. Many teachers, whether new or experienced, find addressing potential cases of academic dishonesty time-consuming and emotionally aversive. Honestly, they are both, but a teacher's ethical responsibility requires addressing potential violations.

Ethical Teachers Use Objective and Fair Assessments

Course assessments of student learning must be objective, valid, fair, and directly related to learning objectives as outlined in the course syllabus or other written materials distributed to students. When designing course assessments (i.e., tests, out-of-class assignments, and even extra credit), ethical teachers are cognizant of assessments that do not match course objectives. For example, ethical teachers assess content objectives, critical thinking, or writing objectives that are specifically stated or emphasized in the course objectives.

Ethical teachers are aware of factors that may affect fairness in grading. They use best practices to design valid and reliable test questions. Teachers should also avoid letting unrelated factors or personal biases affect their grading of student assessments (e.g., a student's attendance or classroom behavior, a theoretical disagreement with a student, grading the expected "best" or "worst" papers first or last).

Ethical Teachers Protect Their Students' Confidentiality

Teachers have a responsibility to maintain confidentiality with respect to student performance, classroom behavior and comments, and personal communications. As Murray et al. (1996, p. 3) argued, "students are entitled to the same level of confidentiality in their relationships with teachers as would exist in a lawyer-client or doctor-patient relationship." The Family Educational Rights and Privacy Act (FERPA) specifically prohibits faculty from revealing student performance to anyone but the student unless there is a compelling reason or legal requirement (U. S. Department of Education, 2011). Ethical teachers are careful to ensure that only individual students have access to their graded assignments. For example, although it may seem convenient and helpful to place graded tests or assignments outside one's office for pickup by students, this tactic potentially allows anyone to see an individual student's grade. In addition, a teacher may be contacted by a student's parents about their child's performance and must be prepared to explain that per FERPA this information cannot be shared with anyone unless the teacher is given the student's express permission.

Another significant challenge is informal discussions among faculty about student academic performance or behavior in the classroom. Students have a right to expect their academic performance, classroom comments, and shared difficulties with their teachers to be confidential, and teachers should respect this right. Any teacher who violates this right strongly risks losing students' respect. Although teachers may want to warn their colleagues about a problematic student with respect to classroom behavior or academic difficulties, they should be extremely careful. Sharing information with others should only occur when it is absolutely necessary to assist a colleague in helping a student succeed or preventing a negative classroom environment from developing.

Ethical Teachers Have Professionally Appropriate Relationships With Their Students

Faculty must be sensitive to maintaining professional and objective relationships with students. First and foremost, all ethical codes for teaching as well as policy statements at most institutions explicitly prohibit dating students. These prohibitions tend to be very specific regarding dating students currently enrolled in class, but sometimes ambiguous about dating after the class is over. Our advice is simple: Teachers should not date currently enrolled students at their institution.

Ethical teachers are also sensitive about engaging in behaviors that take advantage of their power relationship with students. For example, we consider it unethical to incorporate extra credit assignments that reflect their personal, social, or political biases (e.g., giving blood or donating a toy during the holiday season). Although these activities may be laudable, they are often unrelated to course learning objectives and represent an instructor's personal social interests.

Ethical teachers also avoid behaviors that might be construed as discrimination or sexual harassment (e.g., lecture comments that could be interpreted as discriminatory toward a particular religion or race; sexually suggestive comments about a female's/male's appearance; suggesting males are better at mathematics than females, which is both discriminatory and harassing). Not only is it simply wrong, federal law requires institutions to act on charges of sexual harassment and discrimination against teachers who engage in such actions.

Ethical teachers also are sensitive to other situations that may imply an improper student-teacher relationship or the perception of a potential bias because of the interaction. For example, we recommend that teachers not accept gifts from students or hire students to perform personal tasks for them such as home repairs or babysitting. In addition, we suggest avoiding out-of-class personal relationships through social networking media such as Facebook, especially when it may give an appearance of bias.

Conclusions

Although the ethical principles we summarized previously are common to most ethical codes for teachers, the application of a particular principle in a specific situation may not always be clear-cut. Because most ethical codes for teachers constitute behavioral guidelines, not explicit rules of behavior, discussions among teachers as to whether a particular behavior is or is not ethical can often generate diverse opinions and perspectives. Thus, we recommend that teachers take a proactive stance by developing a deeper understanding of ethical teaching and reflecting on these principles and their application to teaching. Some specific strategies we encourage GTAs and new teachers to consider at the outset of their teaching duties include reviewing their institution's faculty handbook for policies and expectations that address the ethics of teaching, doing additional reading on ethical principles and their application to specific situations (e.g., American Association of University Professors, 2001b; Braxton & Bayer, 1999; Keith-Spiegel et al., 2002; Murray et al., 1996; Strike & Soltis, 2009), identifying a mentor with whom to discuss ethical dilemmas as they arise, and participating in discussions on the ethics of teaching that may be scheduled at their university center for teaching or offered at a conference.

References

American Association of University Professors. (2001a). *A statement of the Association's council: Freedom and responsibility.* In AAUP (American Association of University Professors) Policy Documents and Reports (pp. 135–136). Washington, DC: Author.

American Association of University Professors. (2001b). *Statement on professional ethics.* In AAUP (American Association of University Professors) Policy Documents and Reports (pp. 133–134). Washington, DC: Author.

American Chemical Society. (2011). *Academic professional guidelines.* Retrieved from American Chemical Society website: http://portal.acs.org/portal/acs/corg/content?_nfpb=true&_pageLabel=PP_ARTICLEMAIN&node_id=1095&content_id=CNBP_023288&use_sec=true&sec_url_var=region1&__uuid=43cde20a-724a-46da-9ac4-730538157993

American Historical Association. (2005). *Statement on standards of professional conduct.* Retrieved from American Historical Association website: http://www.historians.org/pubs/Free/ProfessionalStandards.cfm#SharedValues

American Psychological Association. (2010). *Ethical principles of psychologists and code of conduct.* Retrieved from American Psychological Association website: http://www.apa.org/ethics/code/index.aspx

American Sociological Association. (1999). *American Sociological Association code of ethics and policies and procedures of the ASA Committee on Professional Ethics.* Retrieved from American Sociological Association website: http://www.asanet.org/images/asa/docs/pdf/CodeofEthics.pdf

Branstetter, S. A., & Handelsman, M. M. (2000). Graduate teaching assistants: Ethical training, beliefs, and practices. *Ethics and Behavior, 10,* 27–50.

Braxton, J. M., & Bayer, A. (1999). *Faculty misconduct in collegiate teaching.* Baltimore, MD: Johns Hopkins University Press.

Davis, B. G. (2009). *Tools for teaching* (2nd ed.). San Francisco, CA: Jossey-Bass.

Donovan, M. S., Bransford, J. D., & Pellegrino, J. W. (Eds.). (2000). *How people learn: Bridging research and practice.* Washington, DC: National Academy Press.

Handelsman, M. M. (1986). Problems with ethical training by "osmosis." *Professional Psychology: Research and Practice, 17,* 371–372.

Keith-Spiegel, P., Whitley, B. E., Jr., Balogh, D. W., Perkins, D. V., & Wittig, A. F. (2002). *The ethics of teaching: A casebook* (2nd ed.). Mahwah, NJ: Lawrence Erlbaum.

Keith-Spiegel, P., Wittig, A. F., Perkins, D. V., Balogh, D. W., & Whitley, B. E., Jr. (2001). Ethical dilemmas confronting graduate teaching assistants. In L. R. Prieto & S. A. Meyers (Eds.), *The teaching assistant training handbook* (pp. 133–155). Stillwater, OK: New Forums Press.

Murray, H., Gillese, E., Lennon, M., Mercer, P., & Robinson, M. (1996). *Ethical principles in university teaching.* North York, Ontario, Canada: Society for Teaching and Learning in Higher Education. Retrieved from Society for Teaching and Learning in Higher Education website: http://www.stlhe.ca/pdf/EthicalPrinciplesInUniversityTeaching.pdf

National Education Association. (2002–2011). *Code of ethics.* Retrieved from National Education website: http://www.nea.org/home/30442.htm

Pusateri, T. (2011). *Journals that publish the scholarship of teaching and learning and address general issues in higher education.* Retrieved from the Kennesaw State University Center for Excellence in Teaching & Learning website: http://www.kennesaw.edu/cetl/resources/journals.html

Strike, K. A., & Soltis, J. F. (2009). *The ethics of teaching* (5th ed.). New York, NY: Teachers College Press.

Tabachnick, B. G., Keith-Spiegel, P., & Pope, K. S. (1991). Ethics of teaching: Beliefs and behaviors of psychologists as educators. *American Psychologist, 46,* 506–515.

U. S. Department of Education. (2011). *Family Educational Rights and Privacy Act (FERPA).* Retrieved from U. S. Department of Education website: http://www2.ed.gov/policy/gen/guid/fpco/ferpa/index.html

Walvoord, B. E., & Anderson, V. J. (2009). *Effective grading: A tool for learning and assessment in college* (2nd ed.). San Francisco, CA: Jossey-Bass.

Chapter 15

Conflict in the College Classroom ❖

Understanding, Preventing, and Dealing With Classroom Incivilities

Mark M. Silvestri and William Buskist

It is your first day of class as a brand-new teacher. Eagerly, you arrive a few minutes early to engage your students in a casual conversation and allay your first-day jitters. You find yourself feeling confident as you speak your first welcoming words to the class. After the initial introductions, icebreakers, and review of the syllabus, you begin with your lesson plan. You use your carefully rehearsed hook to attract the class's attention, and now you are progressing with an excellent first day—until you notice one student texting on her cell phone; another student silently laughing while staring at his laptop screen; yet another student sitting directly in front of you, arms crossed, not taking any notes; and finally, two other students sitting in the back of the classroom engaging in a private conversation.

You had carefully planned every detail of today's lesson, but you did not anticipate these sorts of annoyances. What might happen if you ignore these troubling student behaviors? What might stop these disruptions from occurring the next time you meet the class? Or, more generally, how should you handle these types of situations? In this chapter, we discuss the concept of incivility, how it develops, and how instructors can prevent and address incivilities in their classrooms.

What Is Incivility?

One may understand incivility as "low-intensity deviant behavior with ambiguous intent to harm" (Andersson & Pearson, 1999, p. 457). It often includes displays of rudeness and disrespect. As Feldman (2001) observed, one may also consider incivility as "any action that interferes with a harmonious and cooperative learning atmosphere in the classroom" (p. 137). Classroom incivilities may range in severity from texting, not paying attention in class, and carrying on side conversations to harassment, vulgarity, and physical threats to students and the teacher (Indiana University Center for Survey Research, 2000). For a new teacher or graduate teaching assistant (GTA), the welcomed opportunity of teaching may become dashed once the need to address incivilities presents itself. For all teachers, preparation in handling these incivilities is crucial to effective classroom management as well as to professional development as a teacher. Nilson (2003) noted that preventing and preparing for incivilities may help teachers maintain a positive classroom experience after an incivility occurs. Similar to how teachers prepare and refine their lessons plans, so too should they prepare and refine their plans to maintain a positive classroom environment, especially given that many instructors are not well prepared to deal with incivility (Anderson, 1999; Richardson, 1999; Seidman, 2005).

Identifying Your Perceptions of Incivilities

Prior to identifying and preparing to deal with incivilities, you may benefit from thinking about what constitutes a classroom incivility and how to respond should it occur. As a starting point, consider the two definitions of incivility we presented earlier. Is your thinking about incivility similar to these definitions? If not, how does it differ? Does it fit well with your overall philosophy of teaching? Considering these questions increases the likelihood that your approach to handling incivilities is congruent with your overall approach to teaching. If you have not yet drafted your statement of your teaching philosophy (see Korn's Chapter 8), then reflect on your previous experiences with incivility from your undergraduate education (you may have even committed an incivility as an undergraduate). What sorts of incivilities did you observe (or commit)? How did these incivilities affect your learning and classroom experiences? How did your teachers deal with these incivilities—and were their approaches successful? Reflecting over these questions may help make you more aware of common incivilities, and possibly better prepared for dealing with them.

Thinking about the sorts of classroom incivilities you have encountered as a student is also a good starting point for developing your *incivility philosophy*. Having such a philosophy is important because it will allow you to anticipate classroom incivilities and how to address them. Keep in mind, though, that developing your incivility philosophy is not quite as easy as it may sound. Beyond defining incivility, your philosophy should outline your understanding of its causes (e.g., is it student generated or instructor generated?), the techniques you might use to handle incivilities, and how these techniques might minimize future incivilities and promote more positive student learning experiences. Keep in mind that incivilities are unpredictable. They may occur when you least expect them and may involve only one student or many—thus, it is wise advice to keep an open mind when considering how to approach incivility. As a reasonable starting point for anticipating the potential range of student incivilities, consider Indiana University's Center for Survey Research (2000) survey of Indiana University faculty, in which faculty identified and reported the occurrence of specific incivilities. For example, most faculty considered students teasing or mocking other students as always being a form of classroom incivility. Many faculty perceived chewing gum or eating in class as always being a form of incivility, although some faculty considered these behaviors uncivil only under certain conditions. Over half of the respondents perceived students' reluctance to answer questions directly as an act of incivility in certain circumstances. Most faculty also perceived students' hostility and verbal attacks as being acts of incivility, although, remarkably, a small percentage of faculty never considered these acts as being uncivil.

Thus, faculty in the Indiana survey showed a large degree of consensus on those student behaviors that constitute incivility. This finding raises an interesting question, though: To what extent do students agree with faculty on the nature of incivility? To answer this question, Rehling and Bjorklund (2010) compared faculty and undergraduates from a large midwestern university on their perceptions of classroom incivility. Incredibly, faculty and students agreed on 9 of the top 10 categories of student incivility. In order of the faculty ranking, these incivilities are

- continuing to talk after being asked to stop,
- coming to class drunk or high,
- exhibiting nonverbal disrespect for others,
- talking loudly with others,
- making disparaging remarks,
- swearing,
- cell phone ringing,

- texting,
- sleeping, and
- using computers and other technologies for nonclass activities while in class.

The only student-faculty differences in the top 10 rankings were that students ranked arriving late to class or leaving early as 9th on their list whereas faculty ranked it 13th on their list, and students ranked using technology for nonclass activities as 12th on their list whereas faculty ranked it 10th on their list. Faculty, however, ranked the overall degree of incivility of these and other behaviors much higher than students did, which reflects the fact that, although students and faculty perceive in kind the occurrence of incivility, faculty by and large perceive those behaviors as being more uncivil than students in degree.

As teachers, it is comforting to know that, to a large extent, students share our perceptions of the nature of classroom incivility. Such overlap in perspective empowers faculty to develop policies to prevent incivility, or, should it occur, to reduce its negative impact on the classroom learning environment. Of course, a key element in preventing or reducing incivility is to understand its causes.

Probable Causes of Incivility

One possible cause of incivility is the growing "consumer" orientation among undergraduates—the belief that higher education should cater to students and that they are entitled to a college education without investing much time or effort in the process (Nordstrom, Bartels, & Bucy, 2009). One way to minimize entitlement is to emphasize to students what they stand to gain beyond their grades by being active participants in their education. Nordstrom et al. (2009) suggested providing students with learning goals, rather than letter-grade goals, to reinforce the personal gains they might achieve from college.

A second likely cause of incivility is that some students may not perceive their uncivil behavior as being, in actuality, uncivil. Thus, they may not comprehend the impact of incivility on other students and the learning environment. For example, students who dominate classroom discussion may not realize the negative way in which they impact other students' opportunities for class participation, their willingness to speak up in class, or their enjoyment of the class. According to Nordstrom et al.'s (2009) research, this perspective is a stronger predictor of incivility than students' consumer orientation and warrants careful consideration by teachers in how they reflect and reframe incivilities to their students.

A third likely cause of at least some forms of student incivility is the teacher's behavior. For example, if students perceive a teacher to be unfair in grading or disrespectful toward them in or out of class, then students may respond with apathy or outright anger (or other similar negative emotions) toward that teacher. This sort of student behavior may range from nonverbal cues, such as stern or unhappy facial expressions, to verbal and physical actions, such as talking back hostilely or becoming physically aggressive toward the teacher.

As Rehling and Bjorklund's (2010) data suggest, student incivility, regardless of its causes, is likely to disrupt student learning. Thus, a key priority for all teachers is to prevent or reduce the likelihood of incivility happening in the first place.

Preventing Incivility

According to Meyers (2003, p. 94), "The most effective way to reduce or manage classroom conflict is to prevent it from initially occurring." One way of preventing incivility is for teachers to communicate their enthusiasm for the material and establish a positive climate for the classroom experience by showing a genuine interest in their students' academic welfare from the outset of the semester (Meyers, 2003; Sorcinelli, 1994).

To help establish such a favorable classroom environment, some teachers recommend creating a contract with students at the start of the semester (Nordstrom et al., 2009). The contract emphasizes how incivilities disrupt student learning and affect their motivation for learning (Hirschy & Braxton, 2004). Teachers might even hold a brief open forum during class for students to voice their opinions about behaviors they consider disturbing. Based on this discussion, teachers may then create a written contract, which encourages them and their students to work together in creating and maintaining a civil classroom atmosphere throughout the semester.

The contract should complement the course syllabus, which, of course, serves as the primary source of information about classroom etiquette and faculty expectations of student behavior. When teachers present such a contract to their students, they strengthen the idea that they wish to create a working alliance with their students. This alliance emphasizes the learning and educational goals shared by students and teachers in the classroom and requires faculty to treat "students respectfully despite disagreements" (Meyers, Bender, Hill, & Thomas, 2006, p. 185).

Besides emphasizing the importance of civil behavior at the start of the semester, teachers might also consider the impact of their teaching methods on acts of incivility and whether their behavior contributes to student hostility and incivility (Gonzalez & Lopez, 2001). Teacher behaviors such as cultural faux pas, unintended sarcasm, talking over students, or apparent disinterest in students may lead to student incivility. One way to minimize the occurrence of these sorts of behavior is to seek feedback from students about one's teaching style—after all, it is difficult to modify one's behavior if one is not aware of it or that it is disruptive to students' learning.

Teachers who use active learning strategies and promote class involvement are less likely to experience student incivility relative to instructors who use lecture-only approaches (Meyers et al., 2006). Active learning strategies often capture and maintain students' attention and appear to convey the perception that teachers are genuinely interested in the academic welfare of their students.

Responding to Student Incivility

Although teachers should be proactive in preventing student incivility, it may nevertheless occur, at least occasionally. Teachers can take several actions to ameliorate student incivility once it occurs.

First, no matter how offensive an incivility may seem, it is best to take a deep breath and stay calm (Feldman, 2001). Although offending students may not care about their credibility, teachers may lose their credibility quickly by losing their temper or overreacting to the offense. Second, teachers should deal with the incivility immediately after composing themselves. Ignoring the problem, albeit a common strategy, often results in more classroom conflicts and greater student dissatisfaction with the teacher (Meyers et al., 2006); also, it may convey to students that teachers find such behavior acceptable. Third, teachers should be consistent in responding to student incivilities (Nilson, 2003) by responding to similar incivilities in the same manner each time they occur. Of course, how teachers respond to incivility depends on the nature of the incivility. Table 15.1 offers several suggestions for how to address common classroom incivilities.

Of course, teachers develop and refine good teaching practices through actual classroom experience. Fortunately, graduate students and new faculty can improve their classroom management skills by rehearsing or practicing dealing with various mock incivility scenarios. By familiarizing themselves with specific strategies for addressing various incivilities, teachers may also become comfortable in addressing incivilities immediately rather than avoiding the problem behavior altogether.

In some instances, teachers may not be able to mollify incivilities by themselves. For example, extreme or severe acts of incivility such as physical

Table 15.1   Strategies for Addressing Common Classroom Incivilities

Incivility	Possible Responses
Side conversations	• Break class into groups and have students work on a problem (Svinicki & McKeachie, 2011). • Position yourself by the talkers, make eye contact, or pause until talking stops (Davis, 2009; Nilson, 2003). • Ask a question to someone near the talkers. This strategy will draw attention to the students in that area without putting the talkers on the spot (Sorcinelli, 1994). • For continued offenders, speak with them outside of class (Nilson, 2003).
Cell phone and laptop use	• This issue is related to inattention and may warrant similar approaches as for side conversations. Ask the offending student a question regarding the material or break students into pairs and have them work on a posted problem.
Arriving late/ packing up early	• Schedule mini-quizzes or extra-credit opportunities toward the beginning or end of class (Nilson, 2003).
Argumentative/ hostile students	• Listen respectfully to the offending student, acknowledge his or her position without reinforcing his or her complaining as acceptable behavior (Meyers, 2003; Svinicki & McKeachie, 2011). • Reflect the problem to the class in the attempt to diffuse the issue (Svinicki & McKeachie, 2011). • If further discussion is warranted, invite the offending student to meet with you privately in your office (Davis, 2009).

threats, vulgar verbal assaults, and other threatening acts of incivility may require teachers to seek a higher authority, such as a faculty supervisor, a department chair, or a college dean. (Many colleges and universities have explicit written policies on dealing with student incivilities—teachers should learn what the proper protocol is at their institution and follow it.) As an initial step in this process, many teachers find it useful to keep a detailed paper trail, which might involve keeping notes on the problem and saving e-mail exchanges with the offending student. Keeping good records regarding acts of student incivility will provide valuable background information for any administrators who become involved in helping you resolve the situation.

Final Thoughts

Although incivility is a seemingly easily identifiable behavior in the college classroom, how to deal with it is not likely to be as clear-cut. Incivility threatens the integrity of the classroom learning environment, and teachers should have a plan in mind for how to prevent incivilities from occurring and how to address them if they arise. If an incivility occurs, teachers should deal with it immediately and directly, and escalate their response to it only if milder forms of dealing with it fail.

References

Anderson, J. (1999). Faculty responsibility for promoting conflict-free college classrooms. In S. M. Richardson (Ed.), *Promoting civility: A teaching challenge*. New Directions for Teaching and Learning. No. 77 (pp. 69–76). San Francisco, CA: Jossey-Bass.

Andersson, L., & Pearson, C. (1999). Tit for tat? The spiraling effect of incivility in the workplace. *Academy of Management Review, 24,* 452–471. Retrieved from Business Source Premier database.

Davis, G. B. (2009). *Tools for teaching* (2nd ed.). San Francisco, CA: Jossey-Bass.

Feldman, L. J. (2001). Classroom civility is another of our instructor responsibilities. *College Teaching, 49,* 137–140.

Gonzalez, V., & Lopez, E. (2001). The age of incivility: Countering disruptive behavior in the classroom. *AAHE Bulletin, 53*(8), 3–6. Retrieved from http://www.aahea.org/bulletins/bulletins.htm

Hirschy, A. S., & Braxton, J. M. (2004). Effects of student classroom incivilities on students. In J. M. Braxton & A. E. Bayer (Eds.), *Addressing faculty and student classroom improprieties*. New Directions for Teaching and Learning, No. 99 (pp. 67–76). San Francisco, CA: Jossey-Bass.

Indiana University Center for Survey Research. (2000). *A survey of academic incivility at Indiana University: Preliminary report*. Retrieved from http://www.indiana.edu/~csr/Civility%20PreReport.pdf

Meyers, S. A. (2003). Strategies to prevent and reduce conflict in college classrooms. *College Teaching, 51,* 94–98.

Meyers, S. A., Bender, J., Hill, E. K., & Thomas, S. Y. (2006). How do faculty experience and respond to classroom conflict? *International Journal of Teaching and Learning in Higher Education, 18,* 180–187.

Nilson, L. B. (2003). *Teaching at its best: A research-based resource for college instructors* (2nd ed.). San Francisco, CA: Jossey-Bass.

Nordstrom, C. R., Bartels, L. K., & Bucy, J. (2009). Predicting and curbing classroom incivility in higher education. *College Student Journal, 43,* 74–85.

Rehling, R. L., & Bjorklund, W. L. (2010). A comparison of faculty and student perceptions of incivility in the classroom. *Journal on Excellence in College Teaching, 21*, 73–93.

Richardson, S. M. (Ed.). (1999). *Promoting civility: A teaching challenge.* New Directions for Teaching and Learning, No. 77. San Francisco, CA: Jossey-Bass.

Seidman, A. (2005, Spring). The learning killer: Disruptive student behavior in the classroom. *Reading Improvement, 42,* 40–46.

Sorcinelli, M. D. (1994). Dealing with troublesome behaviors in the classroom. In K. W. Prichard & R. M. Sawyer (Eds.), *Handbook of college teaching: Theory and applications* (pp. 365–373). Westport, CT: Greenwood Press.

Svinicki, M., & McKeachie, W. J. (2011). *McKeachie's teaching tips: Strategies, research, and theory for college and university teachers* (13th ed.). Belmont, CA: Wadsworth.

Chapter 16

Diversity and Diversity Issues in Teaching

❖

Rosemary E. Phelps

Examination of the scholarly literature on teaching and learning across disciplines reveals a sense of urgency for including diversity content in the college curriculum. This literature also provides compelling evidence regarding the benefits of including diversity (e.g., Antonio, 2003). The rationale for including diversity content in all components of the curriculum centers on changes in student demographics in K–12 classrooms and higher education (Drake, 1993), the obligation faculty have to be sensitive to and respectful of all students (Kendall, 1983), and the benefits in attracting diverse faculty (Antonio, 2003). In addition, accrediting agencies often mandate including diversity content in the curriculum and incorporating diversity throughout programs. In some instances, negative consequences, such as loss of accreditation, result if diversity is not addressed in the curriculum and general education programs.

Information on diversity resources for inclusion in the curriculum also abound in the literature. There has been a proliferation of books, articles, and training materials, as well as resources and guides for course-specific diversity readings, films, and activities. There also exists a bounty of information and models for preparing teachers who will be teaching diversity coursework and preparing educators who will be teaching culturally diverse students (e.g., Alexander, 2007; M. Brown, 2007; Chou, 2007).

If the need for including diversity content in the curriculum is recognized and there are resources available on how to include diversity content, research indicating its effectiveness, and literature on how to effectively address the complexities and challenges of teaching diversity content, then why is it that (a) diversity content is not being incorporated routinely into the curriculum, (b) teachers remain reluctant and uncomfortable with diversity as a content area, and (c) students often have unpleasant experiences in the classroom when diversity is addressed (Fishman & McCarthy, 2005; Garner, 2008; Heinze, 2008; Perry, Moore, Edwards, & Acosta, 2009)? Thus, it is important to take a closer look at teaching about diversity and diversity issues.

In this chapter, I will examine key considerations in teaching diversity content and provide a broad perspective on diversity and diversity issues in teaching. I will also provide some general guidelines to consider when preparing to teach diversity content and describe several models for teaching diversity at the college and university level.

General Considerations

A Different Type of Content

Diversity content is different from other types of course content. It can evoke emotions (for both students and teachers) in ways that other content may not because it is often tied to personal beliefs and value systems that people hold dear. Thus, diversity content has an affective component that must be taken into consideration. The manner in which teachers address emotions can have a strong impact on how students make sense of the content (Housee, 2008). Successfully teaching diversity content demands attention to content, process, and affect, which is not necessarily the case with other course content, and doing so can be emotionally draining for teachers in ways that addressing other content are not (Garner, 2008). Indeed, in the diversity literature, one finds accounts of teachers who experience early burnout, negative feelings, and lack of desire to continue teaching diversity content. Thus, it is essential for teachers of diversity and diversity issues to manage their emotions in a healthy manner and avoid personalizing student comments.

Some diversity content must be explained within broader contexts (e.g., historical, sociopolitical) to help students better understand the dynamics that operate in relation to diversity. Teachers must have an accurate understanding of historical events and be comfortable discussing the events and consequences relative to the subject matter (Fishman & McCarthy, 2005; Goodwin, 2004).

Situating Diversity Content

The placement of diversity content within the course is critical because students often make interpretations, sometimes negatively, about the salience of the content depending on where it is discussed in the curriculum. Thus, it becomes an essential aspect of course design for teachers to make sure that diversity is centrally focused and situated such that it sends the message that it is a valuable component of the course. For example, if diversity content is presented only at the end of the term, students may interpret its inclusion as an afterthought on the teacher's part or as the teacher's weak attempt to be "politically correct."

Instructor Preparation and Considerations

Comfort Level

Teachers should not mislead themselves in thinking that they can teach a course with diversity content in the same ways that they teach other courses and still be effective teachers. To teach effectively, teachers must understand their own emotions and reactions to diversity content and deal with their own comfort level in presenting it. Drake (1993) noted that teachers should be aware of their attitudes about culturally diverse students because these attitudes, for better or worse, can carry over to their instructional practices. Kendall (1983) indicated that teachers can intentionally and unintentionally transmit their attitudes to students; thus, teachers must carefully attend to the subtle ways that they may influence their students. Teachers should also be intentional about responding rather than reacting to issues that arise when teaching diversity content, which means that they must be able to think about diversity content from multiple perspectives in their teaching. Such perspective taking is prompted by reflection and introspection, which of course are important dimensions of teacher preparation for any course, especially those including diversity content (Fishman & McCarthy, 2005; Irvine, 1990).

Content Knowledge

Scholars note that teachers may have limited exposure to students from diverse cultures and may lack understanding and knowledge of other cultures (e.g., Chou, 2007). Thus, in addition to dealing with the affective component related to teaching diversity content, there is often the knowledge dimension to which teachers must attend. Chou also indicated that educators must be able to reconcile their intellectual understanding of diversity issues with reality, for example, by engaging in discussion of diversity-related topics with knowledgeable colleagues or by immersing themselves in real-life experiences that deepen and broaden their understanding of diversity in its myriad forms.

Skills

Effectively teaching diversity content often requires a skills set that builds on those skills necessary to teach any subject matter. These skills include the ability to present emotionally laden information in a sensitive manner to facilitate difficult dialogues (Fishman & McCarthy, 2005), deal with conflict, attend and respond to students' nonverbal behavior, provide a balance of challenge and support, engage in perspective taking as a method for presenting diversity material and responding to students' questions and comments about it, respect and model appropriate behavior, and deal with emotions of multiple students as well as one's own emotions.

Instructor Characteristics

Personal characteristics of the teacher (e.g., gender, race) can affect the classroom environment (see, e.g., A. H. Brown, Cervero, & Johnson-Bailey, 2000; Garner, 2008; Housee, 2008; Johnson-Bailey & Lee, 2005). Teachers should be mindful of how these characteristics can influence their students' experiences when teaching diversity content. For example, Perry et al. (2009) described the outsider-within phenomenon for instructors of color whereby, because of their marginality in various social contexts, they are also marginalized in predominantly white institutions and classrooms. A. H. Brown et al. (2000) indicated that teachers' positions in society according to dimensions such as race and gender influence their teaching philosophy, classroom interactions, and teaching strategies. Students' ratings of teaching effectiveness are another area affected by race and gender. For example, Smith (2009) found black facultys' mean teaching evaluation scores were lower than those of white facultys.

Content Considerations

There are several content matters to think through before actually teaching diversity content with respect to learning outcomes emphasizing student attitudes, knowledge, and skills. These considerations include whether to approach diversity from a broad or narrow perspective and being able to clearly articulate one's rationale for the use of either approach. Teachers often choose one perspective or the other based on their choice of which groups to include in diversity discussions. Teachers should be cognizant of presenting material sensitively and aware that various student groups within any class may view the material differently, depending on their life experiences. For example, because constructs such as race, racism, bias, bigotry, power, white privilege, and the study of white culture (Heinze, 2008) can evoke strong emotions in some students, teachers must take care in determining how to address these issues. Strasser and Seplocha (2005) discussed two of Gardner's Multiple Intelligences, interpersonal and intrapersonal, and how activities using both frameworks can be effectively designed to help students understand diversity. Assignments that allow students to work together cooperatively and in small groups can support students who are interpersonal learners. Specific strategies for interpersonal learning include cooperative learning groups, group discussions of a variety of diversity-related material (e.g., music, videos, books), and the opportunity to share personal experiences. Activities that provide opportunities for self-reflection (e.g., individual projects) support learning for intrapersonal learners. Specific strategies related to intrapersonal learning include examining one's own values and beliefs, journaling, and concept mapping.

Student and Audience Considerations

Demographics

The demographic makeup of a class can have a strong impact on classroom dynamics when teaching about diversity content. To create a positive and supportive classroom atmosphere, teachers should develop strategies for managing different dynamics that may arise while teaching about diversity. Use of the reciprocal interview, in which teachers get information from students, and students, in turn, have the opportunity to ask teachers questions to learn more about them, is effective across disciplines in creating a positive environment for learning about diversity (Case, Bartsch, McEnery, Hall, Hermann, & Foster, 2008).

Teachers should also be prepared to deal with how their characteristics sometimes interact with student characteristics in the classroom. For example, in a study of the role of teacher and student characteristics on students' preconceptions of college professors, Anderson and Smith (2005) found that Anglo women professors who had strict teaching styles were rated as warmer than Latina professors with the same style. Latino students evaluated Anglo women professors as more capable than Latina professors and Anglo male professors. In addition, Latino students evaluated Anglo women professors as more capable than African American students did.

Identity Development

Racial and gender identity development also may affect classroom dynamics. Students' worldview, understanding of diversity issues, willingness to engage in diversity-related discussions, and level of resistance are often dependent on their level of racial and gender identity. Because neither type of identity occurs instantly, teachers must be prepared for the opportunities and challenges that go along with growth and questioning of self and others. Thus, it is important that teachers have knowledge and understanding of identity development processes for both students of color and white students. It also is key to take into account students' levels of racial identity development and understand how it can affect students' perspectives and views related to diversity. Helms and Piper (cited in Pope, 2000) conceptualized racial identity development as relevant for all racial groups in terms of understanding one's own racial group and individuals in other racial groups, and having a mature worldview.

Teachers and students often operate with the assumption that diversity is only for groups of color, underrepresented groups, or marginalized groups. Students should understand that white privilege and power, institutional racism, and access and equity are key components in understanding diversity (Elhoweris, Parameswaran, & Alsheikh, 2004; Heinze, 2008). Heinze suggested experiential activities such as "The Benefits of Being White" to help students better understand white privilege. For this activity, students identify as a person of color or white and are divided into small groups based on their identification and discuss the benefits of being white. Further discussion involves the number of benefits identified by each group. When students deal with some of these topics, they experience a variety of emotions, including denial, guilt, shame, and anger. As teachers, it is important not to make students feel guilty or shameful (Heinze, 2008; Tatum, 1992) but instead help them to understand how such things originated and understand that these things do not have to remain the same.

Resistance

Diversity content can elicit resistance and defensiveness in students; thus, it is important for teachers to be prepared to deal with diversity resistance to effectively handle conflict that may arise in the classroom. Types of resistance that may be encountered include denial, questioning the credibility and legitimacy of information or resources, lack of participation in activities, intellectualization, closed nonverbal behavior, and silence (Heinze, 2008; Thomas, 2008). Heinze provided several suggestions for handling resistance, including teachers being sensitive to their own emotions while talking about diversity content, understanding that the content may be uncomfortable for some students, avoiding directly arguing points with students, and not taking oneself so seriously (e.g., using appropriate humor).

Student Experience and Background

In any class, students will differ with respect to their experience with diversity. Thus, teachers are likely to have some students in their courses who have little or no experience with diversity and may be naïve or in denial regarding diversity issues. Some of these students may be operating on preconceived ideas and inaccurate information about these issues. In contrast, teachers will also have students who have had a great deal of experience with diversity, resulting in a solid understanding of diversity issues, dealing with content and emotions, and having a desire to move forward in their growth in this area. Thus, teachers who teach diversity content in their courses must learn to balance their approach so as not to move some students along too fast while at the same time not frustrating other students by moving along too slowly. Johnson-Bailey and Alfred's (as cited in Alexander, 2007) transformational learning paradigm can be instrumental in helping students on both the interpersonal and intrapersonal levels to respond to diversity. One feature of transformational learning is the process adults use to make sense of major life events through reflection and other cognitive processes.

Conclusions

Effectively teaching diversity coursework requires teachers to pay careful attention to affective, interpersonal, and content dimensions of the subject matter as it relates to the course. Although teachers may work hard to teach their students the importance of understanding diversity and diversity issues within the context of their education, the potential impact of such efforts may not be immediately visible in students (Garner, 2008). However, in their discussion of diversity, teachers may plant seeds for future understanding and personal growth. To be sure, teaching diversity coursework is challenging yet can be rewarding.

References

Alexander, I. D. (2007). Multicultural teaching and learning resources for preparing faculty in teaching in higher education courses. In M. Kaplan & A. T. Miller (Eds.), *New directions for teaching and learning* (Vol. 111, pp. 27–33). San Francisco, CA: Jossey-Bass.

Anderson, K. J., & Smith, G. (2005). Students' preconceptions of professors: Benefits and barriers according to ethnicity and gender. *Hispanic Journal of Behavioral Sciences, 27,* 184–201.

Antonio, A. L. (2003). Diverse student bodies, diverse faculties. *Academe, 89,* 14–17.

Brown, A. H., Cervero, R. M., & Johnson-Bailey, J. (2000). Making the invisible visible: Race, gender, and teaching in adult education. *Adult Education Quarterly, 50,* 273–288.

Brown, M. (2007). Educating all students: Creating culturally responsive teachers, classrooms, and schools. *Intervention in School and Clinic, 43,* 57–62.

Case, K., Bartsch, R., McEnery, L., Hall, S., Hermann, A., & Foster, D. (2008). Establishing a comfortable classroom from day one: Student perceptions of the reciprocal interview. *College Teaching, 56,* 210–214.

Chou, H. (2007). Multicultural teacher education: Toward a culturally responsible pedagogy. *Essays in Education, 21,* 139–162.

Drake, D. D. (1993). Student diversity: Implications for classroom teachers. *Clearing House, 66,* 264–266.

Elhoweris, H., Parameswaran, G., & Alsheikh, N. (2004). College students' myths about diversity and what college faculty can do. *Multicultural Education, 12,* 13–18.

Fishman, S. M., & McCarthy, L. (2005). Talk about race: When student stories and multicultural curricula are not enough. *Race Ethnicity and Education, 8,* 347–364.

Garner, P. W. (2008). The challenge of teaching for diversity in the college classroom when the professor is the "other." *Teaching in Higher Education, 13,* 117–120.

Goodwin, A. L. (2004). Exploring the perspectives of teacher educators of color: What do they bring to teacher education? *Issues in Teacher Education, 13,* 7–24.

Heinze, P. (2008). Let's talk about race, baby. *Multicultural Education, 16,* 2–11.

Housee, S. (2008). Should ethnicity *matter* when teaching about "race" and racism in the classroom? *Race Ethnicity and Education, 11,* 415–428.

Irvine, J. J. (1990). Transforming teaching for the twenty-first century. *Educational Horizons, 69,* 16–21.

Johnson-Bailey, J., & Lee, M. (2005). Women of color in the academy: Where's our authority in the classroom? *Feminist Teacher, 15,* 111–122.

Kendall, F. E. (1983). *Diversity in the classroom: A multicultural approach to the education of young children.* New York, NY: Teachers College Press.

Perry, G., Moore, H., Edwards, C., & Acosta, K. (2009). Maintaining credibility and authority as an instructor of color in diversity-education classrooms: A qualitative inquiry. *Journal of Higher Education, 80,* 80–105.

Pope, R. L. (2000). The relationship between psychosocial development and racial identity of college students of color. *Journal of College Student Development, 41*, 302–312.

Smith, B. P. (2009). Student ratings of teaching effectiveness for faculty groups based on race and gender. *Education, 129*, 615–624.

Strasser, J., & Seplocha, H. (2005). How can university professors help their students understand issues of diversity through interpersonal and intrapersonal intelligences? *Multicultural Education, 12*(4), 20–24.

Tatum, B. D. (1992). Talking about race, learning about racism: Application of racial identity development theory in the college classroom. *Harvard Educational Review, 62*, 1–24.

Thomas, K. M. (Ed). (2008). *Diversity resistance in organizations [Applied Psychology Series]*. New York, NY: LEA-Taylor Francis.

Chapter 17

Teaching Controversial Issues, Liberally

❖

Harold L. Miller, Jr., and Diego Flores

Controversy lurks, even in the most benign, pacific classrooms. It also leaps, showing itself unexpectedly and inopportunely. Its appearance in the classroom often unsettles students, graduate teaching assistants (GTAs), graduate-student teachers, and faculty members alike. It brings awkward silences and uneasy feelings that move between outrage and violation. For some, full-blown controversy is entertaining, for others titillating and cathartic. It also can be off-putting, divisive, and dispiriting. These corrosive effects may prompt efforts to purge the classroom agenda of any hint of controversy, to apply a hermetic, controversy-proof seal. Rather than emphasize controversy's downside, we argue here for its merits, confident that teaching controversial issues can invigorate the classroom culture and enliven students' learning.

Controversy arises from difference, from alternative points of view. It may be considered an invitation to students to sample and engage what is unfamiliar or alien. Generally, students perceive the invitation as aversive. Enlarging one's awareness and scope of reference is rarely easy. The reasons are intellectual and emotional. One may have to think in fresh ways and to deal with feelings that oppose such thinking. Both are hard work. One may have to reckon with previously unglimpsed possibilities and oblige distasteful prospects. One may have to turn around on what one traditionally has prized and call it, painfully, into question. Ultimately, what started in controversy may even result in the arduous, draining project of regenerating one's self.

Controversy and the Liberal Ideal of Education

In his classic examination of the wellsprings of personal and collective freedom, John Stuart Mill (1859/1988) gave bold contours to controversy:

> In the case of any person whose judgement is really deserving of confidence, how has it become so? Because he has kept his mind open to criticism of his opinions and conduct. Because it has been his practice to listen to all that could be said against him; to profit by as much of it as was just, and to expound to himself, and upon occasion to others, the fallacy of what was fallacious. . . . No wise man ever acquired his wisdom in any mode but this; nor is it in the nature of human intellect to become wise in any other manner. The steady habit of correcting and completing his own opinion by collating it with those of others, so far from causing doubt and hesitation in carrying it into practice, is the only stable foundation for a just reliance on it; for, being cognizant of all that can, at least obviously, be said against him, and having taken up his position against all naysayers . . . he has a right to think his judgement better than that of any person, or any multitude, who have not gone through a similar process. (p. 80)

Mill's is a tall order and may be considered an ideal, given practical realities. Still, it offers a test of the validity of intellectual (and, by extension, moral and political) authority that installs controversy, that is, the pitting of views, comprehensively. For Mill, authority is best trusted that resolutely remains open to critique.

Mill's liberality underpins pluralist, democratic society and, within it, liberal education. For Richard Rorty (1999), that education is two-step: first, socialization, then individualization. One gives way to the other at the approximate boundary between high school and college. According to Rorty,

> The question, "What should they learn in college?" had better go unasked. Such questions suggest that college faculties are instrumentalities that can be ordered to a purpose. The temptation to suggest this comes over administrations occasionally, as does the feeling that higher education is too important to be left to the professors. From an administrative point of view, the professors often seem self-indulgent and self-obsessed. They look like loose cannons, people whose habit of setting their own agendas needs to be curbed. But administrators sometimes forget that college students badly need to find themselves in a place in which people are not ordered to a purpose, in which loose

cannons are free to roll about. The only point in having real live professors around instead of just computer terminals, videotapes, and mimeoed lecture notes is that students need to have freedom enacted before their eyes by actual human beings. (p. 125)

Although loose-cannon status (as GTA, graduate-student teacher, or faculty member) may accompany flamboyance and stage hogging, they are not necessary companions. What Rorty commends is that the controversy-laced agendas of loose cannons nourish the individualism to which liberal education aspires. Controversy is the medium in which freedom is enacted and modeled.

Gerald Graff (1992) offers his own case study in teaching controversial issues for the same ends to which Mill and Rorty pointed, and for further ends:

I argue that the best solution to today's conflicts . . . is to teach the conflicts themselves, making them part of our object of study and using them as a new kind of organizing principle to give the curriculum the clarity and focus that almost all sides now agree it lacks.

. . . In an important sense, academic institutions are *already* teaching the conflicts every time a student goes from one course or department to another, but they are doing it badly. . . . [S]tudents typically experience a great clash of values, philosophies, and pedagogical methods among their various professors, but they are denied a view of the interactions and interrelations that give each subject meaning. They are exposed to the *results* of their professors' conflicts but not to the process of discussion and debate they need to see in order to become something more than passive spectators to their education. Students are expected to join an intellectual community that they see only in disconnected glimpses. This is what has passed for "traditional" education, but a curriculum that screens students from the controversies between texts and ideas serves the traditional goals of education as poorly as it serves those of reformers. (p. 12)

Graff's (1992) subject matter is English literature, and the controversies belong to culture wars that pit literary canons against each other (often on the continuum of political correctness). But his controversy-centric approach, including the selection of textbooks and classroom methods, is transposable to other disciplines and classrooms.

A final glimpse of controversy-stoked teaching comes from Mark Edmundson's (2002) memoir. Drawing from memories of his senior year of high school, Edmundson assembles the portrait of a teacher, Frank Lears, freshly graduated from college and whose naïvete was initially unnerving to his students. He was a laid-back provocateur who allowed their interests to set the daily agenda while he applied an overlay of controversy. He insisted that the questions and issues they studied be analyzed from more than one perspective, always with an eye to implications for their current lives and futures:

> Really, all he seemed to want was to make us look at ourselves from new angles, become judgmental aliens in our own lives, and then to show us a few alternative roads. If we took them, all to the good. If not, who knows?—maybe something else would turn up for us later. Of all the teachers I have had—some of the world's best known, in fact—Lears was the purest in his evident wish to make his students freer. He would be sorry about the costs, for relative autonomy can have many, but nothing would deter him. (pp. 239–240)

Edmundson's mention of risk is apposite. Teaching controversial issues is risky in at least two ways. In one, the teacher may send her or his students off on protracted personal paths not worth pursuing and that end ignominiously. Alternatively, the encounter with controversy may sour the student sufficiently that she or he ever shies from it. In what follows, we offer advice to GTAs, graduate-student teachers, and new faculty on managing the risk.

Caveats for Those Who Teach Controversial Issues

Depending on one's students and subject matter, it may be possible to predict the controversial issues. In a previous treatment of the topic (Buskist & Davis, 2006), several authors shared experience and insight from teaching the following issues: race and ethnicity (Freeman, 2006), evolutionary psychology (Barker, 2006), human sexuality (Finken, 2006), gender and gender roles (Lloyd, 2006), religion (Hester & Paloutzian, 2006), and drugs and behavior (Bailey, 2006). In addition to specifying potential points of controversy, the authors addressed textbook selection, the syllabus content, classroom etiquette, and techniques for recognizing and accommodating controversial issues in the flow of classroom life, including assignments and other forms of assessment.

Our review of the authors' conclusions and recommendations produced the following caveats (in no particular order of importance):

- Where possible, invoke empirical data in assessing the issue at hand. Students' consideration of data and identification of multiple interpretations of what the data say may result in their deeper appreciation for the complexity of the issue (Freeman, 2006). In turn, this may dispel any notion that the issue already has been decided.
- Encourage students to recognize the difference between what they believe, what they feel, and what they know (Barker, 2006). Being able to draw clearer distinctions among these categories of experience may help them reframe controversial issues more appealingly or at least less defensively.

- Remember that the active use of humility, humor, and goodwill can defuse hostility and suspicion, and promote openness and collegiality (Barker, 2006).
- When preparing for in-class consideration of potentially controversial issues, there is good reason to consult with faculty mentors or other colleagues as to whether the planned-for material and methods are advisable (Finken, 2006).
- Be aware of institutional or departmental policy regarding issues to be avoided, if any. Receiving the department chair's prior approval of material and methods allows a further buffer against impropriety (Finken, 2006).
- Adopt and publicize (in the syllabus, for example) "ground rules" for class conversation. Doing so may prevent or at least reduce felt conflict when controversial issues are considered. For example, students may be asked to (a) refrain from sharing highly personal details, (b) allow someone else to speak before rejoining the conversation, (c) adopt an empathic stance by imagining what others in the conversation are feeling and factors that might have contributed to their perspectives on the issue, and (d) realize that they are under no obligation to state their views or to change them (Lloyd, 2006).
- Maintain an announced availability to students for consultation should they have concerns about the course material or the classroom conversation regarding issues raised by the material (Lloyd, 2006).

In an essay that introduced those referred to above, Pittenger (2006) listed principal student complaints related to the treatment of controversial issues in their classrooms. The list emerged from the author's review of anecdotes posted at a website (www.studentsforacademicfreedom.org) where students reported instances of discrimination by faculty for political views. The complaints were (a) required readings that only present one side of an issue, (b) *ad hominem* derogation of political or religious figures, and (c) assignments that require the student to advocate a point of view that runs contrary to their own. Such missteps on the teacher's part almost always derail otherwise constructive consideration of controversial issues.

Pittenger (2006) also cautioned against unguarded humor—the spontaneous aside that can put even the best-intentioned teachers in the students' doghouse. To avoid such, he urged self-editing to "ensure that expressions of humor are not made at the expense of others" (p. 183).

Teaching Styles and Resources for Teaching Controversies

Several teaching styles are available for teaching controversial issues. Stradling, Noctor, and Baines (1984) identified three: commitment, balance, and neutrality. Using the *committed* style, the teacher informs students of her or his position on the issue, as well as the personal biases that may have been conducive to that position. Teachers may do so when the issue is first broached or subsequently as they consider the best tactics. The *balanced* style obliges teachers to supply alternative viewpoints so that the issue is considered multidirectionally and also to categorize the alternatives in ways that sharpen their differences. The *neutral* style may be the most challenging, because it requires the teacher either to support each of the alternative viewpoints equally (*affirmative neutrality*) or to refrain from supporting any of them (*negative* or *procedural neutrality*).

Although controversial issues are more likely to emerge spontaneously in the course of classroom give-and-take, they also may be included deliberately as part of course design. In courses where the design includes a sequence of weekly topics, for example, a regular component of each topic may be a controversial issue related to it. Alternatively, the issue may be introduced following a series of topics in order to demonstrate their mutual relevance and interconnection.

In addition to classroom conversations (both small-group and whole-class) that introduce and develop controversial issues, teachers can draw from a variety of formal and informal assignments available in graded or nongraded versions. Among written assignments, Miller and Lance (2006) listed progressive papers, multiperspective papers, group papers and projects, reflective writing, interpretive writing, reaction papers, and knowledge maps. Possible oral assignments include mini-lectures and debates. Both types of assignments may be combined in multimedia presentations or in-class poster sessions.

Textbook publishers also are alert to the potential virtue of teaching controversial issues. A popular series titled *Taking Sides* (published by McGraw-Hill/Dushkin) offers a series of volumes across academic disciplines. For example, issues addressed in this series include moral issues (Satris, 2011), educational issues (Noll, 2010), and social issues (Finsterbusch, 2010).

Regular perusal of intellectual media such as newspapers, magazines, documentaries, and blogs, and scholarly media such as journals and books, is sure to yield a more than ample store of controversies for tactical inclusion in lectures, classroom conversation, and assignments. Another dependable source is one's teaching colleagues, who can be consulted for their recent experiences with controversy as well as for time-tested controversies by which they stoke their students' thoughtful, creative engagement with the subject matter.

As already noted, controversy also can emerge spontaneously and unbidden during a class meeting. Innocent as well as intemperate remarks and gestures may promote escalating exchange, whether originating from students or the teacher or both, to trigger a sudden awkwardness, a chilling hush, a sinking feeling of sides setting up all at once. Such moments are inevitable, but they need not be disastrous. Instead, our counsel to GTAs and new teachers caught in them is promptly to recognize them for what they are, take a deep breath, and turn what may be feared as loss into gain. Pose questions: What has just happened? How shall we think about it? What sides showed themselves? How shall we work through it? What is important to learn from what we experienced? Invite several voices to be heard. Ask students to talk together in small groups. Assign them to write about their feelings and their afterthoughts. Assure them that good can come from turning around on differences and contentiousness—good such as civility, the prizing of diversity, deepened understanding, awareness of new and inviting possibilities, and the flush of rapprochement.

Conclusions

There is no sure way to avoid controversy and remain alive. Instead, one strives to do one's best to avoid being upended by it. For those who teach controversial issues, the liberality advocated by J. S. Mill and endorsed, respectively, by Rorty, Graff, and Edmundson in their own way shines a light on personal characteristics—openness to alternatives, never being too sure, empathic regard, appreciation for argument and reason-giving, and goodwill—that will serve the teacher in the joint roles of arbiter and model. Thus supplied, students—learners from controversial issues—someday will look back on their controversy-rich classrooms as microcosms of the unendingly diverse, maddeningly kaleidoscopic experience that now enfolds them. If those classrooms served them well, they eventually will show themselves graceful, even artful, in that experience.

References

Bailey, S. A. (2006). Drugs and behavior. In W. Buskist & S. F. Davis (Eds.), *Handbook of the teaching of psychology* (pp. 214–218). Malden, MA: Blackwell.

Barker, L. (2006). Evolutionary psychology. In W. Buskist & S. F. Davis (Eds.), *Handbook of the teaching of psychology* (pp. 191–195). Malden, MA: Blackwell.

Buskist, W., & Davis, S. F. (Eds.). (2006). *Handbook of the teaching of psychology*. Malden, MA: Blackwell.

Edmundson, M. (2002). *Teacher: The one who made the difference*. New York, NY: Vintage.

Finken, L. L. (2006). Teaching human sexuality. In W. Buskist & S. F. Davis (Eds.), *Handbook of the teaching of psychology* (pp. 196–201). Malden, MA: Blackwell.

Finsterbusch, K. (2010). *Taking sides: Controversial views on social issues* (16th ed.). New York, NY: McGraw-Hill/Dushkin.

Freeman, J. E. (2006). Psychology of race and ethnicity. In W. Buskist & S. F. Davis (Eds.), *Handbook of the teaching of psychology* (pp. 186–190). Malden, MA: Blackwell.

Graff, G. (1992). *Beyond the culture wars: How teaching the conflicts can revitalize American education.* New York, NY: W. W. Norton.

Hester, M. P., & Paloutzian, R. F. (2006). Teaching the psychology of religion: Teaching for today's world. In W. Buskist & S. F. Davis (Eds.), *Handbook of the teaching of psychology* (pp. 207–213). Malden, MA: Blackwell.

Lloyd, M. A. (2006). Psychology of gender and related courses. In W. Buskist & S. F. Davis (Eds.), *Handbook of the teaching of psychology* (pp. 202–206). Malden, MA: Blackwell.

Mill, J. S. (1988). *On liberty.* New York, NY: Penguin. (Original work published 1859)

Miller, H. L., Jr., & Lance, C. L. (2006). Written and oral assignments. In W. Buskist & S. F. Davis (Eds.), *Handbook of the teaching of psychology* (pp. 259–264). Malden, MA: Blackwell.

Noll, J. (2010). *Taking sides: Clashing views of educational issues* (16th ed.). New York, NY: McGraw-Hill/Dushkin.

Pittenger, D. J. (2006). Teaching psychology when everyone is an expert. In W. Buskist & S. F. Davis (Eds.), *Handbook of the teaching of psychology* (pp. 181–185). Malden, MA: Blackwell.

Rorty, R. (1999). Education as socialization and as individualization. In R. Rorty (Ed.), *Philosophy and social hope* (pp. 114–126). New York, NY: Penguin.

Satris, S. (2011). *Taking sides: Clashing views on moral issues* (13th ed.). New York, NY: McGraw-Hill/Dushkin.

Stradling, E., Noctor, M., & Baines, B. (1984). *Teaching controversial issues.* London: Edward Arnold.

Chapter 18

Technology in Higher Education

❖

Christopher R. Howard

Modern technological innovations are changing our lives substantially. The computer has become a permanent fixture in most businesses, schools, and households. Social networking sites allow individuals to develop and maintain friendships without the constraints of physical proximity. Smartphones, netbooks, and iPads allow people to have the power of technology within their reach anytime, day or night. It is not surprising that our students expect technology to play a prominent role in education (Kyei-Blankson, Keengwe, & Blankson, 2009). For some teachers, technology is a welcome tool that serves to enhance existing pedagogical practices and foster the development of new teaching techniques. For other instructors, though, there may be a noticeable absence or minimization of technological integration in the classroom. Researchers (e.g., Black, 2010; Kyei-Blankson et al., 2009) have noted that, despite the increased emphasis on technology in society, students are much more familiar and facile with technology than are college teachers.

Prensky (2001) and Black (2010) have referred to the current generation of college students as "digital natives," a term that implies today's college students have been influenced by technology all of their lives and have difficulty comprehending a world without it. Students often come to college with vastly different technological backgrounds than many of their professors, and bridging the divide can often be challenging for teachers.

In this chapter, I will summarize the use of technology in higher education and discuss important pedagogical considerations for adopting technology in the classroom. I hope to foster dialogue on pedagogy-driven technological inclusion, the currently utilized or promising technologies for higher education, and ways to incorporate those technologies in the classroom. I will discuss technology broadly rather than specifically for two reasons. First, technology is ever-changing and evolving. Instead of detailing programs or resources, I will outline general categories of technology that may be beneficial for teaching courses at the college and university level. Second, the types of classroom technologies teachers might consider adopting for their courses may be course specific, instructor specific, institution specific, or some combination of these. Successfully integrating technology in college and university teaching depends on many factors; some are within the teacher's control and other factors beyond it.

Adopting Technology in the Classroom

Although institutions are developing more initiatives toward integrating technology in higher education, Kirkwood and Price (2006) cautioned that the inclusion of technology does not necessarily lead to increases in student learning. In a similar vein, Staley (2004) suggested that one important question to consider when adopting technology is, "Does technology add some demonstrable pedagogical value?" (p. 22). He argued that technology should be included when, and only when, it demonstrates some learning advantage over the status quo. Kirkwood and Price and Staley both argued that greater inclusion of technology in the classroom has not occurred because institutions have been putting the technological cart in front of the pedagogical horse.

The decision to adopt a specific technology or technologies requires careful consideration of one's goals and objectives for the course, one's teaching strategy or pedagogical plan, and specific ways one can target course objectives with technology. When reflecting over these issues, teachers should consider the following questions:

- How can technology enhance students' understanding of course content or a particular concept?
- Can technology foster the application and transfer of desired skills?
- How can technology be used to reach students who come from diverse backgrounds, have a variety of learning histories, and approach the world perhaps very differently than their instructor?

Technology offers teachers a plethora of tools that allow for greater flexibility, variety, and adaptability in the delivery of course content. For example, technological tools such as computerized simulation programs provide valuable hands-on or experiential training that would otherwise be impossible or impractical. To be sure, in some academic disciplines such as aviation management, engineering, and astronomy, teachers use computer simulations to mimic the real-life conditions under which undergraduates will be making real-life decisions once they graduate and begin working in the field. Nonetheless, some instructors may find that technology will assist with specific course goals and objectives (say, learning to fly a plane), whereas students in other courses (such as philosophy) may not benefit substantially from technological inclusion.

Technology may also allow for greater flexibility in the learning environment and the types of assignments teachers can incorporate into their courses. Some students may benefit more from structured lectures and discussions, while others may find hands-on activities and experiential endeavors more advantageous. Recently, William Buskist and I developed an introductory psychology course where learning was "blended," or split between traditional large lectures or small discussion sections and online activities. The online components included preliminary short-answer assignments for each chapter, videos with corresponding discussion questions, collaborative problem-based learning activities, and multiple-attempt mastery quizzes. Overall, students enjoyed the variety of learning activities and achieved higher final grades in the course than in previous, more traditional sections of the course taught by the authors.

Baron (2008) argued that today's students are not only comfortable with multitasking (engaging in several tasks at the same time) but prefer using multiple modalities. In a study examining podcasting (audio recordings) and vodcasting (video recordings), Parson, Reddy, Wood, and Senior (2009) found that students preferred to use both technologies in conjunction with other course materials (slides, etc.) when studying for exams. Tang and Austin (2009) similarly concluded that the most effective teaching strategies incorporate several different technological approaches.

Social Networking Technology

The last decade or so has seen a considerable rise in social networking sites. The purpose of social networking sites is to facilitate social interaction among users. Sites such as Facebook, MySpace, and Twitter allow users to post personal information, communicate both asynchronously and synchronously with others, and upload content (pictures, text files, etc.) to the Internet. Individuals have the potential to develop friendships with others who share similar interests, hobbies, or goals and who may be geographically distant. The popularity and convenience of social networking sites has led to a surge in the number of people using them. As examples, Facebook (2011) reported that it currently has 500 million users who spend a total of 700 billion minutes logged in per month, and Twitter (2011) has 175 million users who send 95 million tweets (messages of 140 characters or less) per day. Recently, social networking sites have been educationally repurposed in several ways: (a) to allow for social interactions to foster student-teacher or student-student rapport (Mazer, Murphy, & Simonds, 2009), (b) to provide supplemental instructional resources, and (c) to provide teachers with an online classroom space (Baran, 2010).

For example, Baran (2010) developed an online course in distance education using Facebook, in which students added media content (e.g., videos, photos), discussions, and useful links relevant to the particular content domain being covered. She graded students on both the quality and quantity of their contributions to the Facebook page. In postcourse surveys and face-to-face interviews, most students felt that Facebook was a great resource for student-teacher and student-student interactions and that these interactions enhanced student motivation for the course. However, 75% of students believed that Facebook should serve only a supporting role in teaching and 72% questioned the educational value of using such sites. Baran concluded that Facebook can provide an educational environment that is both familiar and educationally advantageous for students.

Course or Learning Management Technologies

Course or learning management technologies (e.g., Blackboard, WebCT, Moodle) offer instructors numerous technological tools conveniently packaged into flexible and often customizable online environments. Typical features of these technologies allow teachers to upload or create course documents (such as syllabi or calendars), build and deliver online assessments (such as quizzes or tests), and provide students supplemental course materials (such as slides, web links, videos, and podcasts). These management systems also can facilitate communication by allowing for discussion posts, blogs, and chat rooms. Successful integration of these systems often requires little technical knowledge and can provide convenient access for the students and teachers. For example, if one is teaching a course in which readings serve as the primary sources of course content, one can simply upload the readings so students can access them anywhere and anytime they desire. Likewise, recording grades online allows students to continually monitor their progress in the course, and again from any place and at any time. Most universities that adopt technologically based educational platforms have information specialists who assist faculty with initial setup and training. Each platform also typically has online guides or tutorials to navigate faculty through the process.

Communication Technologies

Communication technologies are divided into two basic forms: asynchronous and synchronous. Asynchronous communication technologies provide an open channel of communication that is not constrained by being in the same place (real-life or virtual) at the same time as those individuals with whom the teacher is communicating. The most familiar asynchronous technology is e-mail. E-mail provides an easy and accessible way to keep students abreast of current and future activities in their courses. Other forms of asynchronous technology are forums, blogs, wikis, and listservs. Each promotes ongoing dialogue, stresses a collaborative approach to education, and easily allows for the exchange of ideas.

Synchronous communication allows users to communicate simultaneously. The most common forms of synchronous communication are chat and instant messaging. Some instructors hold virtual office hours and answer student questions, advise, and have one-on-one interactions online. Young (2010) suggested that synchronous technology may be used for this purpose because it provides real-time interaction between students and teachers during class. For example, he offered several scenarios in which teachers had integrated Twitter, allowing students to submit questions to their teachers during class. Although the teachers answered the questions face-to-face, technology facilitated the initial stages of the interaction.

Another example of synchronous technology is classroom response systems (also known as "clickers") that allow students to provide, in response to a prompt, an answer choice, word, phrase, or set of numbers. Instructors can either immediately display or summarize the responses in class or save collected responses. Clickers can be used for many purposes, including quizzing or other forms of low-stakes assessment, having students provide feedback about the course or a class activity, and gathering student-generated data for instructional purposes (e.g., teaching statistical analyses). Recently, Shaffer and Collura (2009) found that introductory psychology students who routinely used clickers in class performed better on exams and reported greater course enjoyment and engagement than comparable non-clicker controls.

Communication technology is commonplace in our everyday lives. The challenge, however, is repurposing communication technologies for educational use (Baron, 2008). Students frequently use e-mail, instant messaging, and other forms of real-time interactions when communicating with their friends and family. By incorporating and encouraging the use of these technologies in the classroom, instructors can promote ongoing dialogue and interaction beyond the classroom.

Audio and Visual Technologies

Audio technologies such as podcasting—audio recordings that can be downloaded on portable media devices (e.g., MP3 players, iPods)—allow teachers to provide students with classroom material accessible whenever the student desires. Teachers can use audio technology to capture lecture content, record classroom discussions, and provide supplemental content for the course or for an assignment. For example, a colleague of mine wears a lapel microphone while giving lectures and uploads these lectures to his course web page in case students want to revisit them or missed key notes from class. Most audio recording devices and software are inexpensive and relatively simple to operate.

Visual technologies allow teachers to capture not only audio but also video. Teachers can capture video in real time (live) or record classroom content for later viewing. In recent years, video sharing sites, such as YouTube, have made the distribution and accessibility of videos easier than ever before. Users can upload their original submissions and share them with virtually anyone online. Institutions of higher education, much like other types of organizations, have created special channels, or "YouTube Universities," that provide a convenient interface for educational resources. For example, the Massachusetts Institute of Technology (MIT) has developed a YouTube Channel with over 1,300 videos on topics such as calculus, computer science, and chemistry. The MIT YouTube Channel currently has over 83,000 subscribers and their videos have been viewed over 20 million times (Massachusetts Institute of Technology, n.d.). In addition to providing videos, visual technology allows instructors to stream video in real time. Interactive programs such as Skype allow users to video chat with other users or conference with multiple users. Skype can be used for classroom collaborations and allow instructors to provide online, synchronous instruction. Visual technologies also include presentation software, such as Microsoft PowerPoint, that allows instructors to create visual displays for displaying course content.

Audio and visual technologies are becoming increasingly common in education because teachers find that they are easy to use and students find that they enhance their classroom experiences. As with social technologies, some audio and visual technologies that were not originally designed for educational instruction are finding their way into college and university teaching. Most of the technologies in this category are widely available, easily accessible, cost-effective, and require minimal technical know-how.

Discipline-Specific Technologies

In addition to "general" technologies, many disciplines often have software, applications, or devices that are used primarily, if not exclusively, within that discipline. For example, in my Research Methods classes, students learn how to use specific statistical programs for analyzing quantitative data. Nursing students may use computerized simulations to learn specific medical techniques. Although these two examples are clearly different, the purpose for incorporating technology in the classroom is identical—teaching hands-on skills that students need to learn in their chosen field.

The best way to locate discipline-specific technologies is to consult experts teaching your subject matter. Disciplines have organizations and associations devoted to teaching and instruction that can provide resources or help teachers locate the technological resources they need. Software developers and other technologically related entrepreneurs often market their products through print catalogs, through online sites, and at professional conventions. If adequate technologies are not accessible, then developing, designing, and implementing new innovations can be beneficial for both the classroom and the discipline.

Tips for Successfully Implementing Technology in the Classroom

Successfully implementing technology in the classroom depends on many factors, including the course objectives, the teacher's technological proficiency, the students' technological proficiency, and the type(s) of technology institutions adopt and support. There are, however, some basic tips that can guide any teacher through the process:

• When developing a course that involves technology, teachers should consult the informational technology (IT) department or specialist at their institution early in the planning process. An IT specialist can give teachers an overview of the resources available to them, as well as provide support during development and eventual implementation. In addition, colleagues who have used a particular technology (or a similar one) may be able to offer "insider" knowledge about its benefits, limitations, feasibility, student usage, and student perceptions. An early assessment of the available resources can assist teachers with decisions about what technology-assisted activities are feasible for their courses or allow them time to propose or develop new technologies for their institution. Teachers should keep in mind that the incorporation of some technologies can require a considerable time invest-ment. For example, teachers may need several semesters to build an online course (depending on the course's complexity).

• One of the best strategies for incorporating technology is to build new technology into courses slowly and progressively. Gradually intro-ducing technology into one's courses allows both teachers and students to become familiar and comfortable with the technology without being overwhelmed. Once comfortable, teachers can then adjust the frequency with which they use the technology and their expectations for student use, or begin incorporating other classroom technologies. If, for example, a teacher wants students to collaborate on a writing project using an online discussion board, she might begin by asking students to post a short paragraph on a given topic. After students have successfully posted their paragraphs, she may ask them to reply to or comment on another person's submission. Finally, she can then ask several students to work together on a combined group response to the topic. This example illustrates that the desired outcome is shaped by initially simple tasks and then progresses to more complex ones.

• As with any pedagogical technique, teachers should thoroughly examine the effectiveness of their technological inclusion from their own perspectives as well as the students' perception. Evaluating and reevaluating the technological components of one's courses throughout the semester or across assignments allows one to identify instances where technology has facilitated learning or instances where it has hindered it. Some questions that teachers might consider as they evaluate their use of classroom technol-ogy include the following:

■ Are students mastering the concepts or course better than when previous methods or other technologies were used?
■ Do students feel that the technology is beneficial to their course performance (or activity performance) and understanding?
■ What changes would I or my students make to improve the technology or the usability of the technology as it relates to achieving the course learning objectives?

Answers to these sorts of questions can help reinforce teachers' current practices and provide insight for redesigning the course or activity in the future.

Conclusions

Technology has become a cornerstone in our students' lives and shapes the way they think about their world, the way they interact with others, and how they approach education. As such, teachers should thoroughly examine the potential that technology might have for developing and refining sound pedagogical practices. Considering the incorporation of technology in the classroom is not a decision to be taken lightly, though. It requires conscious planning and careful mapping of technological resources onto one's teaching and learning goals. Technology, in and of itself, cannot replace effective teaching, but it may enable teachers to reach their students in more diverse, engaging, and meaningful ways.

References

Baran, B. (2010). Facebook as a formal instructional environment. *British Journal of Educational Technology, 41*, 146–149.

Baron, N. S. (2008). *Always on: Language in an online and mobile world.* New York, NY: Oxford University Press.

Black, A. (2010). Gen Y: Who they are and how they learn. *Educational Horizons, 88*, 92–101.

Facebook. (2011). *Statistics.* Retrieved from http://www.facebook.com/press/info.php?statistics

Kirkwood, A., & Price, L. (2006). Adaptation for a changing environment: Developing learning and teaching with information and communication technologies. *International Review of Research in Open and Distance Learning, 7*, 1–14.

Kyei-Blankson, L., Keengwe, J., & Blankson, J. (2009). Faculty use and integration of technology in higher education. *Association for the Advancement of Computing in Education Journal, 17*, 199–213.

Massachusetts Institute of Technology. (n.d.). Retrieved from http://www.youtube.com/user/MIT

Mazer, J. P., Murphy, R. E., & Simonds, C. J. (2009). The effects of teacher self-disclosure via Facebook on teacher credibility. *Learning, Media, and Technology, 34*, 175–183.

Parson, V., Reddy, P., Wood, J., & Senior, C. (2009). Educating an iPod generation: Undergraduate attitudes, experiences, and understanding of vodcast and podcast use. *Learning, Media, and Technology, 34*, 215–228.

Prensky, M. (2001). Digital natives, digital immigrants. *On the Horizon, 9*, 1–6.

Shaffer, D. M., & Collura, M. J. (2009). Evaluating the effectiveness of a personal response system in the classroom. *Teaching of Psychology, 36*, 273–277.

Staley, D. J. (2004). Adopting digital technologies in the classroom: 10 assessment questions. *Educase Quarterly, 3*, 20–26.

Tang, T. L., & Austin, M. J. (2009). Students' perception of teaching technologies, application of technologies, and academic performance. *Computers & Education, 53*, 1241–1255.

Twitter. (2011). About. Retrieved from http://twitter.com/about

Young, J. (2009, November 22). Teaching with Twitter. *The Chronicle of Higher Education, 56*, 10.

Chapter 19

Course and Instructor Evaluation ❖

Jared W. Keeley

One of the most vital aspects of learning to teach is to learn how to assess your teaching. In the early stages of learning any task, much less a complex and multifaceted task like teaching, it is important to receive regular feedback on your performance. In a program that trains graduate students, there might be a formal system for providing feedback to them on their teaching. However, part of training a teacher is training that person to function independently. There will not always be faculty members present to provide feedback. Instead, it is important for teachers to learn how to improve on their own. This chapter provides a framework for how to assess one's teaching in order to get the most information possible out of the assessment process. A second purpose of this chapter is to provide a description of the "best practices" in educational assessment to serve as a foundation for good assessment habits for graduate students and new faculty.

We all have moments of weakness. Sometimes, when going to bed, we are so tired that we skip brushing our teeth, even though we know brushing our teeth is good for us. Assessing our teaching can sometimes be similar. We know that there are a variety of things we could do to improve our teaching, but they require a good bit of effort in an already busy schedule, and so we might forgo them. The best way to develop good habits is to be guided to do so from the beginning. Every program that trains graduate student teachers should have a strong system in place to help train them to assess their teaching. However, in the absence of a structured program, conscientious graduate students can learn to implement assessment techniques on their own.

Purposes of Evaluation

It is a truism that your purpose in asking a question will lead to the type of question you ask. The evaluation of teaching is no different. Depending on the purpose for conducting an evaluation, a teacher might choose different methods of evaluation. Thus, it is important that we begin with a review of the main purposes for evaluating teaching.

There are two main purposes for evaluating teaching, broadly termed *summative* and *formative* evaluation. A summative evaluation focuses on feedback for others—department chairs and deans, for example. This sort of feedback is a necessary task for the college or university. It helps ensure a minimal level of educational quality while aiding administrators in personnel evaluation. Summative feedback is an integral part of tenure and promotion decisions, performance evaluations of nontenure line faculty, merit raises, and other personnel decisions.

Formative evaluation focuses on feedback for the individual. This feedback is used for individual improvement in one's teaching over time. All teachers can benefit from continual feedback about their performance in the classroom. However, formative feedback is especially crucial early in one's teaching career. It can direct a new teacher to problems in his or her presentation style, to ways of altering assignments or course policies, and to improving many other vital aspects of teaching.

Summative and formative feedback are not mutually exclusive. In fact, the same evaluation process could serve both purposes simultaneously. For example, a student evaluation at the end of an academic term is a summative requirement at many institutions, but course instructors can also use that evaluation for reflective improvement of their next course offering. Nonetheless, there might be times when information for one type of evaluation may not be useful for the other. Using the same example of a student evaluation of instruction, the form required by your institution may not tap all of the dimensions on which a teacher wants—and needs—students' feedback. Perhaps the course includes a substantial group project, but the form has no means of assessing this sort of work.

Sources of Information

Applied fields have long advocated the use of multimodal, multisource assessments (Martin, 1988; Merrell, 2003). When attempting to gain information about an assessment target, that information will vary across different informants and methods. Consider, for example, a disruptive child. A teacher may complain that a student is constantly out of his seat, talking out of turn, and generally creating a nuisance. However, the child's parents report that he is a "perfect angel" at home. A professional conducting an evaluation of this child would not capture a complete picture of the child by relying on only one source of information. Similarly, the method by which a question is asked may lead to different information, even from the same source. The teacher above may complain at length about the student in an open-ended interview but rate the child's behavior as being within a normal range on a behaviorally anchored rating scale. For that reason, it is important to consider the sources of information about teaching and the methods teachers use to assess it. When evaluating teaching, either for summative or formative purposes, the most informative practice will be to include as many sources of information across as many methods as feasible in order to capture as complete a picture as possible and to look for ways in which the disparate sources provide converging information.

Source 1: Students

The most obvious source of information about teaching is students. They are the direct "consumers" of teaching and are in a unique position to comment on its effectiveness. However teachers might conceptualize the goals of their teaching, a common denominator of all effective teaching is that it produces change in students. The change students perceive (e.g., their judgments of how much they learned in a course) does not always equal the amount of change measured by other methods (e.g., teacher-developed measures of learning, such as exams). Students may perceive themselves as having learned more than they demonstrate to their teachers, or they may perceive themselves as not having changed substantially despite evidence to the contrary. In any event, student perceptions are an important part of any evaluation because they can provide valuable information about the degree to which those perceptions align with teacher-developed measures of learning. Student perceptions influence important variables like motivation, engagement, and satisfaction, all of which are related to the ultimate goal of learning (Goodboy & Bolkan, 2009; Goodboy & Myers, 2008; Greimel-Fuhrmann & Geyer, 2003; Klein, Noe, & Wang, 2006).

Source 2: Peers

Peers are a valuable but often underutilized source of information about instructors' teaching. Students simply are not qualified to comment on some aspects of a course. For instance, they may not be able to comment on a teacher's academic qualifications or adequacy of coverage of course material, especially if they are new to the discipline. However, fellow instructors would be able to assess these and other dimensions—for example, how well course content reflects the current state of the field. Peers can also comment on a teacher's method of delivery from a perspective different than that of students. Peers can evaluate classroom presentation skills from the perspective of a fellow professional who also engages in these activities (e.g., pace, use of PowerPoint). More senior colleagues may be able to recount times they have encountered problems in their own teaching and how they addressed these issues.

Source 3: Self-Reflection

Self-reflection is an important source of information for teachers, and its value should not be underestimated. Instructors have a unique perspective from which to judge their performance over time and to consider changes they have, or have not, made. Regular time spent evaluating various aspects of one's teaching is a valuable formative experience.

Source 4: Time

One important dimension on which to evaluate one's teaching is time. In fact, the only way to track improvement in teaching is across time. The time frame of comparisons will vary. A teacher might measure student learning before and after a new class activity, which is a span perhaps of only a single class period. Teachers might measure changes in their behavior from midsemester to the end of the semester to assess how effectively they responded to the midsemester feedback. Teachers might measure change from year to year as they repeat a course and change aspects of it. Finally, teachers might reflect upon their teaching philosophy and how it changes across their career (see Korn's Chapter 8).

Methods of Assessment

There are a variety of techniques to use when assessing teaching, some of which are more specific than others. As always, the purpose of evaluation will help guide the choice of assessment methods. Some methods are only appropriate for one of the sources of information discussed in the preceding paragraphs (e.g., student evaluations of instruction, by definition, must come from students), but other methods might appropriately be evaluated through multiple sources (e.g., a teacher and a peer might both evaluate the content of a syllabus). Teachers should tap multiple sources of information when selecting methods, not just one method.

Student Evaluations of Instruction

Student evaluations of instruction are the most common measure of teaching effectiveness as well as the most controversial. Most postsecondary institutions use a formal process of evaluating teachers, and that process often includes a formal rating of instructors by students. The instruments used to collect students' evaluations of teachers vary widely. Some measures contain just a few items; some encompass a broad range of assessment targets. Many are home-grown and the measurement properties of the instruments are often unknown (Barnes et al., 2008; Keeley, Smith, & Buskist, 2006). To be useful, a measurement instrument must show reliability, both internal consistency and consistency over time, and validity. The validity of student evaluations of instructions has been widely debated for many years (e.g., see Greenwald, 1997). Particular issues have been the perceived (and sometimes measured) effect of grade leniency on student ratings and how well those ratings correspond to other outcomes such as student learning (Ellis, Burke, Lomire, & McCormack, 2004; Marsh & Roche, 2000). The jury is still largely out on these issues, but student evaluations of instruction are still widely used in many institutions.

There are a number of well-developed instruments in existence. Some institutions (e.g., University of Washington) have developed broad systems that utilize many adaptable measures (e.g., separate forms for labs versus lectures). Other empirically supported instruments are available, such as the Teacher Behavior Checklist (Keeley et al., 2006), the Student Evaluation of Educational Quality (Marsh, 1982), and an instrument developed by Barnes et al. (2008).

Mini-Assessments

In *Classroom Assessment Techniques: A Handbook for College Teachers*, Angelo and Cross (1993) provided detailed information about and suggestions for the use of a variety of assessment tools that teachers can use in their courses. A frequently used assessment technique is the minute paper, which is simply a response that teachers ask students to write within a purposefully short time frame, often a minute. Students hand in their responses, which provide feedback to the teacher. Student responses may address a substantive topic, such as a summary of what was covered in lecture, or an assessment of critical thinking regarding a point made in class. The minute paper can also be an assessment of teaching. For example, the topic of the paper could be students' perceived effectiveness of a class demonstration.

Graded Assignments and Tests

One assessment measure is so obvious that some faculty might overlook its value. All graded assignments and tests provide potentially rich sources of feedback to teachers (and to students). First, these assignments are one definition of student learning in a course. As noted earlier, student learning is an invaluable benchmark regarding course outcomes and, although it may not be the only outcome of interest, it is usually a major one.

Graded assignments can also be an indirect source of feedback about one's teaching. There are many factors that contribute to how an individual student performs on an assignment like a test. First, there is student motivation—a motivated student will put forth more effort than an unmotivated student. Second, there is student ability—students with stronger academic ability or relevant background knowledge in a subject will tend to perform better, all other things being equal. Other factors, such as study skills, educational history, family influences, and many other factors, all contribute to an individual's performance on a test. These factors vary across students, and as such, change test scores in nonsystematic ways—essentially washing out their effects when examining the whole class's performance. A teacher's presentation of the material and the structure of the course will have an impact on students' performance in a systematic way, meaning that most students will be affected. For example, if a course goal is that students learn a particular concept, but all students seem to show a fundamental misunderstanding of that concept, that is valuable feedback.

Syllabus and Materials Review

Not all teaching occurs in the classroom. Teachers log many hours preparing for their class time. Thus far, we have not discussed how one might assess these aspects of teaching. The best way to do so is through a systematic review of a course's syllabus and other materials. For the purpose of assessment, it is useful to think of a syllabus as the outline for a course. It should include course goals, how those goals will be assessed (assignments and grading), what topics will be covered, and so on. Over successive offerings of a course, those goals might change or a teacher might devise new assignments. It is important to review periodically how well the syllabus reflects these changes and how well the goals match the assignments. Peers can also help evaluate the content of a syllabus, the amount of material a course covers, and the nature of the assignments. Individuals and organizations in some disciplines post syllabi for different courses for public comment and review, for a broader perspective.

Teaching Philosophy Review

Ideally, everything teachers do related to their courses flows logically from their personal philosophy of teaching. Reflecting on one's teaching philosophy is another form of assessment, as teachers periodically update their philosophy and change the way they view the discipline (see Korn's Chapter 8). It is a good practice to keep old versions of teaching philosophies and periodically review them to track changes over time.

Student Focus Groups

It may be beneficial to obtain feedback from students in more depth than would be feasible to gather from an entire class. When the teacher is the person conducting the evaluation, students might not be forthright in their answers—for example, they might not want to say anything critical about the class because they like the teacher. A student focus group is run by an outside consultant who gathers a set of information from a representative subset of students enrolled in a course. If an institution has a teaching and learning center or a similar entity, a staff person may be able to conduct a focus group for a course. Teachers can work with the consultant to determine what they want to learn from the focus group and the nature of the feedback desired.

In Vivo Assessments

As scary as it might be, obtaining samples of actual teaching behavior can provide an invaluable source of information. A peer might sit in for a class or two and offer feedback about style, class dynamics, and so on. The feedback a peer can offer from a sample of teaching is far more specific than from other methods, such as materials review or an informal discussion of teaching. Another option to consider is videotaping class sessions. Then, reviewers (both the teacher and others) may review the video at their leisure. The teacher might even have multiple peers evaluate the same lesson to see whether their reactions converge on the same issues.

Conclusions

Good habits, like brushing your teeth, are difficult to maintain but well worth the effort in the long run. This chapter has highlighted a number of ways that instructors can assess their teaching. This information will serve new graduate students and new faculty learning to teach as well as those faculty training graduate students to teach (and maybe even teach some old dogs new tricks). The purpose of evaluating teaching should guide the methods and informants chosen. The best information comes not from any single source or method, but from examining many sources in combination. In that way, one will gather a rich set of data regarding one's performance that can guide continual improvement in one's teaching.

References

Angelo, T. A., & Cross, K. P. (1993). *Classroom assessment techniques: A handbook for college teachers* (2nd ed.). San Francisco, CA: Jossey-Bass.

Barnes, D., Engelland, B., Matherine, C., Martin, W., Orgeron, C., Ring, J, . . . & Williams, Z. (2008). Developing a psychometrically sound measure of collegiate teaching proficiency. *College Student Journal, 42,* 199–213.

Ellis, L., Burke, D. M., Lomire, P., & McCormack, D. R. (2004). Student grades and average ratings of instructional quality: The need for adjustment. *Journal of Educational Research, 9,* 35–41.

Goodboy, A. K., & Bolkan, S. (2009). College teacher misbehaviors: Direct and indirect effects on student communication behavior and traditional learning outcomes. *Western Journal of Communication, 73,* 204–219.

Goodboy, A. K., & Myers, S. A. (2008). The effect of teacher confirmation on student communication and learning outcomes. *Communication Education, 57,* 153–179.

Greenwald, A. G. (1997). Validity concerns and usefulness of student ratings of instruction. *American Psychologist, 52,* 1182–1186.

Greimel-Fuhrmann, B., & Geyer, A. (2003). Students' evaluation of teachers and instructional quality: Analysis of relevant factors based on empirical evaluation research. *Assessment & Evaluation in Higher Education, 283,* 229–238.

Keeley, J. W., Smith, D., & Buskist, W. (2006). The Teacher Behaviors Checklist: Factor analysis of its utility for evaluating teaching. *Teaching of Psychology, 33,* 84–90.

Klein, H. J., Noe, R. A., & Wang, C. (2006). Motivation to learn and course outcomes: The impact of delivery mode, learning goal orientation, and perceived barriers and enablers. *Personnel Psychology, 59,* 665–702.

Marsh, H. W. (1982). SEEQ: A reliable, valid and useful instrument for collecting students' evaluations of university teaching. *British Journal of Educational Psychology, 52,* 77–95.

Marsh, H. W., & Roche, L. A. (2000). Effects of grading leniency and low workload of students' evaluations of teaching: Popular myth, bias, validity, or innocent bystanders? *Journal of Educational Psychology, 92,* 202–228.

Martin, R. P. (1988). *Assessment of personality and behavior problems.* New York, NY: Guilford Press.

Merrell, K. W. (2003). *Behavioral, social, and emotional assessment of children and adolescents* (2nd ed.). Mahwah, NJ: Lawrence Erlbaum.

Chapter 20

Assessing the Effectiveness of GTA Preparatory Activities and Programs

Cecilia M. Shore

One purpose of this book is to help faculty members who may be interested in starting or improving graduate teaching assistant (GTA) training programs for their departments or institutions. In these days of heightened attention to accountability in higher education, it is important to evaluate program quality. The first question is, "Is the GTA program following best practices?" This question subsumes two other questions, "What do other GTA programs do?" and "Is the program making use of practices that have been demonstrated to be effective?" A third question is, "What data from the GTA program can provide evidence of its effectiveness?"

Best Practices

One indicator of quality for a GTA program is that it follows best practices. It offers training that is comparable to other GTA programs and that has been demonstrated to be effective. Eison and Vanderford (1993) provided a list of qualities of good departmental GTA programs: a substantive orientation, a comprehensive set of written materials, instruction in discipline-specific instructional skills, classroom observations with feedback, and reflection by GTA supervisors on the effectiveness of GTA training efforts. They provided specific questions for self-assessment. Buskist, Tears, Davis, and Rodrigue (2002) provided a review of the typical contents of a teaching of psychology course, including such topics as delivering lectures, leading class discussion, test construction, grading, and ethics. An overview of pedagogy courses offered to GTAs was provided by Marincovich (1998). In another view on common practice, Meyers and Prieto (2000) catalogued the training opportunities or activities offered by psychology departments. Their list included elements such as readings and discussions on teaching theory and practice, watching one's own performance on video, reviewing student evaluations with the supervisor, and the supervisor observing teaching or microteaching.

What training activities or opportunities appear to be effective? Smith (2003) conducted a longitudinal, qualitative, multicase study in which she used GTA discussion boards, surveys, and interviews to learn about the development of teacher-scholars in graduate school, through the job search, and into their early careers. Thus, the data primarily represented the participants' attributions about what factors had supported or hampered their professional growth. Participants reported that they had been helped by support for GTAs to develop six areas of teaching competency: scholastic, planning, management, presentation/communication, evaluation/feedback, and interpersonal. Smith concluded that the developmental framework used in the GTA program was a key factor in the success of these junior colleagues. Finally, participants reported that confidence they gained from reflective practice, embodied in their teaching portfolio, had been beneficial.

Chism (1998) presented an overview of the research literature on specific training effects—for example, training in the asking of questions and consultations around midterm analysis of teaching. Lewis (1997) and Abbot, Wulff, and Szego (1989) conducted reviews of the literature on the effectiveness of GTA training. The studies they reviewed overlapped considerably and relied heavily on pre-post measures of student ratings of teachers and teaching observations as outcome variables. In general, they both concluded that the evidence supported the effectiveness of GTAs reviewing videotapes of their teaching and of receiving consultations with a faculty member about their student evaluations. The finding that video review and consultation with a faculty member were effective in improving teaching accords with McElroy and Prentice-Dunn's (2005) self-report data. This research indicated that GTAs in their teaching courses perceived the most useful component of the course to be the consultation session, in which the advisor and the student tried to interpret the undergraduate student ratings in light of video or advisor observation.

Collecting Data for Assessment

The best evidence for the quality and effectiveness of a GTA program is provided by collecting data from the program itself. But what information should be collected? Chism (1998) indicated that assessors could focus on a number of questions:

- To what extent is the program used?
- How satisfied are the GTAs who participate?
- What effects does the program have on their teaching?
- What effects does the program have on learning by the GTA's students?

Chism observed that, as is the case generally with faculty development programs, administrators of GTA programs often report GTA usage of the program and GTA satisfaction with the program, and less often report effects of the program on teaching. Generally, assessing impacts on student learning is not feasible because there are too many uncontrolled variables. In other words, undergraduates who are learning in classes taught by GTAs differ in many ways besides whether the GTA has received training. Gaining either experimental or statistical control of these variables is generally impractical for most GTA program assessors. Chism noted that the selection of methods for assessment depends on whether the assessor needs information for improvement, information for accountability, or a formal experimental design. Finally, she reminded assessors of GTA programs to keep it simple. Leaders of GTA programs generally need methods that are easily usable in natural settings; that do not require a great deal of background in research methods; and that, while simple to interpret, lead to clear understanding of what is or is not working.

GTA programs vary in scope and thus may call for different types of assessment. Multiyear departmental or university "certificate in college teaching" programs could examine undergraduate student ratings, job placement, and alumni rankings of graduate experiences (see, e.g., Benassi & Fernald, 1993). In her 10-year longitudinal study, Smith (2003) made use of qualitative information from entering GTA mentor interviews, observations of their teaching, and discussions on their GTA mentor listserv. As the GTAs moved into academic careers, the researchers replaced direct observations with surveys, but continued to monitor the GTA mentor listserv and to do individual interviews with the former GTAs.

A likely outcome of a multiyear program would be a teaching statement or portfolio. Kaplan, Meizlish, O'Neal, and Wright (2008) and Schönwetter, Sokal, Friesen, and Taylor (2002) provided examples of rubrics for reviewing teaching statements. Bernstein et al. (2009) provided an example of a rubric for evaluating portfolios. For formal program evaluation purposes, program leaders may desire an external peer review (Chism, 1998).

Leaders of informal peer social support programs, such as that described by Verges, Spitalnick, and Michels (2006), often assess program success by means of a satisfaction survey. Their survey is typical in being simple and straightforward. University teaching and learning centers that offer services and workshops could assess their effectiveness during the sessions by using classroom assessment techniques, or CATs (Angelo & Cross, 1993). CATs allow leaders to find out what workshop participants are learning by asking them to use or reflect on the information. Chism (1998) suggested that leaders conduct a brief discussion at the end of the session about participants' perceptions of how well the conversation had gone. Center staff members often send surveys a short time after their workshops or services for assessment purposes. However, surveys or interviews that take place after more elapsed time may reveal longer-term outcomes of the center's services than do surveys immediately following an event. For example, Jacobson, Wulff, Grooters, Edwards, and Friesem (2009) provided an example of a survey they used to assess the impact of consultations with their center on TAs and faculty. The survey included open-ended questions to probe for ways the work with the center had affected teaching. Similarly, Way, Piliero, and Carlson (2001) provided questionnaires that they used to measure GTAs' perceptions that their department or course or supervisor encouraged them to make use of the workshop. As another example, Barnett and Hodges (2009) provided a qualitative analysis of follow-up interviews with GTAs about a series of workshops on learning.

Faculty who teach courses on college teaching often assess participants' responses by means of course evaluations (see, e.g., McElroy & Prentice-Dunn, 2005). However, rather than evaluating the teacher of the pedagogy course, one could instead evaluate the teaching of the GTAs. If the assessor defines effective teaching (by the pedagogy course teacher) as effective learning (by the GTAs), then the GTAs ought to perform better as teachers. Assessors need to be mindful that GTAs may be anxious about having their teaching evaluated. Nyquist and Wulff (1996) provided some useful guidelines for assessing GTA effectiveness in a sensitive way. Specifically, they suggested that the assessor clarify the purpose of the assessment to the GTAs, provide a written description of the assessment process to the GTAs, and involve GTAs in the process. They also argued that the assessment should be framed as supportive of the GTAs, and provide the GTAs with information about both strengths and weaknesses of their teaching. Nyquist and Wulff indicated that assessment should be an ongoing process, such that the supervisor and GTAs establish goals and strategies pertaining to the GTAs' teaching and check on the GTAs' progress. They suggested that if these guidelines are followed, assessment would become feedback to help the GTA progress as a teacher, as well as be a source of information about the effectiveness of the program.

If the faculty member assesses the effectiveness of a given GTA program or course by examining GTA teaching effectiveness, then the sources for assessment information are the same as the sources for any teaching evaluation: the instructor, a supervisor/peer, and undergraduate students (Bernstein et al., 2009). Assessors can make use of the self-perceptions of GTAs (Abbot et al., 1989; Lewis 1997; Nyquist & Wulff, 1996). One self-perception measure is teaching self-efficacy (Komarraju, 2008; Prieto & Meyers, 1999). Komarraju assessed the effectiveness of her pedagogy course by administering Gibson and Dembo's (1984) self-efficacy questionnaire as well as a self-designed measure of liking for teaching. Technology is often a specific concern for novice instructors; Lieberman and Reuter (1996) provided a useful technology self-assessment measure.

Information about GTA effectiveness can also come from supervisors or peers who review teaching materials such as syllabi and exams (Nyquist & Wulff, 1996) or who observe teaching behavior, live, via microteaching, or on video (Abbot et al., 1989; Lewis 1997). Frameworks for reviewing teaching materials and doing class observations can be found in Chism's (2009) book on peer review of teaching. A teaching observation checklist with good psychometric properties was presented by Keeley, Smith, and Buskist (2006). An alternative framework for peer review was provided by Paulsen (2001), who listed teaching behaviors that address students' motivation, their ability to reflect on their own thoughts and actions, and the social environment of the classroom.

Finally, undergraduate students can provide assessment information about GTA teaching effectiveness. Researchers studying the effectiveness of teaching programs on GTA teaching often report results of student ratings of GTAs (Abbot et al., 1989; Lewis, 1997). Ideally, of course, effective teaching is related to student learning. Nyquist and Wulff (1996) suggested that GTAs use CATs (Angelo & Cross, 1993) as well as other measures of student performance to determine what students are learning.

Conclusions

Assessing the effectiveness of the department's or institution's GTA program is, of course, important for both accountability and improvement. However, even more important is that, by doing so, the program coordinator provides a model for the GTAs of scholarly and reflective teaching practice. Generally, GTA programs encourage GTAs to take a scholarly approach to their teaching. They often encourage GTAs to set student learning outcomes, search the literature for effective means of helping students reach those goals, assess student learning, and reflect for improvement. Leaders of GTA programs should model scholarly teaching by following scholarly practices themselves.

References

Abbott, R. D., Wulff, D. H., & Szego, C. K. (1989). Review of research on TA training. In J. D. Nyquist, R. D. Abbott, & D. H. Wulff (Eds.), *Teaching assistant training in the 1990s*. New Directions for Teaching and Learning, No. 39 (pp. 111–124). San Francisco, CA: Jossey-Bass.

Angelo, T. A., & Cross, K. P. (1993). *Classroom assessment techniques* (2nd ed.). San Francisco, CA: Jossey-Bass.

Barnett, P. E., & Hodges, L. C. (2009). Teaching learning processes to students and teachers. *To Improve the Academy, 27*, 401–424.

Benassi, V. A., & Fernald, P. S. (1993). Preparing tomorrow's psychologists for careers in academe. *Teaching of Psychology, 20*, 149–155.

Bernstein, D., Addison, W., Altman, C., Hollister, D., Komarraju, M., Prieto, L., Rocheleau, C. A., & Shore, C. (2009). Toward a scientist-educator model of teaching psychology. In D. Halpern (Ed.), *Undergraduate education in psychology: A blueprint for the future of the discipline* (pp. 29–45). Washington, DC: American Psychological Association.

Buskist, W., Tears, R. S., Davis, S. F., & Rodrigue, K. M. (2002). The teaching of psychology course: Prevalence and content. *Teaching of Psychology, 29*, 140–142.

Chism, N. (1998). Evaluating TA programs. In M. Marincovich, J. Prostko, & F. Stout (Eds.), *The professional development of graduate teaching assistants* (pp. 249–262). Boston, MA: Anker.

Chism, N. (2009). *Peer review of teaching: A sourcebook* (2nd ed.). San Francisco, CA: Jossey-Bass.

Eison, J., & Vanderford, M. (1993). Enhancing GTA training in academic development: Some self-assessment guidelines. *To Improve the Academy, 12*, 53–68.

Gibson, S., & Dembo, M. H. (1984). Teacher efficacy: A construct validation. *Journal of Educational Psychology, 76*, 569–582.

Jacobson, W., Wulff, D. H., Grooters, S., Edwards, P. M., & Friesem, K. (2009). Reported long-term value and effects of teaching center consultations. *To Improve the Academy, 27*, 223–246.

Kaplan, M., Meizlish, D. S., O'Neal, C., & Wright, M. C. (2008). A research-based rubric for developing statements of teaching philosophy. *To Improve the Academy, 26*, 242–262.

Keeley, J., Smith, D., & Buskist, W. (2006). The teacher behaviors checklist: Factor analysis of its utility for evaluating teaching. *Teaching of Psychology, 33*, 84–91.

Komarraju, M. (2008). A social-cognitive approach to training teaching assistants. *Teaching of Psychology, 35*, 327–334.

Lewis, K. G. (1997). *Training focused on postgraduate teaching assistants: The North American model*. Retrieved from www.ntlf.com/html/lib/bib/backup/lewis.htm

Lieberman, D. A., & Reuter, J. (1996). Designing, implementing and assessing a university technology-pedagogy institute. *To Improve the Academy, 15*, 231–249.

Marincovich, M. (1998). Teaching teaching: The importance of courses on teaching in TA training programs. In M. Marincovich, J. Prostko, & F. Stout (Eds.), *The professional development of graduate teaching assistants* (pp. 145–162). Boston, MA: Anker.

McElroy, H. K., & Prentice-Dunn, S. (2005). Graduate students' perceptions of a teaching of psychology course. *Teaching of Psychology, 32,* 123–125.

Meyers, S. A., & Prieto, L. R. (2000). Training in the teaching of psychology: What is done and examining the differences. *Teaching of Psychology, 27,* 258–261.

Nyquist, J. D., & Wulff, D. H. (1996). *Working effectively with graduate assistants.* Thousand Oaks, CA: Sage.

Paulsen, M. B. (2001). After twelve years of teaching the college teaching course. *To Improve the Academy, 19,* 169–192.

Prieto, L. R., & Meyers, S. A. (1999). Effects of training and supervision on the self-efficacy of psychology graduate teaching assistants. *Teaching of Psychology, 26,* 264–266.

Schönwetter, D. J., Sokal, L., Friesen, M., & Taylor, K. L. (2002). Teaching philosophies reconsidered: A conceptual model for the development and evaluation of teaching philosophy statements. *International Journal for Academic Development, 7,* 83–97.

Smith, K. S. (2003). Assessing and reinvigorating a teaching assistant support program: The intersections of institutional, regional, and national needs for preparing future faculty. *To Improve the Academy, 21,* 143–159.

Verges, M., Spitalnick, J., & Michels, K. (2006). Soapbox sessions: A graduate student teaching forum. *Teaching of Psychology, 33,* 123–125.

Way, D., Piliero, S., & Carlson, V. (2001). Evaluating teaching workshops: Beyond the satisfaction survey. *To Improve the Academy, 20,* 94–106.

Chapter 21

Preparing Graduate Students for the Political Nature of the Academy

❖

Randolph A. Smith and Stephen F. Davis

As graduate students prepare for entry to the world of academia, there are many activities in which they may engage to help prepare for that new world. For example, they may have served as graduate teaching assistants to help them learn how to teach and they may have had research assistantships to help prepare them for their research careers. Graduate students can talk to their professors about their early experiences as new faculty members. They can consult sources in the literature (e.g., Benson & Buskist, 2005; Boice, 2000; Buskist & Irons, 2006; Clifton & Buskist, 2005; Darley, Zanna, & Roediger, 2004; Irons & Buskist, 2008) to help them be better prepared for their first faculty position. However, none of these sources, with the possible exception of talking to faculty colleagues, can prepare them for the political climate they are likely to experience in the academic world.

Just like other careers, academia is susceptible to political considerations. The important point about politics in academia is making certain that graduate students and beginning faculty do not allow politics to sabotage their academic careers. Henry Kissinger is often credited with saying "academic politics are so bitter because the stakes are so small." When it comes to a person's job and career, those stakes are *not* small, so it pays to be prepared for future situations.

There are a few oft-cited book chapters dealing with academic politics (Capaldi, 2004; Penner, Dovidio, & Schroeder, 2004; Salancik, 1987). Capaldi's (2004) chapter focused primarily on classification of colleges and the power hierarchy in colleges, so it provides little in the way of practical advice for new faculty. Salancik (1987) focused on power relationships, with some attention given to individual faculty members. Penner et al. (2004) provided some useful practical advice for new faculty about important topics such as becoming known and well known, self-protection, and what to do if things go bad. However, their focus was primarily on the new faculty member's relationship with the department chair. Although these chapters offer some useful information, they seem to be aimed primarily at faculty members who work at large research universities, which make up a minority of higher education institutions in the United States (see http://classifications.carnegiefoundation.org/). Many new faculty, of course, begin their academic careers at smaller colleges and universities that have a greater emphasis on teaching. In this chapter, we attempt to fill the void and focus on political considerations that are relevant to the academic lives of most new faculty.

Bloom and Bell (1979) wrote an article dealing with "superstars" in graduate school. They listed five traits of graduate students who excelled in their graduate programs: visibility, hard working, reflection of program values, professor attachment, and the "W Factor" (being easy to teach, not complaining, receiving feedback well). We believe that some of these traits also are relevant to six issues that we have identified as important political considerations for new faculty.

Political Considerations Dealing With Professor Attachment

One set of important political considerations for graduate students is selecting people who can help them guide their graduate careers. Bloom and Bell (1979) wrote that graduate superstars found at least one professor with whom to work during their graduate careers. Although there are critical differences, new faculty can also benefit from forming relationships with other professors early in their professional careers. In particular, these colleagues can help with important issues ranging from "learning the ropes" in the particular department, college, and university to forming research collaborations to providing career advice. Likewise, seasoned faculty can be invaluable in helping new faculty "find their way" through the maze of academia—they can help you get the most out of your new faculty experience.

Selecting a Local Guide

For new faculty, it can be important to find colleagues who can help guide them through the intricacies of a new job. These faculty, especially those who are untenured, can serve as mentors in helping make new faculty aware of and understand the politics within the department. Some of the issues new faculty may have to confront include the following: What is the best way to prepare for several classes at once (you may have taught only one course at a time as a graduate student)? How should you develop a class presentation for an entry-level course? An upper-level undergraduate course? A graduate course (if you have any to teach)? What does it mean to be a research mentor for students? How do faculty meetings run, and what is the new faculty member's role during these meetings? Does the department have less-than-cordial relations with any other department on campus? How should new faculty interact with the dean or president (a question that could refer to protocol, substance, or chain of command)? And so forth. Yes, politics are going to be part of any academic career, and new faculty need to be prepared to deal with them effectively. Senior faculty have already been down the road new faculty are traveling. By using their knowledge wisely, new faculty in turn can be prepared to share their insights with new faculty who join the department in subsequent years. Most faculty members are more than happy to *pay forward* (Hyde, 1999) the kind of help and assistance they have received.

Although a local guide can help new faculty with most of the issues they encounter as they adjust to new roles in a new environment, they may wish to seek more specialized advice from particular individuals regarding research issues. Although faculty evaluation typically encompasses teaching, research, and service, the research component is especially critical as new faculty work toward tenure and promotion, or toward securing a long-term contract.

Selecting a Research Guide

New faculty should look for a research guide for at least three reasons. First, however, let us assure you that we do not mean that new faculty need someone to tell them how to do research—new faculty will obviously already have those skills and abilities. One reason a research guide can be helpful is to acquaint new faculty with the ins and outs of research at their new institution. There are probably a number of issues new faculty dealt with in graduate school about which they need information in their new context—how to find research participants, how the IRB process works, how to get access to research space (if one doesn't have laboratory space), and so on. Second, a research guide may be helpful in providing information about the importance of research to one's new institution. There is quite a range of possibilities to this issue, and the most accurate perspective is likely to come from someone who has observed the retention and promotion process firsthand. Although the size of a college and a department can be important determiners of research importance, they are probably not perfect predictors. Even knowing that one's school is teaching oriented does not mean that research is unimportant to progression through the academic ranks. Some institutions that are quite strongly oriented toward teaching also have high scholarship expectations. A third reason that one might benefit from finding a research guide is that one might be able to find a research collaborator through this process. Particularly if new faculty are teaching at a smaller school, they may broaden their research endeavors beyond their graduate school specialties when they become a faculty member.

Quite possibly, the faculty member who serves as a local guide for learning about the nature of one's new department and institution will not be a good choice to also serve as one's research guide. A senior faculty member may know all the local information but may not be as invested in the intricacies of tenure and promotion as a younger faculty member (particularly one who has recently experienced the tenure/promotion process). Another advantage of having a research guide who is different from the local guide is that the new faculty member will establish a relationship with an additional department member. Although friendship should not play a role in professional decisions such as tenure and promotion, it is still a good idea to establish some sort of personal tie or link with multiple department members. Having more resources is almost always better than having fewer.

Do You Need a Mentor?

Faculty members usually think of a mentor as a person who helps a student during graduate school days. As Cronan-Hillix, Gensheimer, Cronan-Hillix, and Davidson (1986) pointed out, a mentor is more than an advisor—a mentor goes beyond simply providing information and training. Perlmutter (2008) indicated that graduate students view the ideal mentor as someone who

> is respected within the field and has contacts; can help you with publications and jobs; is knowledgeable about the university and its politics and policies; takes the time to help with your studies and your career; does not exploit you; is not a disinterested observer of your career but cares about you as a person and is supportive—like a coach cheering you on. (p. C1)

Graduate students may use their mentor as a role model. Mentors typically help their graduate students gain visibility with the mentors' professional colleagues, thus often leading to academic opportunities such as jobs or research and writing opportunities.

Many early-career faculty members end up finding a mentor who fills some roles that are quite similar to those just described. For example, it is possible that new faculty get their first job in a region of the country that is new to them. Thus, someone who serves as a mentor for them could introduce them to professional colleagues in the state or region, which can lead to opportunities for scholarship and other professional development. A mentor could also introduce them to colleagues outside of the region who may have opportunities for professional involvement that are ideal for new faculty members. For example, thanks to mentors early in our careers, we received invitations to serve as manuscript reviewers for professional journals and coauthors of book chapters, make presentations at professional meetings, and serve on task forces or committees of professional organizations. All of these opportunities had profoundly important impact on our careers.

Political Considerations Dealing With Reflecting Program Values

Bloom and Bell (1979) reported that graduate school superstars consistently reflected program values dealing with research and scholarly excellence. Early career faculty also can become recognized and valued members of their departments by endorsing the values of their programs.

Developing a Teaching Orientation

One challenge that many new faculty must confront is developing teaching skills and caring about teaching within an environment that may stress research over teaching (sometimes almost to the exclusion of teaching). In writing about reflection of program values, Bloom and Bell (1979) indicated that graduate superstars also recognized the importance of having broad contact with their discipline even though their graduate program might be highly specialized. Given that many new faculty will begin their careers in schools that emphasize teaching (Buskist & Irons, 2006), it is important that they develop both their teaching skills and an attitude of caring about teaching. Unfortunately, in today's academic climate, faculty may receive or perceive mixed messages about the value of teaching. It is our impression (which is difficult or impossible to quantify) that even teaching-centered colleges and universities are placing greater emphasis on scholarship today. To the extent that the department or college (or faculty peers) emphasizes research over teaching, it may be difficult for new faculty to develop their teaching skills or a positive attitude about teaching. In some departments, it might even be politically unwise for a faculty member to show that he or she cares "too much" about teaching (Buskist & Irons, 2006).

What should new faculty who find themselves in such environments do? Although research accomplishments might be more prestigious or valued at some institutions, if new faculty know that they want to teach, they should strive to develop their teaching skills. Research-oriented universities, like many teaching-oriented institutions, often have a teaching/learning center that offers faculty myriad professional development opportunities. New faculty should seek out such centers and take advantage of these opportunities. Some research-oriented professors may disagree with this advice. Nonetheless, as related to that first job, more teaching experience gives one the opportunity for more practice and skills development.

The attitude of caring about teaching may be harder to develop in a research-oriented department. However, we would stress that competent professionals care about what they do, always striving to do their best. New faculty should adopt this attitude and develop pride in being the best possible teacher they can be. Likewise, most teachers (at *any* level) can look back at their student days and point to a teacher or teachers who made an important difference in their lives. This difference might have been an encouraging word, a challenging class, extra help with a project or question, or any number of other things. We endorse the concept of "paying it forward" (Hyde, 1999), in which people repay the kindness and encouragement from important people in their lives by helping other people who come into their lives. This approach is a perfect rationale for new faculty to develop a positive and caring attitude about teaching.

Dealing With Cliques

It seems that cliques are inevitable in any group with more than two people. In a typical job environment, joining a clique may be hazardous to your "job health." It is natural that new faculty will gravitate to some faculty members more than others—particularly those who are in the same specialty program or research area as them. However, they should realize that other faculty have much to offer them in terms of informal faculty education. Remember that Bloom and Bell (1979) emphasized the broad view of the discipline that graduate superstars took. The perspectives that faculty from other programs or labs have to offer can be invaluable in one's teaching career. It is rare that new faculty will find themselves being such a narrow specialist in their first (or subsequent) teaching job as they are when they were in graduate school. Thus, avoiding faculty cliques provides the opportunity for more breadth in a new department.

We are not suggesting that faculty cliques are an inevitable part of academia, but they do occur commonly. The best advice we can give is to "be wary of faculty politics!" The problem with cliques is that often one side wins, or at least gains more than its fair share of power. If new faculty cast their lots with a clique that ends up on the losing side, they may end up doing irreparable harm to their new careers. Hinchey and Kimmel (2000) recounted stories of power struggles among faculty on dissertation committees in which students got caught in the middle. Faculty cliques and politics are typically ugly—they are even worse when they claim innocent victims such as this example. New faculty should do their best to *not* go there— they should run from faculty cliques if at all possible.

Interacting With the Department Chair

New faculty members may have a range of opportunities for interacting with the department chair that varies from limited to numerous. An important point to remember during such interactions is that any meeting with the department chair has the possibility of turning political. A comment that one makes offhandedly may be interpreted in a different light by the chair. Remember that faculty colleagues have a vested interest in virtually anything that new faculty say to the department chair. Thus, new faculty members should have an idea of what they are going to say and think about the possible implications of such a conversation. For example, if a new faculty member mentions to the chair that she and a colleague are struggling to get a research project started, might that information cast the colleague in a negative light with the chair? Even worse, might that statement cast the new faculty member in a negative light with the chair? Using common sense, weighing one's words carefully, and perhaps consulting with one's colleague before discussing matters with the chair may be a wise political move.

Conclusions

Although new faculty may be politically naïve, we believe that it will pay for them to become more politically astute in short order. Being wise and political in one's department may make a significant difference in one's career. We encourage new faculty to attend to the important political considerations that we have raised in this chapter.

References

Benson, T. A., & Buskist, W. (2005). Understanding "excellence in teaching" as assessed by psychology faculty search committees. *Teaching of Psychology, 33,* 47–49.

Bloom, L. J., & Bell, P. A. (1979). Making it in graduate school: Some reflections about the superstars. *Teaching of Psychology, 6,* 231–232.

Boice, R. (2000). *Advice for new faculty members: Nihil nimus.* Boston, MA: Allyn & Bacon.

Buskist, W., & Irons, J. (2006, September). Teaching matters: The truth about the job market in academic psychology. *APS Observer, 19*(9), 14–17.

Capaldi, E. D. (2004). Power, politics, and survival in academia. In J. M. Darley, M. P. Zanna, & H. L. Roediger III (Eds.), *The compleat academic: A career guide* (2nd ed., pp. 245–257). Washington, DC: American Psychological Association.

Clifton, J., & Buskist, W. (2005). Preparing graduate students for academic positions in psychology: Suggestions from job advertisements. *Teaching of Psychology, 32,* 265–267.

Cronan-Hillix, T., Gensheimer, L. K., Cronan-Hillix, W. A., & Davidson, W. S. (1986). Students' views of mentors in psychology graduate training. *Teaching of Psychology, 13,* 123–127.

Darley, J. M., Zanna, M. P., & Roediger, H. L., III. (2004). *The compleat academic: A career guide* (2nd ed.). Washington, DC: American Psychological Association.

Hinchey, P., & Kimmel, I. (2000). *The graduate grind: A critical look at graduate education.* New York, NY: Falmer Press.

Hyde, C. R. (1999). *Pay it forward.* New York, NY: Simon & Schuster.

Irons, J. G., & Buskist, W. (2008). Preparing the new professoriate: What courses should they be ready to teach? *Teaching of Psychology, 35,* 201–204.

Penner, L. A., Dovidio, J. F., & Schroeder, D. A. (2004). Managing the department chair and navigating the department power structure. In J. M. Darley, M. P. Zanna, & H. L. Roediger III (Eds.), *The compleat academic: A career guide* (2nd ed., pp. 259–276). Washington, DC: American Psychological Association.

Perlmutter, D. D. (2008, April 18). Are you a good protégé? *Chronicle of Higher Education, 54*(32), C1, C4.

Salancik, G. R. (1987). Power and politics in academic departments. In M. P. Zanna & J. M. Darley (Eds.), *The compleat academic: A practical guide for the beginning social scientist* (pp. 61–84). New York, NY: McGraw-Hill.

Chapter 22

Preparing for the Future

❖

Undergraduates as Teaching Assistants

Thomas P. Hogan and John C. Norcross

All the other chapters in this book focus on the use of graduate students as teaching assistants (GTAs). Understandably so. Using GTAs is a long-established and much-valued practice in American higher education. Virtually any institution offering graduate programs has graduate assistants, and serving in a teaching assistant role is a common responsibility for them (Norcross, Hanych, & Terranova, 1997).

Many institutions do not have GTAs, and instead rely on using undergraduates as teaching assistants (UTAs). In some departments, UTAs work alongside GTAs, while in other departments, particularly those without graduate programs, UTAs function *sui generis*. In this chapter, we explore various uses of UTAs, benefits of their use, and differences between UTAs and GTAs, and we conclude with recommendations for instituting programs that utilize UTAs.

Varieties of Use of UTAs

Reviews of the published literature, as well as anecdotal reports, reveal two distinct reasons for using UTAs; the reasons, in turn, flavor subsequent activities of the UTAs. On the one hand, some programs and professors use UTAs for specific, targeted roles, primarily in connection with large introductory courses. In this mode, UTAs typically serve as discussion section leaders or mark the huge number of assignments that may be generated in the large-enrollment course (see, e.g., Bernstein, 1979; Boeding & Vattano, 1976; Civilky-Powell & Wulff, 2002; Deithloff, 2002; Egerton, 1976; Fremouw, Millard, & Donahoe, 1979; Goolkasian & Lee, 1988; Janssen, 1976; McAdam, 1987; McKeegan, 1998; Whitbourne, Collins, & Skultety, 2001; White & Kolber, 1978). Professors report that they instituted UTAs in these circumstances to avoid the oft-lamented practice of lecturing to 500 students followed by strictly multiple-choice exams. Utilizing UTAs helps these professors to increase student engagement and diversify course assignments. In this mode, professors may employ both GTAs and UTAs or only UTAs.

On the other hand, some programs and professors use UTAs primarily for the educational benefit to UTAs, although shifting some responsibilities from the professor to UTAs adds a much-appreciated incidental benefit for the professor. In this mode, UTAs enjoy a much wider scope of activities. UTAs may serve as discussion leaders and may grade work, either that requiring judgment or objectively scored tests. But UTAs also may occasionally make brief presentations in class, assist with copying materials, keep track of assignments, maintain the electronic grading book, serve as peer facilitator in problem-based learning (PBL) groups, and provide feedback to the professor about how things are going in the course. Some courses may involve tracking an assortment of class-related materials (e.g., kits, specimens, samples) with UTAs distributing and collecting such materials. In assignment-intensive courses, for example, math courses with frequent homework problems, UTAs log in assignments and return them. For examples of this wider use of UTAs, see Gurung (n.d.); Hogan, Norcross, Cannon, and Karpiak (2007); and Wortman and Smyth (1997).

For any of the uses of UTAs, we should distinguish between the role of a UTA and that of a tutor. The tutor, widely used in American higher education, typically works with another student one-on-one or in small groups, often without any direct contact with the professor in the relevant course. In many institutions, tutors are employed by a university-wide office to which students in need of help apply for assistance. UTAs, as we describe them here, may serve some functions of a tutor, but that is not their primary role. UTAs work directly with and under the supervision of the professor for a particular course.

UTAs and URAs

The second, fuller use of UTAs seems to spring from the same soil as the use of undergraduates as research assistants (URAs). This practice has burgeoned in recent years, even spawning its own organization, the Council on Undergraduate Research (n.d.), and a companion journal, *The CUR Quarterly*, containing articles on undergraduate students as research assistants. This use of URAs emphasizes the benefits of the experience to the students, although professors certainly derive multiple benefits from using URAs, for example, in collecting data.

Serving as a URA is a significant factor in graduate school admissions. That has not occurred, at least yet, for serving as a UTA. Most of the research on this topic developed within psychology and related disciplines but likely would generalize to other academic fields. (For a discussion of the relative value of research experience and teaching experience in graduate school admissions in psychology, see Keith-Spiegel, 1991; Keith-Spiegel & Wiederman, 2000; and Norcross, Kohout, & Wicherski, 2005.)

Involving undergraduates in research is much better established than involving undergraduates in the teaching enterprise. However, we believe that experience as a UTA will increase in importance as the practice becomes more widespread, although it is unlikely to rival research experience for purposes of graduate admissions.

Facing the Grading Issue

In our experience, the first question administrators and faculty raise about using UTAs is whether they will be involved in grading other undergraduates' work when the grading requires judgment in evaluating work. Such grading is normal activity for GTAs. But what about for UTAs? Three positions emerge on this contentious point.

First, institutions or professors may take the position that UTAs should never grade materials requiring judgment. UTAs may review the work and offer comments but grading authority rests with the supervising professor. Hogan and colleagues (2007) described a program that adopts this position.

Second, professors may hold that it is possible for UTAs to grade other undergraduates' work as long as the process ensures anonymity: UTAs do not know whose work is being graded and the person being graded does not know who did the grading. The system can apply checks on the UTAs grading. Bernstein (1979) provided an example where 35 UTAs (and 3 GTAs) were trained to grade short-answer questions for a large introductory course. The test responses were identifiable only by a code number. Using UTAs allowed Bernstein to assign frequent short-answer items in a course with enrollments of 400–600 students.

Third, some institutions and professors may take the position that UTAs, with proper training, will evaluate other students' work in a manner that affects grading, although the process requires careful monitoring by the supervising professor. The UTA never has the same overall authority as would a GTA.

We do not recommend which position to adopt. We strongly recommend that teachers face this issue forthrightly. We also recommend, even more strongly, that whatever position teachers take, they should emphasize to UTAs the centrality of professional ethics regarding confidentiality with respect to information they receive in their roles.

Contracting and Compensating UTAs

GTAs are routinely compensated with tuition waivers, monetary stipends, or both, for their activities, which are contractually regulated for a certain number of hours per week (Norcross et al., 2005). No such clear patterns of contract or compensation exist for UTAs.

For the limited-role type of UTA, examples in the literature suggest that an hourly pay rate and/or academic credit may serve as compensation (e.g., Boeding & Vattano, 1976; Deithloff, 2002; Janssen, 1976). For academic credit, UTAs typically receive some version of independent study credit. In this limited role model, for example, serving as discussion leader, students would expect tangible compensation.

In contrast, for the more broadly based UTA role, involving a variety of teaching-related duties, compensation may or may not occur. When it does, it is almost always in the form of academic credit. But this broader UTA role may be undertaken purely for the value of the experience and enhancing entry into baccalaureate-level employment or graduate school admission. In this sense, the UTA role is more like the URA role, which usually does not involve direct compensation but is undertaken for the experience itself.

Crucial Differences Between GTAs and UTAs

Anyone having experience with GTAs and now contemplating the use of UTAs should be alerted to crucial, practical differences between the two categories. First, UTAs typically do not bring the same total commitment to the enterprise as do GTAs. Almost by definition, GTAs have committed to a field of study, and likely think of their role as a first career step. Not so for typical UTAs. UTAs devote most of their coursework outside the field in which they serve as assistants. For example, during an academic term a UTA in psychology may take 6 credits of psychology courses and 12 credits in other fields. Generally being active students, UTAs frequently engage in a range of extracurricular activities: athletics, drama, band, school newspaper—things that GTAs would hardly ever think of doing. UTAs also typically disappear during any break in the academic calendar, whereas GTAs interminably haunt the hallways.

Second, GTAs have a reasonable degree of stability and continuity. Once recruited, they will usually work in the department for 2 or more years, often working with the same supervising professor. In contrast, recruiting UTAs is a nearly continuous process: Their turnover for a single professor can be complete from semester to semester.

Third, utilizing UTAs often entails extra paperwork for the individual professor. An office of graduate studies or dean's office typically handles such paperwork for GTAs, usually in the form of a contract. We do not know of any instances where a single university office handles paperwork for UTAs. Typically, it's up to the individual professor to complete such paperwork and, in conjunction with the point about UTA turnover, this continual process constitutes a real nuisance.

Fourth, GTAs and UTAs differ in degrees of responsibility. GTAs may have complete responsibility for teaching a course, a lab section, or a significant part of a course. That would never hold for a UTA. A UTA may handle part of one class meeting or a discussion section. In a related vein, GTAs may have complete or nearly complete authority to grade students, whereas UTAs may grade only objective tests.

Finally, we confront the ubiquitous concern about confidentiality. How much does or should the UTA know about fellow undergraduates? Of course, GTAs need to be alerted to the professional ethics of confidentiality, but they occupy a higher step in the hierarchy with respect to undergraduates, much like faculty do. Supervising professors need to deal with the ethics of confidentiality forthrightly with UTAs. The chapter on the ethics of teaching in McKeachie's classic "teaching tips" book (Svinicki & McKeachie, 2011), although intended primarily for full-time faculty, may be a useful read for UTAs.

Training UTAs

There exists an extensive literature and much experience on GTA training. The extent and quality of GTA training might be lamented, but at least we have many examples of courses and other training models for GTAs (see Bernstein et al., 2010; Buskist, Beins, & Hevern, 2004; Meyers & Prieto, 2000; Prieto & Meyers, 2001). By contrast, the literature on training UTAs is thin—but it is beginning to develop. Prieto (2010) offered a comprehensive model for UTA training, a spinoff from his model for GTA training. Gurung (n.d.) referenced a full course for UTA training. Hogan et al. (2007) described a 1-credit seminar covering many of the same topics as Gurung's course. Both of the latter courses mimic typical GTA training courses and seminars, covering such topics as grading, conducting discussion groups, lecturing techniques, and ethical issues in teaching. Training needed for the more focused use of UTAs, for example, serving only as discussion leaders or for grading, obviously requires more targeted preparation. Civikly-Powell and Wulff (2002) provided a detailed discussion of such training needs. Prieto (2010) recommended 1 hour per week of faculty supervision for UTAs.

Evaluating UTAs

Evaluation of UTAs has taken two paths: Evaluating the impact on the UTAs themselves and evaluating the impact on students in courses served by UTAs. In general, results have been positive on both fronts. UTAs gain knowledge of the subject matter and regard their experiences as very positive (Fremouw et al., 1979; Hogan, 2010; Hogan et al., 2007; Weidert, Roethal, & Gurung, 2010; Wortman & Smyth, 1997). Students in courses served by UTAs rate the UTAs' contribution favorably, with UTAs often outranking GTAs (White & Kolber, 1978; Wortman & Smyth, 1997), perhaps because UTAs resonate better than do GTAs with undergraduate students.

Benefits of UTAs

At scattered places in this chapter, we have mentioned the benefits of using UTAs. Here we assemble a concise summary of these advantages for UTAs, professors, and students in courses served by UTAs.

- UTAs gain valuable experience and knowledge in ways they would not gain through ordinary coursework, which probably enhances their prospects for employment or graduate admissions.
- UTAs gain experience that helps to decide in favor of (or against) pursuing a teaching career.
- UTAs may benefit by making money or acquiring credit for a meaningful experience.
- Professors teaching courses with large enrollments find that UTAs allow for enriching the courses with varied assignments and activities.
- Professors teaching courses with any level of enrollment benefit from UTAs' handling course-related chores, continuing engagement with a lively group of students, and an invaluable source of information about "what's really going on."
- Students in courses served by UTAs usually find them helpful and easier to approach than their professor or GTA.

Increased student engagement in the academic enterprise, the holy grail of process variables for success in higher education (Pascarella & Terenzini, 2005), represents the common thread running through reports of benefits for both UTAs and students in courses served by UTAs.

Suggestions for Starting a UTA Program

Suppose you do not use UTAs at present but think you might like to try it. Here are six suggestions for getting started.

- Decide whether to adopt the limited-role or broader activity for the UTAs (as described earlier), as this decision will inform your subsequent preparation. You may desire the focused, single-use approach. Or, you may want the more broadly based approach where UTAs engage in many different functions.
- Squarely address the question of whether UTAs will engage in grading that requires judgment and whether they will see confidential information about students, for example, test grades.
- Decide the reward structure for the program. Will UTAs receive academic credit or a monetary stipend? If so, how much? Obviously, pay has budget implications and credit entails a course or quasi-course structure. Remember that some programs operate without pay or credit: UTAs participate because it is a good learning experience for them and may assist with their graduate school admissions and/or career placement.
- Legitimize the UTA function through appropriate institutional structures. This step may entail a dean's office, the registrar, or any number of other campus units, varying from one institution to another. Establishing these structures may take time and entail bureaucratic frustrations, but it is an important step. It gives recognition to the program and it provides an important legal safeguard by formally defining the role(s) taken by UTAs within the institutional structure.
- Decide how you will recruit UTAs. Will you have a formal application process? Or will individual professors make ad hoc decisions on whom to use as UTAs? Remember that recruiting UTAs presents a continuous task—semester after semester—so develop an efficient process for handling this task.
- Consider a training process for your UTAs. Every source emphasizes the importance of such training (e.g., Civikly-Powell & Wulff, 2002; Hogan, Norcross, Cannon, & Karpiak, 2007). The type of training depends heavily on the approach decided in the first step described earlier. If UTAs serve only as discussion leaders, training will focus on that task. If UTAs fulfill a broader set of roles, training will cover a wider set of skills. Think of the training process as encompassing both formal experiences, such as a seminar, and informal contacts, such as weekly meetings between the UTA and the supervising professor. Include ethical issues in teaching, especially respecting confidentiality and avoiding dual relationships.

If your institution does not boast a UTA program, you may find it helpful to review existing programs. Here are websites for three programs that provide an assortment of forms, descriptions, and policies.

- University of Wisconsin–Green Bay, a midsize, nondoctoral public university: www.uwgb.edu/gurungr/Classes/TA/TA.htm
- Stony Brook University, a 25,000 enrollment, doctoral-level institution: sb.cc .stonybrook.edu/bulletin/2010/spring/policiesandregulations/special_ academic_op/undergrad_teaching_assistantships.php
- University of Scranton, a midsize, nondoctoral, private university: matrix .scranton.edu/academics/ctle/student-faculty-teaching-mentorship-program/ index.shtml and http://academic.scranton.edu/faculty/hogant1/

Conclusions

Virtually all professors who have used UTAs express enthusiasm about the experience. In addition, UTAs derive substantial benefits from the experience, benefits that probably cannot result from any other type of undergraduate experience. Students in courses served by UTAs report enhancement of their own learning. We encourage readers who have not used UTAs to try it and those who have tried it to think of possible expansions of the practice. We hope the analysis and recommendations in this chapter will facilitate accomplishing those goals.

References

Bernstein, D. J. (1979). Reliability and fairness of grading in a mastery program. *Teaching of Psychology, 6*, 104–107.

Bernstein, D. J., Addison, W., Altman, C., Hollister, D., Komarraju, M., Prieto, L., Rocheleau, C.A., & Shore, C. (2010). Toward a scientist-educator model of teaching psychology. In D. F. Halpern (Ed.), *Undergraduate education in psychology: A blueprint for the future of the discipline* (pp. 29–45). Washington, DC: American Psychological Association.

Boeding, H. C., & Vattano, F. (1976). Undergraduates as teaching assistants: A comparison of two discussion methods. *Teaching of Psychology, 3*, 55–59.

Buskist, W., Beins, B. C., & Hevern, V. W. (2004). *Preparing the new psychology professoriate: Helping graduate students become competent teachers.* Syracuse, NY: Society for the Teaching of Psychology. Retrieved from http://teachpsych .org/resources/e-books/pnpp/index_pnpp.php

Civikly-Powell, J., & Wulff, D. H. (2002). Working with teaching assistants and undergraduate peer facilitators to address the challenge of teaching large classes.

In C. A. Stanley & M. E. Porter (Eds.), *Engaging large classes: Strategies and techniques for college faculty* (pp. 109–122). Bolton, MA: Anker.

Council on Undergraduate Research. (n.d.). *Council on Undergraduate Research.* Retrieved from http://www.cur.org/

Deithloff, L. F. (2002). Maintaining intimacy: Strategies for the effective management of TAs in innovative large classes. In C. A. Stanley & M. E. Porter (Eds.), *Engaging large classes: Strategies and techniques for college faculty* (pp. 123–137). Bolton, MA: Anker.

Egerton, J. (1976). Teaching learning while learning to teach. *Change, 8*(2), 58–61.

Fremouw, W. J., Millard, W. J., & Donahoe, J. W. (1979). Learning-through-teaching: Knowledge changes in undergraduate teaching assistants. *Teaching of Psychology, 6*, 30–32.

Goolkasian, P., & Lee, J. A. (1988). A computerized laboratory for general psychology. *Teaching of Psychology, 15*, 98–100.

Gurung, R. (n.d.). *Teaching assistantship—Psych 495.* Retrieved from http://www.uwgb.edu/gurungr/Classes/TA/TA.htm

Hogan, T. P. (2010, August). *Utilization of undergraduates as teaching assistants at the University of Scranton.* Paper presented at the meeting of the American Psychological Association, San Diego, CA.

Hogan, T. P., Norcross, J. C., Cannon, J. T., & Karpiak, C. P. (2007). Working with and training undergraduates as teaching assistants. *Teaching of Psychology, 34*, 187–190.

Janssen, P. (1976). With a little help from their friends. *Change, 8*(2), 50–53.

Keith-Spiegel, P. (1991). *The complete guide to graduate school admission: Psychology and related programs.* Hillsdale, NJ: Lawrence Erlbaum.

Keith-Spiegel, P., & Wiederman, M. W. (2000). *The complete guide to graduate school admission: Psychology, counseling, and related professions* (2nd ed.). Mahwah, NJ: Lawrence Erlbaum.

McAdam, D. (1987). Bringing psychology to life. *Teaching of Psychology, 14*, 29–31.

McKeegan, P. (1998). Using undergraduate teaching assistants in a research methodology course. *Teaching of Psychology, 25*, 11–14.

Meyers, S. A., & Prieto, L. R. (2000). Training in the teaching of psychology: What is done and examining the differences. *Teaching of Psychology, 27*, 258–261.

Norcross, J. C., Hanych, J. M., & Terranova, R. D. (1997). Teaching opportunities for graduate students in psychology: Commonly available but (still) rarely required. *Teaching of Psychology, 24*, 265–267.

Norcross, J. C., Kohout, J. L., & Wicherski, M. (2005). Graduate study in psychology: 1971 to 2004. *American Psychologist, 60*, 959–975.

Pascarella, E., & Terenzini, P. (2005). *How college affects students (Vol. II): A third decade of research.* San Francisco, CA: Jossey-Bass.

Prieto, L. R. (2010, August). *Supervising undergraduate teaching assistants: A developmental model.* Paper presented at the meeting of the American Psychological Association, San Diego, CA.

Prieto, L. R., & Meyers, S. A. (2001). *The teaching assistant handbook.* Stillwater, OK: New Forums Press.

Svinicki, M., & McKeachie, W. J. (2011). *McKeachie's teaching tips: Strategies, research, and theory for college and university teachers* (13th ed.). Belmont, CA: Wadsworth.

Weidert, J., Roethal, A., & Gurung, R. (2010, August). *Benefits of being a UTA: Hard data and critical reflection.* Paper presented at the meeting of the American Psychological Association, San Diego, CA.

Whitbourne, S. K., Collins, K. J., & Skultety, K. M. (2001). Formative reflections on service-learning in a course on the psychology of aging. *Educational Gerontology, 27,* 105–115.

White, K. M., & Kolber, R. (1978). Undergraduate and graduate students as discussion leaders. *Teaching of Psychology, 5,* 6–9.

Wortman, C. B., & Smyth, J. M. (1997). Using one's own passion and undergraduate TAs to transform the large-lecture introductory psychology course. In R. J. Sternberg (Ed.), *Teaching introductory psychology: Survival tips from the experts* (pp. 163–180). Washington, DC: American Psychological Association.

Chapter 23

Useful Resources for Preparing the New Professoriate

❖

Jennifer J. Stiegler-Balfour and Catherine E. Overson

Although matriculation at the graduate level may prepare individuals for a career in research, simply completing an advanced degree program is no guarantee of future success in the classroom. In order to establish themselves as productive researchers and confident teachers, junior faculty members must quickly acclimate to their new professional roles and responsibilities. Of particular challenge is the ability to maintain a balance among teaching, research, service to the institution, and perhaps beyond.

For many years, providing graduate students with structured training programs to better prepare them for their teaching responsibilities was not a priority of the professoriate. Beginning in the early 1990s, though, institutions began to recognize that new faculty members need to excel not only in the laboratory, but in the classroom as well. Today, an increasing number of graduate programs are placing a greater emphasis on offering students a variety of resources and opportunities as a means of preparation for the demands of academia. This new emphasis on preparation is a welcomed—and much needed—change of thinking, and has emerged as an important element in professional development (e.g., Wulff & Austin, 2004).

The focus on professional development is particularly important in light of the rapidly changing nature of today's student body. Filling the classrooms of colleges and universities is a new breed of student: individuals who have grown up online with much of the world's knowledge a mouse-click away. Although these tech-savvy students present new challenges for faculty, the effective use of technology in the classroom has the potential to make teaching and learning more impactful and fulfilling. With the rapid evolution of technology, it has perhaps never been more important to remember that professional development does not end with the completion of graduate school. Instead, it is a lifelong process that requires individuals to stay abreast of pedagogical research developments and implement teaching methods that promote high levels of student learning.

The goal of this final chapter is to provide a summary of available resources for preparing future faculty. Our intent is to offer guidance to graduate students and new and experienced faculty alike on best practices and current research related to college teaching. This chapter should also be helpful for faculty and administrators considering how to best prepare graduate students for current and future teaching assignments. In the following paragraphs, we describe resources that are dedicated to preparing graduate students and junior faculty to become more effective in their teaching duties and readying them to become successful faculty. The annotated bibliography includes texts addressing teaching and professional development, teaching resources, graduate teaching assistant training programs, journals, and online resources. Although some of the resources appear dated, many are considered by professional development experts to be "classics," and therefore are worthy of inclusion in this chapter.

Teaching and Professional Development

Boice, R. (1992). *The new faculty member: Supporting and fostering professional development*. San Francisco, CA: Jossey-Bass.

Written for new faculty seeking to start their career on the right foot, this text discusses collegiality, teaching, publishing, and obstacles facing most new faculty members and approaches for overcoming them. Although written almost 2 decades ago, the content of this reference is still relevant to today's new faculty members. Boice offers helpful suggestions about joining campuswide programs for nurturing newcomers and mentoring programs that foster collegiality through social networking. Advice on establishing basic teaching skills and specific techniques (e.g., time and stress management techniques) for helping new faculty find the time to write and deal with editorial evaluations and rejections is also provided.

The book concludes with a discussion about building an institutional support system to achieve promotion and tenure. The book provides accounts from faculty that enhance the main points of discussion.

Boice, R. (2000). *Advice for new faculty members: Nihil nimus*. Needham Heights, MA: Allyn & Bacon.

Boice provides practical suggestions for making a smooth transition from graduate school to the academic world. The theme in this book is *nihil nimus* (nothing in excess). The three sections in this book are titled "Moderate Work at Teaching," "Write in Mindful Ways," and "Socialize and Serve With Compassion." Boice advocates for new faculty members approaching their duties and responsibilities in moderation as a path to ensuring long-term success.

Darley, J. M., Zanna, M. P., & Reodiger, H. L. (Eds.). (2004). *The compleat academic: A career guide* (2nd ed.). Washington, DC: American Psychological Association.

This book offers a wide-ranging, practical guide for junior faculty or academics in the making. Beginning with primary decisions facing new graduates, such as the type of position one may choose (postdoctoral fellow or faculty), the text navigates a range of faculty responsibilities and expectations and explores the academic environment in general, including inter- and intradepartmental political frameworks. Recognizing that many new graduates enter academia underprepared for teaching, the editors offer a chapter exploring issues faculty members encounter, such as choosing a textbook, syllabus preparation, lecturing, and student- and self-evaluations. Issues regarding self-presentation and authority are also explored, as well as unique challenges facing women in academia.

Gibson, G. W. (1992). *Good start: A guidebook for new faculty in liberal arts colleges*. Bolton, MA: Anker.

Filled with practical information about how to navigate the application, interview, and negotiation processes for faculty positions, readers will find much of the content in *Good Start* relevant to today's academic environment. Gibson provides insightful tips on orienting oneself at a new college or university and provides an in-depth review of faculty duties, including teaching, scholarship, and service.

Lucas, J. C., & Murry, J. W. (2002). *New faculty: A practical guide for academic beginners*. New York, NY: Palgrave.

A detailed resource for new faculty looking for advice on teaching, student advising, publishing, grant writing, and professional service. The importance of faculty mentoring to obtain a better understanding of the climate at each institution is also discussed, along with many other important topics (e.g., balancing teaching and research, and legal issues).

Menges, R. J. (1999). *Faculty in new jobs: A guide to settling in, becoming established, and building institutional support.* San Francisco, CA: Jossey-Bass.

This book covers all phases of the faculty career—from settling into one's first position and becoming socially and academically established to building an institutional support system. The author addresses the needs and concerns of new faculty, offering a wealth of information and strategies for faculty developers, senior colleagues, and administrators.

Teaching Resources

Books

Ambrose, S. A., Bridges, M. W., DiPietro, M., Lovett, M. C., & Norman, M. K. (2010). *How learning works: 7 research-based principles for smart teaching.* San Francisco, CA: Jossey-Bass.

Based on research evidence, this book is an invaluable resource for teachers of all levels. It addresses new ways of thinking about teaching and bridges the gap between pedagogical research and teaching practices. Drawing on new research in psychology, education, and cognitive science, the text lays out powerful learning principles that can be applied in college courses, including how students' prior knowledge affects learning, how students' intellectual and social identity development is influenced by course climate, and how students become self-directed learners.

Davis, B. G. (2009). *Tools for teaching* (2nd ed.). San Francisco, CA: Jossey-Bass.

A bestseller when originally published in 1993, *Tools for Teaching* is an accessible and empirically based reference for teachers in any discipline. Davis presents the latest teaching strategies relevant for college teachers, including discussion strategies, managing large classes, using student feedback to improve teaching, and techniques to strengthen students' writing and problem-solving skills. Among the many new additions to this edition is the inclusion of information about the effective use of the latest presentation technologies as well as broader concerns, such as diversity in the classroom. Using the latest research on teaching and learning, this book is an outstanding resource for teachers who want to increase their teaching effectiveness.

Fink, L. D. (2003). *Creating significant learning experiences: An integrated approach to designing college courses.* San Francisco, CA: Jossey-Bass.

Fink is an advocate for shifting from a content-centered teaching approach to a more learning-centered approach that takes into consideration what kind of learning is most significant for students. To accomplish this goal, he interjects new concepts such as the taxonomy of significant learning into widely held perspectives on teaching, and, as a result, shows how courses can be transformed into powerful learning experiences for students. Fink not only introduces a new and exciting vision of higher education but also indentifies the types of institutional and national support faculty members will require to sustain these changes in teaching.

Gurung, R. A. R., & Schwartz, B. M. (2009). *Optimizing teaching and learning: Practicing pedagogical research.* Malden, MA: Wiley-Blackwell.

Offering instructions on how to design, conduct, analyze, and write pedagogical research, *Optimizing Teaching and Learning* is an excellent resource for graduate students and faculty seeking to improve student learning while contributing to the overall scholarship of teaching. The text includes questionnaires and checklists that instructors can integrate into their research practices or the classroom. The authors also explore a variety of pedagogical practices in different disciplines and provide a comprehensive list of discipline-specific scholarship of teaching and learning journals.

Nilson, L. B. (2010). *Teaching at its best: A research-based resource for college instructors* (3rd ed.). San Francisco, CA: Jossey-Bass.

This comprehensive, best-selling handbook offers an array of practical teaching strategies, formats, and classroom exercises, all of which can easily be implemented into any course. The latest edition includes updated information for instructing the millennial generation, current research in cognition, and legal options on copyright issues, as well as how to best use new technology such as blogs, podcasts, and clickers. Chapters added to this edition cover topics such as helping students write in specific academic disciplines, matching teaching methods with learning outcomes, and accommodating different learning styles.

Svinicki, M. & McKeachie, W. J., (2011). *McKeachie's teaching tips: Strategies, research, and theory for college and university teachers* (13th ed.). Belmont, CA: Wadsworth Cengage Learning.

This 13th edition of *McKeachie's Teaching Tips* continues the approach of earlier editions by providing teachers with an abundance of teaching strategies, research, and theories. The authors recognize that faculty differ in how they prepare and present course material and offer teaching tips for a variety of instructors and learners without being prescriptive. The book covers a full range of topics, including course preparation, facilitating active learning, student learning assessment, ethics of teaching, and dealing with problem students, as well as teaching culturally diverse students and controversial topics. What stands out in this book is the inclusion of chapters dedicated to teaching with technology and distance learning, two topics of increasing importance to how today's teachers and students interact. *Teaching Tips* continues to be the gold standard in this genre.

Weimer, M. (2010). *Inspired college teaching: A career-long resource for professional growth*. San Francisco, CA: Jossey-Bass.

Inspired College Teaching is a hands-on resource that can help teachers at all levels understand and plan what it takes to sustain teaching excellence throughout a career. The premise is that faculty must play a central role in their own professional development. Weimer also provides a description of those characteristics required of good teachers, such as creative approaches and vigilance, and helpful advice on how teachers can maintain their intellectual stamina over the course of their academic careers.

Graduate Teaching Assistant Training Programs

Allen, R. R., & Rueter, T. (1990). *Teaching assistant strategies: An introduction to college teaching*. Dubuque, IA: Kendall/Hunt.

Teaching Assistant Strategies explores the nature of the GTA's role at colleges and universities. This book helps GTAs develop a sense of who and what kind of GTA they will be. The authors note the importance of effective interpersonal relationships between GTAs and their students, and present a hands-on primer of how to work with a range of student "personalities." The remainder of the book emphasizes course preparation and presentation. These sections cover the particulars of generating course objectives, syllabi, and teaching plans, as well as common presentation styles.

Gaff, J. G., Pruitt-Logan, A., Sims, L. B., & Denecke, D. D. (2003). *Preparing Future Faculty in the humanities and social sciences: A guide for change*. Washington, DC: Council of Graduate Schools.

This book reports on the Preparing Future Faculty (PFF) cross-discipline initiative to promote a program of study for graduate students incorporating the varied roles of the professor. The authors emphasize the fundamental philosophy of such a program and the specific strategies used to meet program objectives. Included in the book is a review of graduate programs that have been revised according to the PFF standards and input from graduate faculty who report they are well-positioned to prepare students for academic careers.

Gaff, J. G., Pruitt-Logan, A., & Weibl, R. A. (2000). *Building the faculty we need: Colleges and universities working together*. Washington, DC: Association of American Colleges and Universities.

Building the Faculty We Need reports on the PFF cross-discipline initiative to promote a program of study for graduate students that incorporates the varied roles of the professor. Notably, the teaching role has come under focus as an area increasingly regarded as an essential component of doctorial preparation. Some of the potential challenges include using technology in the classroom, the implementation of a variety of teaching approaches, and working with diverse student populations. This report describes the philosophy underlying such a program, along with outlines describing specific strategies to meet the needs of future faculty.

Lambert, L. M., & Tice, S. T. (1993). *Preparing graduate students to teach: A guide to programs that improve undergraduate education and develop tomorrow's faculty*. Washington, DC: American Association for Higher Education.

This book stresses the importance of preparing the professoriate for their teaching duties and outlines the steps that need to be taken to accomplish this goal. Among the books referenced in this bibliography, it is unique as it describes a variety of GTA programs and practices at American universities that stand out for their excellence in preparing future faculty. Disciplines dealt with in this book include biological sciences, chemistry, English and composition, foreign languages, mathematics, psychology, social sciences, and speech communication.

Marincovich, M., Prostko, J., & Stout, F. (1998). *The professional development of graduate teaching assistants*. Bolton, MA: Anker.

This book addresses the training and professional development of GTAs to prepare them for full-time teaching responsibilities. The chapters cover topics such as the role of centralized and discipline-specific GTA training, preparing GTAs to respond to the needs of a diverse student body, helping GTAs to improve undergraduate writing, the use of teaching portfolios in training GTAs, international GTA programs, and the evaluation of GTA training programs.

Nyquist, J. D., Abbott, R. D., Wulff, D. H., & Sprague, J. (Eds.). (1991). *Preparing the professoriate of tomorrow to teach: Selected readings in TA training.* Dubuque, IA: Kendall/Hunt.

The authors describe different approaches to GTA training (both campuswide and discipline specific). This book features a description of six successful GTA training programs in disciplines including psychology, engineering, writing, Spanish, chemistry, and biology and describes their approaches to preparing future faculty for teaching. A section is dedicated to resources, tools, and strategies to prepare GTAs to work with undergraduates. The authors discuss effective supervision strategies of GTAs and special needs of international GTAs and the support they need as they learn to teach in a different culture using a second language.

Prieto, L. P., & Meyers, S. A. (2001). *The teaching assistant training handbook: How to prepare TAs for their responsibilities.* Stillwater, OK: New Forums Press.

Ideally suited for faculty or staff who train TAs, this book provides the reader with information about designing, implementing, and improving GTA training in departments and university-wide. The book provides resources on multiple strategies to prepare GTAs for their teaching responsibilities, such as workshops, orientation programs, courses, and ongoing supervision. Critical topics in college teaching, including increasing GTAs' awareness of ethical issues and diversity in the classroom and sensitivity to issues of gender and race/ethnicity, are also addressed in this book.

Wulff, D. H., & Austin, A. E. (2004). *Paths to the professoriate: Strategies for enriching the preparation of future faculty.* San Francisco, CA: Jossey-Bass.

This book provides graduate students, faculty, and administrators with research-based findings and strategies intended to help graduate students become better prepared for faculty life. The book first presents an overview of the changes that have occurred in higher education, such as new expectations for faculty work and new types of faculty appointments. Also included is a summary about a national study on the professional development of graduate students in their roles as GTAs. Examples of innovative programs that have responded to the need to reform graduate education are also given in this book.

Journals

To stay current on the latest research on teaching and learning, many faculty subscribe to journals dedicated to increasing teaching effectiveness and to faculty development. Academic journals, which exist for nearly every discipline of pedagogy, provide fast and easy access to the latest research findings and practices. The journals listed in this section are peer reviewed and relevant for instructors at every level of their career, regardless of their discipline.

Cognition and Instruction. Philadelphia: Taylor & Francis.

Peer-reviewed articles published in *Cognition and Instruction* focus on how learning and intellectual practices work. This journal is known for the rigorous study of important issues concerning mental and sociocultural processes, as well as exploring various conditions of learning and intellectual competence.

International Journal for the Scholarship of Teaching and Learning (online only). Statesboro, GA: Georgia Southern University Press.

IJ-SoTL is an international, peer-reviewed journal published twice a year by the Center for Teaching, Learning & Scholarship at Georgia Southern University. Content focuses on examining the scholarship of teaching and learning to improve classroom effectiveness, student learning outcomes, and the continuous development of the academic culture.

Journal of the Learning Sciences. New York, NY: Routledge.

This journal provides a multidisciplinary forum for the dissemination of research on education and learning. Emphasis is placed on ideas that can change our understanding of learning as well as the practice of education. Articles come from various disciplines such as artificial intelligence, cognitive science, cognitive and educational psychology, cognitive anthropology, and education.

New Directions in Teaching and Learning. San Francisco, CA: Jossey-Bass.

New Directions in Teaching and Learning offers a wide range of ideas and techniques aimed at improving college teaching based on the experience of instructors and the latest research in education and psychology. Published quarterly, each issue is devoted to a singular topic such as experiential education or evidence-based teaching. Issues are edited by a guest editor, whose job it is to bring together a set of experts to share their collective research, theory, experience, and wisdom on these respective topics.

The Journal on Excellence in College Teaching. Oxford, OH: Miami University Press.

A peer-reviewed journal published at Miami University, *The Journal of Excellence in College Teaching* is dedicated to increasing students' learning through effective teaching, enthusiasm for the teaching profession, and sharing best practices among faculty.

Online Resources

The Internet offers an abundance of teaching resources available for teaching graduate students and faculty. The appeal of using online resources is apparent, as they are typically free of charge and can easily be accessed from any computer that is connected to the Internet. Following are two particularly helpful e-books and websites that focus on PFF programs and offer a variety of helpful teaching tips.

E-books

Buskist, W., Beins, B. C., & Hevern, V. W. (Eds.). (2004). *Preparing the new psychology professoriate: Helping graduate students become competent teachers*. Syracuse, NY: Society for the Teaching of Psychology. Retrieved from http://teachpsych.org/resources/e-books/pnpp/index_pnpp.php

This e-book consists of 31 chapters and can be downloaded at no cost from this website. In addition to reviewing various methodologies for preparing graduate students, the book discusses an array of effective methods for preparing graduate students in master's and PhD-level programs across the United States for their teaching responsibilities. Skills and qualifications a successful job applicant should possess are also discussed at length (e.g., qualities and abilities desired for positions at community colleges, religiously affiliated institutions, small liberal arts colleges, and research universities). The last part of this e-book offers advice on making the transition from graduate student to assistant professor and includes a bibliography of resource books.

Howard, C., Buskist, W., & Stowell, J. (Eds.). (2007). *The STP guide to graduate student training in the teaching of psychology*. Syracuse, NY: Society for the Teaching of Psychology. Retrieved from http://teachpsych .org/resources/e-books/gst2007/gst07.php

This e-book is a free online resource containing descriptions of almost 50 graduate programs in 25 states that offer graduate student teaching training in psychology at both the master's and PhD levels. The programs highlighted in this e-book offer a variety of methods to prepare graduate students for their teaching duties at colleges and universities. The various chapter authors offer insightful ideas on the preparation, training, and supervision of graduate students who are pursuing academic careers.

Websites

Preparing Future Faculty. Retrieved from http://www.preparing-faculty.org

This website provides information about the nationwide PFF initiative regarding the breadth of roles and responsibilities (teaching, research, and service) that the academy expects from its faculty. An outline detailing the progressive phases of the PFF development is included, along with listings of participating institutions. The "Related Resources" tab provides links to relevant material on emerging faculty roles, effective new faculty mentoring, teaching resources, and career and job search information.

Association of American Colleges and Universities (AAC&U). Retrieved from http://www.aacu.org/pff

The AAC&U is an association dedicated to providing a liberal arts education to all students, regardless of major, with an aim toward personal growth, scholarly achievement, integrative learning, and social engagement. Preparing current and future faculty to meet these challenges is among the top priorities of the AAC&U. This website reports on the PFF cross-discipline initiative to promote a program of study for graduate students that incorporates the varied roles of the professor (i.e., teaching, research, and service). A link titled "Updates and Resources" opens a page containing more links to information and articles ranging from the current status of doctoral programs with regard to preparing future faculty to meet the demands of comprehensive faculty work to cross-discipline responsibilities and integrating facets of a liberal arts focus into program design.

Conclusions

This bibliography provides ample resources and guidance for enhancing teaching skills and professional development for graduate students as well as new and seasoned faculty. These resources will also prove useful to graduate program coordinators seeking to improve their graduate students' preparedness for the challenges that await them as first-time faculty. Rather than view this bibliography as a list of resources that should be consumed cover to cover, readers will be better served by viewing them as valuable references that could be consulted as specific situations and scenarios arise. The collective wisdom of the authors referenced in this bibliography will prepare the next generation of faculty for successful academic careers.

Index

About the Editors

William Buskist is the Distinguished Professor in the Teaching of Psychology at Auburn University and a Faculty Fellow at Auburn's Biggio Center for the Enhancement of Teaching and Learning. He has published over 40 articles and coedited a dozen books on teaching and learning in higher education, especially in the realm of the teaching of psychology. His recent book publications include *The Teaching of Psychology: Essays in Honor of Wilbert J. McKeachie and Charles L. Brewer* (with Stephen F. Davis; Lawrence Erlbaum, 2003); *The Handbook of the Teaching of Psychology* (with Davis; Blackwell, 2005); and *Evidence-Based Teaching* (with James Groccia; New Directions in Teaching and Learning, 2011); along with several e-books (http://teachpsych.org/resources/e-books/index.php). His many teaching awards include the Society for the Teaching of Psychology's Robert S. Daniel Teaching Excellence Award (2000); Auburn University's highest teaching honor, the Gerald and Emily Leischuck Presidential Award for Excellence in Teaching (2005); and the American Psychological Foundation's Charles L. Brewer Award for Excellence in Teaching (2009). He is a past president of the Society for the Teaching of Psychology and currently serves as the Society's Editor-in-Chief for e-books. He is a Fellow of both the American Psychological Association and the Association for Psychological Science. His teaching at Auburn focuses heavily on preparing graduate students to teach at the college and university level, and his research addresses issues related to excellence in teaching. Six of his former graduate students have been awarded national teaching awards. (e-mail: buskiwf@auburn.edu)

Victor A. Benassi is a professor of psychology and faculty director of the University of New Hampshire (UNH) Center for Excellence in Teaching and Learning. He has taught courses in college teaching and supervised over 100 graduate students' teaching of psychology since the early 1980s. In addition to research on teaching and learning, his publications have addressed such topics as judgment of personal control, belief in alleged paranormal phenomena, and depression. Professor Benassi is involved in developing and implementing Preparing Future Faculty programs at UNH, including the university's formal academic program in college teaching that is available to graduate students and faculty from UNH and other institutions. In recent years, he has been developing an online course titled Preparing to Teach a Psychology Course. To date, over 350 graduate students and faculty from the United States and nearly a dozen other countries have completed the course. Dr. Benassi also has appointments as Professor of Psychology (Psychology Department) and Professor of College Teaching (Graduate School). He has received several UNH awards—the Excellence in Teaching Award, the Outstanding Use of Technology in Education Award, and the College of Liberal Arts' Lindberg Outstanding Scholar/Teacher Award. In 2003, he received the American Psychological Foundation's Distinguished Teaching of Psychology award. (e-mail: Victor.Benassi@unh.edu)

About the Contributors

Robert Bubb is a Teaching Fellow and doctoral candidate in industrial and organizational psychology at Auburn University. He received a master's degree in psychology from Brigham Young University in 2008, and his current research focuses on the efficacy of digital learning products in the classroom. (e-mail: robb.bubb@auburn.edu)

Brennan D. Cox is an Aerospace Experimental Psychologist with the U.S. Navy. His research interests include individual differences, personnel selection, and training design and evaluation. (e-mail: cox.brennan@gmail.com)

David B. Daniel is a Professor of Psychology at James Madison University. His research focuses on the application of psychological science to positively affect both student learning and teacher performance, especially in ecologically valid contexts. (e-mail: danieldb@jmu.edu)

Stephen F. Davis is Roe R. Cross Professor Emeritus at Emporia State University and Distinguished Guest Professor at Morningside College. His research on academic dishonesty spanned three decades and culminated in the book *Cheating in School: What We Know and What We Can Do*. (e-mail: davis122@suddenlink.net)

Diego Flores has been an adjunct faculty member at Utah Valley University in International Business and Organizational Behavior and is currently pursuing a PhD in behavioral economics at Brigham Young University. (e-mail: diegogfloresg@hotmail.com)

Peter J. Giordano is Professor and Chair of Psychological Science at Belmont University in Nashville, TN. A Fellow of the Society for the Teaching of Psychology, he has served as National President of Psi Chi and as the Methods and Techniques Editor for *Teaching of Psychology*. (e-mail: pete.giordano@belmont.edu)

Gary S. Goldstein is Associate Professor of Psychology at the University of New Hampshire at Manchester, where he is Chair of the Division of

Social Sciences and Program Coordinator of Psychology. He has 30 years of experience teaching in the college classroom and is a recipient of the UNH Manchester Excellence in Teaching Award. His research interests focus on various dimensions of college teaching. (email: gsg@unh.edu)

Elizabeth Yost Hammer is the Director of the Center for the Advancement of Teaching and a Kellogg Professor in Teaching at Xavier University of Louisiana in New Orleans. Her research interests focus on the scholarship of teaching and learning, and she is a coauthor of *Psychology Applied to Modern Life*. (e-mail: eyhammer@xula.edu)

G. William (Bill) Hill IV is Professor Emeritus of Psychology and former Executive Director of the Center for Excellence in Teaching and Learning at Kennesaw State University. His professional interests and research focus on faculty development and effective teaching. (e-mail: bhill@kennesaw.edu)

Thomas P. Hogan is Professor of Psychology and Distinguished University Fellow at the University of Scranton, where he served for 10 years as Dean of the Graduate School and now teaches psychological testing, research methods, and statistics. His specialization is psychometrics, and he is author of numerous articles, chapters, and books related to testing, as well as coauthor of several nationally standardized tests. (e-mail: Thomas. Hogan@Scranton.edu)

Christopher R. Howard is an Assistant Professor of Psychology at Husson University. His current research focuses on educational applications of cognitive psychology and the scholarship of teaching and learning. (e-mail: howardc@husson.edu)

Krisztina Varga Jakobsen is an Assistant Professor in the Department of Psychology at James Madison University. In addition to studying cognitive development, she examines the effectiveness of team-based learning. (e-mail: vargakx@jmu.edu)

Jared W. Keeley is an Assistant Professor of Psychology at Mississippi State University. He has won several teaching-related awards and has a strong interest in improving the quality of graduate student teaching training. (e-mail: jkeeley@psychology.msstate.edu)

James H. Korn was Professor of Psychology at Saint Louis University and now is retired. Since receiving his PhD at Carnegie-Mellon University (1965), his interests have included physiological psychology, program evaluation, adult development, research ethics, and the history of psychology; his current interest is the development of college teachers. He is the coauthor of the Society for the Teaching of Psychology e-book, *A Guide for Beginning Teachers of Psychology*. (e-mail: kornjh@earthlink.net)

Sandra Goss Lucas is the retired Director of Introductory Psychology at the University of Illinois, Urbana-Champaign, although she continues to teach. She is the author of two books on teaching psychology at the college level and a codeveloper of the University of Illinois Psychology Department's new TA orientation. (e-mail: gossluca@cyrus.psych.illinois.edu)

Mark A. McDaniel is a Professor of Psychology at Washington University in St. Louis, with a joint appointment in education. His research is in the general area of human learning and memory, with an emphasis on prospective memory, encoding and retrieval processes in episodic memory, and applications to educational contexts. (e-mail: mmcdanie@artsci.wustl.edu)

Steven A. Meyers is Professor of Psychology and Mansfield Professor of Social Justice at Roosevelt University in Chicago, IL. His research interests include faculty development, effective college instruction, and parent-child relations. (e-mail: smeyers@roosevelt.edu)

Harold L. Miller, Jr., is Professor of Psychology at Brigham Young University. His scholarly interests include behavioral economics (the relative effects of gains and losses), evolutionary psychology, computer-based educational assessment, and education reform. (e-mail: harold_miller@byu.edu)

John C. Norcross is Professor of Psychology and Distinguished University Fellow at the University of Scranton, where he teaches courses in career development, clinical psychology, and field experience. Among his recent books are the second editions of the *History of Psychotherapy* and *Psychotherapy Relationships That Work,* along with the seventh edition of *Systems of Psychotherapy: A Transtheoretical Analysis.* (e-mail: Norcross@Scranton.edu)

Catherine E. Overson earned her PhD in social psychology from the University of New Hampshire in 2011. She is interested in individual differences related to judgment of performance in academic settings, and her research is aimed at identifying theoretically based individual differences in self-efficacy and study behaviors related to academic performance. (e-mail: coverson@unh.edu)

Rosemary E. Phelps is Professor and Chair of the Department of Counseling and Human Development Services at the University of Georgia, and Director of the University of Georgia Preparing Future Faculty in Psychology program. She is the 2010 recipient of the American Psychological Association's Award for Distinguished Contributions to Education and Training in Psychology. Research interests include racial and ethnicity identity, experiences of students and faculty of color at predominantly white institutions, and mentoring relationships. (e-mail: rephelps@uga.edu)

Steven Prentice-Dunn is a social psychologist at the University of Alabama. He investigates preventive health behaviors and has taught the Teaching of Psychology course for more than 20 years. (e-mail: sprentic@bama.ua.edu)

Rebecca G. Ryan received her PhD in life-span developmental psychology from West Virginia University. She is currently a teacher and researcher at Georgia Southern University. Her interests include social and cognitive development, psychology and law, and effective teaching through service learning. (e-mail: rgryan@georgiasouthern.edu)

Bryan K. Saville is an Associate Professor in the Department of Psychology at James Madison University. He is an Associate Editor for *Teaching of Psychology* and studies evidence-based teaching methods. (e-mail: savillbk@jmu.edu)

Cecilia M. Shore is Professor of Psychology and Director of the Center for the Enhancement of Learning, Teaching, and University Assessment at Miami University. She has received teaching awards from the university and college and has led Preparing Future Faculty and Graduate Student Teaching Effectiveness programs. (e-mail: shorec@muohio.edu)

Mark M. Silvestri is currently a graduate student at Auburn University pursuing a PhD in clinical psychology. Beyond teaching, his research interests also include substance abuse issues among college students. (e-mail: mms0016@auburn.edu)

Randolph A. Smith is Professor of Psychology and Department Chair at Lamar University, where he teaches research methods and is Associate Director of the Center for Teaching and Learning Enhancement. He is actively involved in the scholarship of teaching and learning, edited *Teaching of Psychology* for 12 years, and is current Editor of the *Psi Chi Journal of Undergraduate Research*. (e-mail: rasmith@lamar.edu)

Jennifer J. Stiegler-Balfour is an Assistant Professor of Psychology at the University of New England. Her research investigates cognitive processes that support learning and memory within the context of reading comprehension. She earned her PhD in cognitive psychology and a Master of Science for teachers in college teaching from the University of New Hampshire. (e-mail: jstiegler@une.edu)

Janie H. Wilson teaches and conducts research at Georgia Southern University. She received her PhD from the University of South Carolina in 1994. In the teaching realm, she conducts research on student-teacher rapport. (e-mail: jhwilson@georgiasouthern.edu)

Cynthia Wooldridge is a PhD candidate in psychology at Washington University in St. Louis. Her research interests involve human learning and memory, specifically visual perspective in autobiographical memory and applications to educational contexts. (e-mail: Cynthia.wooldridge@ wustl.edu)

Tracy E. Zinn is an Associate Professor in the Department of Psychology at James Madison University. She conducts research on effective teaching practices at the university level, focusing particularly on interteaching and other behavioral methods of instruction. (e-mail: zinnte@jmu.edu)

Dorothy D. Zinsmeister is Professor Emeritus of Biology and former Interim Executive Director of the Siegel Institute for Leadership, Ethics & Character at Kennesaw State University. She also served as an Assistant Vice Chancellor for Academic Affairs, University System of Georgia. (e-mail: dzinsmei@kennesaw.edu)

SAGE Research Methods Online

The essential tool for researchers

An expert research tool

- An **expertly designed taxonomy** with more than 1,400 unique terms for social and behavioral science research methods

- **Visual and hierarchical search tools** to help you discover material and link to related methods

- Easy-to-use navigation tools
- Content organized by complexity
- Tools for citing, printing, and downloading content with ease
- Regularly updated content and features

A wealth of essential content

- The most comprehensive picture of quantitative, qualitative, and mixed methods available today

- More than **100,000 pages of SAGE book and reference material** on research methods as well as editorially selected material from SAGE journals

- More than **600 books** available in their entirety online

Launching 2011!

$SAGE research methods online